THE NEW KNOWLEDGE
MANAGEMENT

About KMCI Press
Powerful Knowledge for Knowledge Professionals

KMCI Press is an exciting publishing partnership that unites the Knowledge Management Consortium International (KMCI), the leading organization for knowledge management professionals, and Butterworth–Heinemann's Business group and Digital Press imprints, one of the premier publishers of knowledge management books.

KMCI Press publishes authoritative and innovative books that educate all knowledge management communities, from students and beginning professionals to chief knowledge officers. KMCI Press books present definitive and leading-edge ideas of the KMCI itself, and bring clarity and authoritative information to a dynamic and emerging profession.

KMCI Press books explore the opportunities, demands, and benefits knowledge management brings to organizations and defines important and emerging knowledge management disciplines and topics, including:

- Professional roles and functions
- Vertical industry best practices and applications
- Technologies, including knowledge portals and data and document management
- Strategies, methodologies, and decision-making frameworks

KMCI is the only major not-for-profit member organization specifically for knowledge management professionals, with thousands of worldwide members including individuals in the professional and academic fields as well as leading companies, institutions, and other organizations concerned with knowledge management, organizational change, and intellectual capital.

For information about submitting book proposals, please see our website at http://www.kmci.org.

Titles from KMCI Press:

THE NEW KNOWLEDGE MANAGEMENT

Complexity, Learning, and Sustainable Innovation

MARK W. MCELROY

KNOWLEDGE
MANAGEMENT
CONSORTIUM
INTERNATIONAL

BUTTERWORTH
HEINEMANN

An imprint of Elsevier Science
Amsterdam   Boston   London   New York   Oxford   Paris
San Diego   San Francisco   Singapore   Sydney   Tokyo

Library of Congress Cataloging-in-Publication Data

McElroy, Mark W.
   The new knowledge management : complexity, learning, and sustainable innovation / Mark W. McElroy.
      p.   cm.
   Includes bibliographical references and index.
   ISBN 0-7506-7608-6 (pbk. : alk. paper)
   1. Knowledge management.   2. Organizational learning.   I. Title.

   HD30.2 .M396 2002
   658.4′038—dc21

                                                        20022071720

British Library Cataloguing-in-Publication Data
A catalogue record for this book is available from the British Library.

The publisher offers special discounts on bulk orders of this book.
For information, please contact:

Manager of Special Sales
Elsevier Science
200 Wheeler Road, 6th Floor
Burlington, MA 01803
Tel: 781-313-4700
Fax: 781-313-4882

For information on all Butterworth-Heinemann publications available, contact our World Wide Web home page at: http://www.bh.com

10 9 8 7 6 5 4 3 2 1

Printed in the United States of America

Cover art and all figures courtesy of Svend Filby of Svend Design (www.svend.com).

CONTENTS

2

INTEGRATING COMPLEXITY THEORY, KNOWLEDGE MANAGEMENT, AND ORGANIZATIONAL LEARNING

PART II PRACTICE IMPLICATIONS

3

A FRAMEWORK FOR KNOWLEDGE MANAGEMENT

4

DOUBLE-LOOP KNOWLEDGE MANAGEMENT

5

WHERE DOES KNOWLEDGE MANAGEMENT BELONG?

6

The Policy Synchronization Method 92

The Stork Theory of Knowledge, 93
A Life Cycle View, 95
Too Theoretical?, 100
An Executable Process Model for Creating Sustainable
    Innovation, 103
Conclusion, 119

PART III   SUSTAINABLE INNOVATION

7

The Principle of Sustainable Innovation 125

Unsustainable Innovation, 126
The Politics of Knowledge, 127
The "Knowledge Drive," 129

8

Managing for Sustainable Innovation 133

Second-Generation Knowledge Management, 133
A Social Process, 134
First Principles, 136
Policies As Leverage, 138
Practice Implications, 138
Conclusion, 141

9

Sustainable Innovation and the "Learning Drive" 144

Framing the Debate, 147
Complexity Theory and Organizational Learning, 149

PART IV THE ECONOMICS OF
KNOWLEDGE MANAGEMENT

10

SOCIAL INNOVATION CAPITAL   169

11

RETURNS ON INVESTMENT FROM
KNOWLEDGE MANAGEMENT   187

APPENDIX: A PRESENTATION ON SECOND-
GENERATION KNOWLEDGE MANAGEMENT   211

FOREWORD

Knowledge management (KM), new as it is, is changing. There are at least three theories about how it is changing and about how we should view the new knowledge management (TNKM). One theory sees KM as a field that was originally driven by information technology, the World Wide Web, best practices, lessons learned, and most importantly, knowledge sharing. This theory sees a second stage of KM being about human factors, systems thinking, and knowledge creation viewed as the conversions among tacit and explicit knowledge. The third stage of KM is the arrangement and management of content through taxonomy construction and use, and like the first, is also heavily biased toward information technology.

The second theory of change in KM is a bit more subtle than the first. According to this theory (put forth mainly by David Snowden of IBM), the first age of knowledge management is one in which the word "knowledge" itself was not problematic, and in which the focus was on distributing information to decision-makers for timely use in decisions, usually through technology. The second age replaced the focus on information technology with one on tacit/explicit knowledge conversion that was inspired by Ikujiro Nonaka's SECI (Socialization-Externalization-Combination-Internalization) model. The third age is one in which all of the following pertain: (1) knowledge is viewed paradoxically as both a thing and a flow; (2) context, narrative, and content management are central to our view of KM; (3) there is an understanding of organizations as being engaged in sense-making through the utilization of complex adaptive systems phenomena that are constrained by human acts of free will attempting to order them; and finally, (4) there is a rejection of scientific management and its mechanistic models as relevant for knowledge management.

This book of Mark McElroy's presents the third and best of these reconstructions. It is the one that has had the longest gestation period (since late 1998) and the most careful underlying conceptualization.

ix

It is the one that distinguishes two, not three, generations (or ages or stages) of KM. It is the one that makes a clear distinction between knowledge management and knowledge processing, and between these two and knowledge use. It is the one that provides the tightest integration of organizational learning and complex adaptive systems theory. It is the one that uses the clearest definition of different primary types of knowledge and that clearly distinguishes knowledge in minds from knowledge embedded in cultural products. It is the one that views knowledge production and creation as a response to business problems and as an essential object of knowledge management. It is the one that avoids logical inconsistency, the confusion of process with products (or outcomes), and the embrace of "mystery" or "paradox" in characterizing knowledge. It is the one that emphasizes sustainable innovation as an important goal in knowledge management. It is the one that views Information Technology not as a driver, but as an enabler of broader KM and knowledge processing goals. And it is the one that provides a new outlook on intellectual capital, emphasizing process-based (social innovation) capital. In short, it is the one that offers a coherent and understandable, but not overly simplistic, foundation for building a mature knowledge management discipline.

This book is full of new ideas and novel perspectives for KM. There is no other book like it in the field right now. With uncommon clarity, it puts forward a fundamental conceptual framework and relates it to practice, to new types of learning organizations, to complex adaptive systems, to organizational learning, to management, to intellectual capital, to return on investment, and to innovation. It defines certain concepts, such as the new knowledge management, second-generation knowledge management, sustainable innovation, social innovation capital, the open enterprise, and the knowledge life cycle for the first time in book form.

If you're looking for a short, well-written, easy to understand account of knowledge management that deals with the central issues of its scope as a professional field, this is the one book you need to read. It represents a reorientation of KM that is rather fundamental. Whether or not the field moves toward the position sketched out here, *The New Knowledge Management* will still stake out a position that people will want to discuss whenever they are considering the question of what their fundamental orientation toward KM should be. In other words, this book presents a "paradigm." The paradigm will be as relevant for discussion five years from now as it is now, whether or not you or others accept it. If you do accept it, it will define the boundaries of your inquiry and practice in KM. If you don't accept it, it will provide a good benchmark or foil against which to formulate your own view of KM. It is that provocative, that clearly stated, and that nuanced. So read it! Enjoy it! And use it to form your own version of TNKM.

Joseph M. Firestone, Ph.D.
Executive Vice President
Education, Research, and Membership
Knowledge Management Consortium International
Alexandria, VA

PREFACE

In the fall of 1998, I made a fateful trip to attend an organizational meeting of the Knowledge Management Consortium International (KMCI), which was being held against the backdrop of the annual KM World event in Chicago. KMCI had attracted my attention because of its avowed focus on the convergence of knowledge management and complexity theory. Today, four years later, I am the president of KMCI and have emerged as one of its most active conceptual developers.

What I and several others at KMCI, most notably Joseph M. Firestone and Steven A. Cavaleri, both Ph.D.s, have managed to do over the past four years is to recast KM in a form that we call second-generation KM. This is actually a term I first coined when Chapter 1 of this book was published as an article in 1999.[1] But despite this achievement, it occurred to me this past year that there are no texts out there yet that chronicle the unfolding evolution of thinking behind the new KM in its contemporary form. Having written many papers on the subject along the way, I decided to assemble a collection of them that would help to explain the concept using the paper trail itself as a means of doing so.

What I would like to say more than anything else, up front, is that what makes the new KM so different from the old KM is not just its balanced emphasis on knowledge *making* and knowledge *sharing*, but its recognition of the presence of *learning systems* in human organizations. I am reminded of a seemingly perennial argument (more like a friendly debate) that I have been having over the past two years with colleagues of mine at the Sustainability Institute (SI) in Hartland, Vermont, where until recently I served as Chairman of the Board. The mission of SI is to study, and to try to resolve, intractable problems of sustainability, or *un*sustainability, in the behavior of whole industries in the commodities arena. In particular, SI has been focusing on unraveling the sources of unsustainable behaviors in the corn, forestry, and shrimp industries for the past few years. This remains a work in progress.

My friendly debate with my friends at SI, however, has been carried out at the challenging level of the *level of analysis level* at which SI's work should occur. For example, when we focus on the global performance of an industry, we are aiming our analysis at its visible *operational level*. But this is not the same as focusing our analysis of an industry's workings at, say, its *learning level*. How people and groups in complex social systems organize themselves around learning and problem-solving—or even to *detect* problems—may have nothing to do with how and what they do at their operating level, and usually doesn't. So what does this have to do with KM, you ask?

The problem of unsustainable performance is at least an *operating level* problem. Sure, we can potentially solve the problem by changing operating-level behaviors. People can stop using so much chemical fertilizer, or chopping down so many trees, or catching so many shrimp. But the fixes are never that simple. We know, for example, that global behaviors in complex systems often arise from the structure of the system itself, and even the best intentions of a group within the system won't solve the problem. This is classic systems thinking, a hallmark of our work at SI over the years, thanks largely to the legacy of its founder, and my friend, the late Donella H. Meadows.

But what is the source of behavior in a human social system? And what is the reason for its failure to detect and correct problems, even when those problems threaten its very existence? Why can't unsustainable systems correct themselves? And what does this have to do with KM?

One source of behavior in a social system is its knowledge and the manner in which it learns. If you want to know what an organization knows, observe its behavior. Behavior is knowledge in practice. Next, examine its learning regime. How does it come to acquire its knowledge? How does learning *happen* inside the system? Is its *learning system* helpful? Is it serving the needs of its host? Is the host system adaptive, or is it maladaptive? How can a social system that seems so hell-bent on running itself into the ground, like modern agriculture or forestry, be seen as anything less than *mal*adaptive? Neither of these industries are adapting successfully to their conditions. They're arguably in a free-fall plunge to their deaths, and yet they don't seem to have the capacity to learn from their current predicaments in ways that can change their behaviors. Why?

I believe that the answer to the puzzle lies in the makeup of a social system's *learning regime*, not its *operating* system (i.e., in its learning system behaviors, not its instrumental ones). To point to the operating system is to beg the question. We know which behaviors are dysfunctional in most cases; they're plainly visible. But we can't say why *knowledge* of that behavior, even by actors within such systems, fails to induce changes in behavior. Or can we?

In a profound piece of work published in 1982 by Larry L. Kiser and Elinor Ostrom, *The Three Worlds of Action: A Metatheoretical Synthesis of Institutional Approaches*,[2] the authors make the distinction between three levels of analysis in trying to unravel the behavior of human social systems (see Figure P-1). The first level in the hierarchy is the Operational Level, such as observable business processing behaviors in a firm. Next is the Collective Choice Level, at which decisions are made about actions to take or rules to apply in the Operational Level. Third is the Constitutional Choice Level, at which rules for making decisions (and rules) at the Collective Choice Level are made—in other words, the Constitutional Choice Level is where meta-rules are made.

In the context of the essays contained in Kiser and Ostrom's book, the *new knowledge management* is a management discipline that embraces the notion of a Collective Choice Level as the *learning system* of an enterprise, the machinations of which can be identified, changed, and enhanced. Further, the *rules for making rules* found at the Constitutional Choice Level offer an even deeper source of leverage in our attempts to help firms learn better and make smarter choices at the Collective Choice Level. Interventions made at these levels, in turn, give rise to changes in the behaviors found at the Operational Level, especially in such rare cases as whole industries that seem intent on self-destruction. But the same principles apply in smaller social systems, like businesses and other sorts of organizations.

Without even knowing as much, KMCI has been developing its own conception of what Kiser and Ostrom defined as the Collective Choice Level so many years ago, except that the collective choices of interest to us have been *knowledge* processing choices, not *business* processing ones (i.e., how organizations should go about producing and integrating their knowledge, and how knowledge managers can help them do so). In my own work, I have taken the additional step

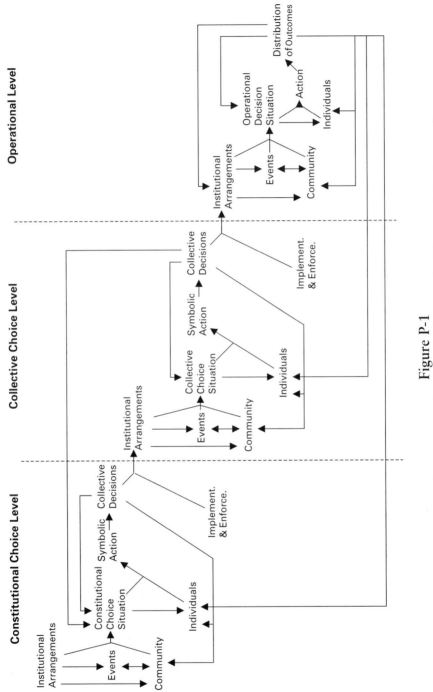

Figure P-1

Three Levels of Institutional Analysis (Source: L. Kiser and E. Ostrom[3])

backwards, or up, the hierarchy and have formulated an approach, along with my colleague Dr. Steven A. Cavaleri, for changing the rule-making rules (meta-rules) at the Constitutional Choice Level using *policy* as a lever to do so. I call this the Policy Synchronization Method.[4]

All of these themes are variously discussed and emphasized in the essays collected in this book, but I urge readers to bear in mind, above all, that the central vision of the so-called *new*, or second-generation, knowledge management school of thought is that learning systems of varying degrees of health can be found in all human social systems, and that the behavior of a system, whether it be the struggle to adapt in a business or the performance of an entire industry, can ultimately be traced to the quality and condition of its learning system. No amount of well-meaning interventions aimed at changing behaviors at the instrumental or operating level of an organization can have impact on its learning system. And insofar as dysfunctional systems are concerned, without having an impact on the learning system, management is reduced to the practice of treating the symptoms, not the disease.

We must learn to *look through* the behaviors we see in the operating levels of organizations, such that the *learning behaviors*, and the meta-rules that lie behind them, come sharply into focus. There we will find the proper ground for KM and its interventions, and nowhere else. In the new KM scheme of things, we call this the knowledge life cycle, or KLC, of an organization. The target of KM interventions is mostly the KLC in a firm and the rules that lord over it. It is the KLC that gives rise to operating behaviors, both good ones and bad ones, and it is the KLC that holds them in place.

I have often said that unsustainable industries suffer from broken or missing learning systems. I believe the same is true in organizations and social systems at any level of scale. Understanding the presence and crucial role of learning systems in human collectives of all kinds is the central, immutable insight at the heart of the new KM. This changes everything.

ENDNOTES

1. M. W. McElroy, "The Second Generation of Knowledge Management," *Knowledge Management* (October, 1999), pp. 86–88.

2. Larry L. Kiser and Elinor Ostrom, "The Three Worlds of Action: A Metatheoretical Synthesis of Institutional Approaches." In *Strategies of Political Inquiry*, edited by Elinor Ostrom. (Beverly Hills, CA: Sage Publications, 1982), pp. 179–222.
3. Ibid., p. 207.
4. The Policy Synchronization Method is the subject of a U.S. patent application filed with the Patent and Trademark Office in September, 2000 by Macroinnovation Associates, LLC of Windsor, VT (www.macroinnovation.com). It currently holds patent-pending status.

ACKNOWLEDGMENTS

Jim Britell, an environmental activist and consultant, made a memorable remark in his review of Daniel Quinn's book, *My Ishmael*, a sequel to Quinn's unforgettable *Ishmael: An Adventure of the Mind and Spirit*: "From now on I will divide the books I have read into two categories—the ones I read before Ishmael and those read after" (*Whole Earth Review*). I, too, find that I am indelibly influenced by Quinn, whose story of a man whose discovery of his own subjugation to the myths of modern (and unsustainable) culture is at once as liberating as it is disturbing. It was Quinn's *Ishmael* that—for the first time—allowed me to separate myself from the cultural story in which I live and to see it objectively, and for that I will always be grateful. But it was also *Ishmael* that allowed me to see my duty in the world as well. Thank you for that, Daniel Quinn!

Soon after my experience with *Ishmael*, I had the good fortune to attend a course at Schumacher College in Devon, England on Gaia Theory, an experience that I think also changed me forever. At Schumacher under the tutelage of Stephan Harding, Brian Goodwin, and James Lovelock himself, the primary developer of Gaia Theory, I began for the first time to make the connections between complexity theory, evolution, organizational learning, environmental ethics, management, and sustainability. This was a watershed event for me. It was Schumacher's influence that set me on the path I've traveled ever since, a path marked by the recognition of, and reverence for, self-organization and its implications for choices about how we should live our lives, manage our organizations, and come to terms with our place in the universe. For that, too, I will always be grateful.

Next in my streak of good fortune was my friendship and close working relationship with Donella H. Meadows (Dana), whose towering mastery of system dynamics and environmental studies is, and was, legendary in the field. For three years I served as a board member at Dana's Sustainability Institute here in Hartland, Vermont, including the year in which she died. It was largely through dialogue with Dana in the years I knew her that I began to see the application of system dynamics to knowledge processing behaviors in organizations. And it was through that experience that I also began to see the connections between healthy organizational learning and healthy (i.e., sustainable) outcomes. I will always savor and appreciate that seemingly eternal moment of shared insight we had one day, when in one of our discussions about what seems to cause and lock in unsustainable behaviors in human social systems, we suddenly acknowledged the possibility that things may have more to do with dysfunctional learning systems than with instrumental behaviors. I have been working on that insight ever since, and I will always be indebted to Dana for the role she played—and continues to play—in my thinking about it.

Almost last, but not least, is my gratitude to an extraordinary cast of contrarian thinkers I fell in with in 1998 at the Knowledge Management Consortium International (KMCI). This unusual group of individuals from business, government, and academia truly self-organized in late 1997 for no other reason than to take on the development of a complexity-theory-inspired brand of knowledge management. How could I resist! Currently, I am the President of KMCI, but my experience there has paid other, more rewarding dividends that will no doubt have a more lasting and important effect on my life—not least of which is my affiliation with Dr. Steven A. Cavaleri, Professor of Management at Central Connecticut State University, with whom I eventually collaborated in the development of the patent-pending Policy Synchronization Method (discussed variously throughout this book). Steve's depth of knowledge in the field of organizational learning, and his tireless patience in putting up with so many basic questions from me about the subject, its history, and its conceptual twists and turns over the past hundred years or so, endowed me in ways that have made all the difference. Indeed, I attribute most of what I know about organizational learning and the history of thought behind it to Steve. I thank him for that.

Finally, there is no question that if it were not for the extraordinary generosity—and just sheer good will—of Joseph M. Firestone, another of my KMCI colleagues, I wouldn't be here writing these words today. Say what you will about the quality of my work, without Joe, it wouldn't be half as good as it is. My affiliation with him has been by far the most fruitful collaboration of my life. I think

I have learned more from him over the past four years than I did in the preceding forty. His uncommon tolerance of what must surely seem at times to be my insufferable naivete continues to humble me. At the same time his acceptance of my ideas and his willingness to collaborate with me in their development and improvement is a gift. Everything I know about the joy and rewards of openly and respectfully sharing knowledge and collaborating with one's peers, I learned from my association with Joe. There is not one line of text in this book that hasn't been influenced by my affiliation with him, and for that—and for our *future* collaborations as well—I owe him a tremendous debt.

Hartland, VT

INTRODUCTION

Knowledge management (KM) is a field that can easily be described as having two sides to it: one that tends to focus on knowledge *sharing*, and the other that tends to focus on knowledge *making*. It is the latter side that accounts for the connections between KM and innovation management (IM), and the former one which accounts for the ties between KM and organizational learning (OL).

In truth, however, it is the former group (the knowledge sharers) who tend to get the most attention in the marketplace. The value proposition of KM, according to their view, is that it helps make old learning more accessible and reusable for current-day workers, thereby improving their performance. To get a better feel for the logic here, listen to the following statement made by a well-known management guru as he discussed one of four types of interventions that he felt managers should make to improve the performance of their workers:

The first of these four groups of duties taken over by the management is the deliberate gathering on the part of those on the management's side of all of the great mass of traditional knowledge, which in the past has been in the heads of the workmen, and in the physical skill and knack of the workmen, which he has acquired through years of experience. The duty of gathering all this great mass of traditional knowledge and then recording it, tabulating it, and, in many cases, finally reducing it to laws, rules, and even to mathematical formulae, is voluntarily assumed by the scientific managers. And later, when these laws, rules, and formulae are applied to the everyday work of all the workmen of the establishment, through the intimate and hearty cooperation of those on the management's side, they invariably result, first, in producing a very much larger output per man, as well as an output of better and higher quality; and, second, in enabling the company to pay much higher wages to their workmen; and, third, in giving to the company a larger profit.

The first of these principles, then, may be called the development of a science to replace the old rule-of-thumb knowledge of the workmen; that is, the knowledge which the workmen had, and which was, in many cases, quite exact as that which is finally obtained by the management, but which the workmen nevertheless in nine hundred and ninety-nine cases out of a thousand kept in their heads, and of which there was no permanent or complete record.[1]

The speaker above is, of course, Frederick Taylor, who in the early twentieth century developed his so-called Scientific Management system, which he advocated for machine shops and other industrial settings around the country. The occasion upon which he uttered the words above, however, was a somewhat inauspicious one. This proclamation took place in a Congressional hearing on January 25, 1912, in which Taylor's method and others were being investigated by a House Committee because of their controversial reputations in the marketplace. Being "scientifically managed" apparently did not set well with labor at the time.

What's so interesting about Taylor's remarks is that he refers to the process of capturing, codifying, and sharing knowledge as a "science to replace the old rule-of-thumb knowledge of the workmen." And he concludes by making reference to what we, today, would recognize as a formal process of capturing knowledge held by individual workers—tacit or otherwise—for widespread use. Indeed, Taylor's passage is vintage knowledge-sharing dogma, and he may very well deserve the title, "the Father of Knowledge Management."

Taylor's perspective, in today's terms, has become known as "supply-side KM," a term I first coined in 1999.[2] Supply-side KM is the practice of KM in any way that is designed to enhance the supply of existing knowledge to workers in an enterprise. It is typically associated with two well-known phrases that have become the mantras for advocates of the knowledge-sharing side of KM: (1) *It's all about capturing, codifying, and sharing valuable knowledge,* and (2) *It's all about getting the right information to the right people at the right time.* These two phrases, more than any others, neatly sum up the essence of supply-side KM, which has also come to be known as first-generation KM.

Second-generation KM, on the other hand, introduces "demand-side KM," which instead of focusing on the supply of existing knowledge to a workforce, seeks instead to enhance their capacity to produce it. The mission of demand-side KM, then, is to enhance an organization's capacity to satisfy its *demand* for new knowledge. But second-generation KM includes supply-side thinking, as well, and prefers to think of KM in a more cyclical, holistic way. It's not just knowledge sharing or knowledge making that matters—it's *both* that matters. There's a knowledge life cycle at work in human social systems, and it is the job of the knowledge manager to manage the *whole* cycle, not just the parts that happen to be of interest to one school of thought or another.

Having personally been involved in the conceptual development of second-generation KM over the past several years, I wrote frequently on the topic and published several papers in magazines, online "e-zines," and academic journals. The collective publication of these articles in book form struck me as an effective way of presenting the evolution of second-generation KM (also known as the new KM) to the profession. Although several of the chapters in this book have been published before, others have not, and are printed here for the first time. Those that have been published before have been substantially revised and updated to reflect the latest thinking in the field.

This collection of essays begins with two chapters in Part I that consist of previously published papers that introduced the theory of second-generation KM to the profession. Both include treatment of the so-called *knowledge life cycle*, or KLC, and the all-important distinction now being made between first- and second-generation KM. It is second-generation KM, of course, that is the namesake of this book, although I have chosen to refer to it in the title as the new KM. I introduced the term second-generation KM in a paper I wrote under the same title, which was published in *Knowledge Management Magazine* (then published in print as well as online) in October, 1999.[3] It proved to be one of the most popular papers I ever wrote and is presented in Chapter 1.

Chapter 2, "Integrating Complexity Theory, Knowledge Management, and Organizational Learning," was originally published in the fall of 2000 in a journal in the United Kingdom entitled the *Journal of Knowledge Management*.[4] In that paper, I sought to reinforce the connections I saw between KM and OL, while adding a new theoretical twist to the mix: *complexity theory*. I initially addressed the connections between KM and complexity theory in the paper presented in Chapter 1, but only barely so. This second paper, then, was designed to offer up a new theoretical foundation for the practice of both KM and OL that would rest heavily upon the view of human social systems as *complex adaptive systems*, or CASs, complexity theory's term for adaptive, living systems. The production, diffusion, and use of knowledge in such systems is their most conspicuous activity.

Although I was certainly not the only practitioner in the new field of second-generation KM to recognize the connections between KM and CAS theory, I was among the few in the field (especially at Knowledge Management Consortium International) who sought to develop its implications with gusto and determination. This second paper was my own attempt to specify the basis of the alleged connections between KM and CAS theory in some detail, in a way that would help pave the way for a new body of practice. If organizations are CASs, I argued, then our KM interventions crafted accordingly. This paper eventually received a literary award from the Literati Club in London following its publication in the fall of 2000.[5]

Having helped lay the theoretical groundwork for second-generation KM, I then started to focus on the implications for practice and methodology. If human social systems are adaptive in nature, relying as they do on the dynamics of shared learning cycles, I then asked myself what role can or should KM play in helping to improve their performance? It was in contemplating this question that I and several others began to recognize the now critically important distinction we make between *knowledge management* and *knowledge processing*. Knowledge *processing*, we argued, is a social process that organizations follow in order to produce (make) and integrate (share) their knowledge.

Knowledge *management*, on the other hand, is what a particular class of managers do as they attempt to enhance knowledge processing. Out of this realization came the view that if knowledge management is in any way a misnomer—or a bad choice of words for a very legitimate field—it was because what knowledge managers do is manage *knowledge processes*, not knowledge. A more correct, albeit awkward, term for KM would be *knowledge process management*. Putting terminology issues aside, I and several others began to develop practice frameworks for the new KM that were true to this vision. What we started to formulate, then, were tools and methods designed to have an impact on knowledge processing in organizations, as defined in a model developed by me and several others at KMCI—a conceptual framework that we referred to as the knowledge life cycle, or KLC.

Part II of this collection continues with four papers of mine in which the practice implications of second-generation KM were laid out in some detail. The first one (Chapter 3), "A Framework for Knowledge Management," published in March of 2002,[6] provides a fairly comprehensive framework for practice that practitioners can use to put their strategies and interventions in context. The approach described in this paper begins by grounding its focus in the supply-versus demand-side distinctions earlier discussed, and then proceeds to acknowledge the various social and technological interventions practitioners can make to improve the KLC, as well as the style of their interventions (e.g., making *policy* interventions versus *program* interventions).

Chapter 4 presents the second paper, "Double-Loop Knowledge Management," first published in *The Systems Thinker* in October 1999,[7] which firmly established the connections between second-generation KM and the closely related field of organizational learning (OL). Central to OL theory and practice is a model that makes the distinction between single-loop learning and double-loop learning. According to that model, single-loop learning amounts to choosing behaviors in accordance with rote sets of rules, whereas double-loop learning involves the production of new rules. Here, the connections between supply-side and demand-side KM were obvious to me, so I took steps to cast second-generation KM as an implementation methodology for OL, a view that I still hold to quite strongly today.

Chapter 5, "Where Does KM Belong?"[8] is the next paper, which I wrote in 2001. Here I attempted to resolve issues concerning the proper positioning of KM in an enterprise. My argument, in sum, was that KM is an organizational function that transcends strategy, temporal management regimes, and even the value chain itself. Its proper placement in a firm, therefore, is analogous to the finance function: it should coordinate with management but report to the board. In the wake of the Enron scandal here in the United States, this advice seems even more appropriate today than it did when I wrote it. If organizations are knowledge processing systems, and the purpose of KM is to enhance knowledge processing, then KM should not be subordinated to the dictates of strategies or to their itinerant creators. Strategy is itself a knowledge processing *outcome*, and its creators are not above learning. Moreover, strategies and managers change over time, but knowledge processing is persistent and should be managed as independently as possible from the potential interference of parochial management regimes, be they scrupulous or otherwise.

Chapter 6, the fourth paper in this group, "The Policy Synchronization Method," was actually first published in KMCI's *Knowledge and Innovation* journal in late 2000 under a different title: "The New Knowledge Management."[9] It describes a second-generation KM methodology that I developed earlier that year with the assistance of my friend and colleague, Dr. Steven A. Cavaleri. As of this writing, the Policy Synchronization Method (PSM) holds patent-pending status in the United States. The PSM method is based on the view (from complexity theory) that human social systems or organizations are self-organizing in their knowledge production and integration affairs. You don't *manage* the KLC, you have impact on it.

According to the PSM method, one can improve the performance of the KLC (hence, knowledge *making* and *sharing*) by adopting policies of several specific types that support, strengthen, and reinforce its dynamics but that can never *determine* them. This is because knowledge making and sharing in organizations is a self-organizing process that does not respond well to deterministic management interventions. The KLC is an emergent phenomenon, not subject to deterministic control or explainable in terms of a random model. Under the rubric of the PSM method, *desired behaviors* do not follow from policy interventions; rather, *desired policy interventions* follow from behavioral tendencies. Understanding the behavioral tendencies of people in organizations to engage in knowledge production and sharing, as well as the pattern of their behaviors, inspires the choice of policies that, in turn, reinforce the very same behaviors. That's the PSM method in a nutshell.

Next in this intellectual journey was the short hop from the inspiration behind the PSM method to the companion idea of "sustainable innovation." If the manner in which people in organizations innovate (i.e., how they make and share their knowledge) is self-organizing in its ontogeny, then only KM strategies and interventions that support, strengthen, or reinforce related patterns of behavior can be seen as sustainable. Strategies or interventions that in any way contravene the tendencies of people to make and share knowledge in their own particular ways are *un*sustainable, by contrast, because they will conflict with them (i.e., with self-organizing behaviors related to knowledge production and integration), and the knowledge processing performance of the whole social system will, as a result, be hampered and degrade over time.

Part III of this collection, then, includes four papers of mine in which I explore this topic further and lay out a prescription for achieving sustainable innovation. Not surprisingly, the basis of this prescription rests heavily on many of the ideas covered above, especially those that relate to the knowledge life cycle, CAS theory, and the PSM method. In all cases, I appeal to the self-organizing nature of knowledge production and sharing activities in human social systems, and the importance of deferential policy-making to achieving sustainable innovation. By "deferential" I mean to say that the learning- and innovation-related policy environment of a firm should be determined in deference to the social behavioral predispositions of its members, and not in accordance with some ad hoc or administrative view of how learning and innovation *should* work.

Only one of the three chapters in Part III of the book has been previously published (Chapter 8, "Managing for Sustainable Innovation"), although its title at the time (October 2000 in *Knowledge Management Review*) was different: "Using Knowledge Management to Sustain Innovation."[10] Chapter 7, "The Principle of Sustainable Innovation," and Chapter 9, "Sustainable Innovation and the 'Learning Drive,'" both appear here for the first time.

Last in this collection of essays is Part IV, which deals with the business case, or economic, aspects of the new KM. Of particular interest here is the connection between second-generation thinking and the field of intellectual capital (IC) management. In the spring of 2001, I was invited by New York University's Professor Baruch Lev, the well-known authority on measuring the value of "intangibles," to participate as a panelist at his annual conference on the subject. The invitation to attend was based upon his review of my paper, "Social Innovation Capital" (Chapter 10), which was later published in a special collection of papers from that event in the *Journal of Intellectual Capital* (February 2002).[11]

In my own survey of the literature on IC management, I had earlier discovered that none of the mainstream, competing schema for measuring intangible or intellectual capital made any provisions for the value of *social* capital, much less the kind of social capital that leads to innovation. By contrast, the knowledge life cycle is nothing if not a form of social capital, which specifically gives rise to innovation, hence the term I coined: *social innovation capital*. I further argued that the only thing more valuable than valuable intellectual capital is the capacity to produce it—and sustainably so. In making this argument, I took the essence of second-generation KM and intentionally put an IC spin on it, in such a way that investments in KM could be seen as adding value to the balance sheet. If the social capacity to innovate has material value, then investments in KM can be seen as adding direct value to a firm's balance sheet of a sort that yields increasing returns, because the capacity to innovate leads to open-ended innovation.

The second paper in Part IV (Chapter 11, "Returns on Investment from KM") was developed as a consequence of my role as a co-developer and co-instructor of KMCI's market-leading KM certification program (i.e., its Certified Knowledge and Innovation Manager, or CKIM, program). It is a short paper that attempts to show the trajectory of returns from investments in KM, spun from the perspective of supply- versus demand-side thinking. Its content generally shows that balanced investments in supply- and demand-side KM (also known as second-generation KM) lead to higher returns on investment than do isolated investments on either side, and also that supply-side-only investments either lead to delayed returns or to diminishing ones.

For the Appendix I decided to include a slide presentation that I gave at the KM World conference last year in California (October 2001) on second-generation KM.[12] As readers of my work will soon discover, I often experiment with different ways of describing the essence of second-generation KM using key principles and other means to convey its meaning. In the KM World presentation, I employed this technique by reducing the concept to ten principles of second-generation KM. There's nothing sacred about this particular formulation; it just seemed like the right way to go at the time. I hope readers find it useful and informative.

Finally, a word or two about the manner in which the Policy Synchronization Method is formulated throughout the chapters of this book is warranted. When Dr. Cavaleri and I first developed the method, we organized the targets of policy interventions specified by the method into four categories: embryology, politics, intellectual diversity (or *ethodiversity*), and connectedness. Later on, however, we decided to drop what many had complained was our confusing and cryptic language in favor of recasting our model into two simpler categories: structural dimensions and operational dimensions. With this in mind, readers should not be confused when they see the model behind the method described in these alternative ways. It is the same system throughout—a practitioner's methodology for achieving sustainable innovation in human social systems!

ENDNOTES

1. F. W. Taylor, *Scientific Management* (New York: Harper & Brothers Publishers, 1947), pp. 40–41.
2. M. W. McElroy, "The Second Generation of Knowledge Management," *Knowledge Management* (October, 1999), pp. 86–88.
3. Ibid.
4. M. W. McElroy, "Integrating Complexity Theory, Knowledge Management, and Organizational Learning," *Journal of Knowledge Management* Vol. 4, No. 3 (2000), pp. 195–203.
5. I received the "Highly Commended Award" in 2001 from the Literati Club in the United Kingdom, which is affiliated with MCB University Press.
6. M. W. McElroy, "A Framework for Knowledge Management," *Cutter IT Journal* Vol. 15, No. 3 (March, 2002), pp. 12–17.
7. M. W. McElroy, "Double-Loop Knowledge Management," *The Systems Thinker* Vol. 10, No. 8 (October, 1999), pp. 1–5.
8. M. W. McElroy, "Where Does KM Belong? A Better Solution," *Knowmap: The Knowledge Management, Auditing and Mapping Magazine* Vol. 1, No. 4 (2001) (www.knowmap.com).
9. M. W. McElroy, "The New Knowledge Management," *Knowledge and Innovation: Journal of the KMCI* Vol. 1, No. 1 (October 15, 2000), pp. 43–67.
10. M. W. McElroy, "Using Knowledge Management to Sustain Innovation," *Knowledge Management Review* Vol. 3, Issue 4 (Sept./Oct., 2000), pp. 34–37.
11. M. W. McElroy, "Social Innovation Capital," *Journal of Intellectual Capital* Vol. 3, No. 1 (2002), pp. 30–39.
12. This presentation was given at the Knowledge Management World conference on October 30, 2001 in Santa Clara, CA. It is included here in an edited, updated form.

Part I

THE NEW
KNOWLEDGE
MANAGEMENT

"The science of complexity [theory] presents us with a completely different metaparadigm. Through this lens, the world of organization is seen as a system held far from equilibrium, at the edge of chaos, by the paradoxical dynamic of competition and self-organizing cooperation. In this fundamentally paradoxical world, the links between actions and their long-term outcomes is lost, and what remains predictable is the system dynamic and the archetypal behavior it produces: predictability is possible at the general level but not the specific, the opposite of the conclusion reached with the aid of [conventional management thinking]."

—*Ralph D. Stacey*

1

SECOND-GENERATION KNOWLEDGE MANAGEMENT[1]

At a conference on knowledge management (KM) not too long ago, attendees could be heard grumbling about what they felt was the event's myopic obsession with technology. "Document management and imaging—that's all I've seen and heard about here," one man complained. He then amplified his discontent and shared his broader disappointment with knowledge management as a whole: "an idea that amounts to little more than yesterday's information technologies trotted out in today's more fashionable clothes." Point well taken.

Indeed, at the heart of most KM strategies to date can be found data warehousing, groupware, document management, imaging, and data mining. By continuing to promote that kind of narrow, technocentric brand of thinking, the nascent field of knowledge management places its own credibility at risk. Merely re-labeling yesterday's technologies in the sexy new name of today's KM brings nothing new to the table. And businesses won't stand for it. As reported above, evidence of the backlash is already apparent. We, the community of KM practitioners, can do much better than that.

3

As an advocate and strong supporter of KM, I and many others hold an entirely different view of the field compared to what we typically see in the press and at trade shows. Recently, a new name for this, we hope, more enlightened brand of KM has emerged: "Second-Generation KM"[2] (also known as, "the new knowledge management"). Unlike first-generation KM, in which technology always seems to provide the answer, second-generation thinking is more inclusive of people, process, and social initiatives. I believe we should embrace this term, along with its expanded perspectives, as a way of differentiating *the new KM* from its technology-minded ancestry. A comparison of these two competing frameworks follows below.

THE FUNDAMENTALS

The arrival of second-generation KM includes the introduction of new terms, new concepts, and new insights, which together give second-generation KM some real depth and distinction when compared to first-generation models. These concepts, of which there are many, include the following ten (10) key ideas:

1. The Knowledge Life Cycle (KLC)
2. KM versus Knowledge Processing
3. Supply-Side versus Demand-Side KM
4. Nested Knowledge Domains
5. Containers of Knowledge
6. Organizational Learning
7. The Open Enterprise
8. Social Innovation Capital
9. Self-Organization and Complexity Theory
10. Sustainable Innovation

Each of these concepts is defined and discussed in more detail below.

THE KNOWLEDGE LIFE CYCLE (KLC)

The conventional practice of knowledge management—if there is such a thing—is often associated with the following common phrases:

- *It's all about getting the right information to the right people at the right time.*
- *If we only knew what we know.*
- *We need to capture and codify our tacit and explicit knowledge before it walks out the door.*

Most of us in KM have heard these expressions many times before. In a very real way, they speak volumes about our assumptions concerning the purpose and value of KM, as well as its scope. In particular, the unspoken assumption behind each of these statements is that *valuable knowledge exists*—all we need to do is capture it, codify it, and share it. According to this view of knowledge management, the practice of KM begins sometime after knowledge is produced. Ergo, the purpose of KM is not to enhance knowledge production; rather, the purpose of KM is to enhance the deployment of knowledge into practice (i.e., by taking steps to diffuse it throughout an organization and into the minds of individuals and groups who need it). This is a view of KM that we shall call "first-generation KM"— a view that places its emphasis not on knowledge production but on knowledge integration.

Although practitioners of first-generation KM tend to begin with the rather convenient assumption that valuable knowledge already exists, practitioners of second-generation KM do not. Instead, they— or *we*—take the position that knowledge is something that we produce in human social systems, and that we do so through individual and shared processes that have regularity to them. We can describe this process at an organizational level in the form of what is now being referred to as *the knowledge life cycle*, or *KLC* (see Figure 1-1). This is perhaps the single most important foundation of second-generation thinking, since most of what we do in KM, according to this view, is designed to have impact on the KLC. If it doesn't have impact on the KLC, or if it is not *intended* to have impact on the KLC, then it is not KM. This is a view of KM that we shall call "second-generation KM"—a view that emphasizes *both* knowledge production and integration.

The KLC shown in Figure 1-1, and referred to variously throughout the remainder of this book, was conceived of and developed by a handful of active members at the Knowledge Management Consortium International (KMCI), especially Joseph M. Firestone and me. In presenting this model, we often take care to point out that the

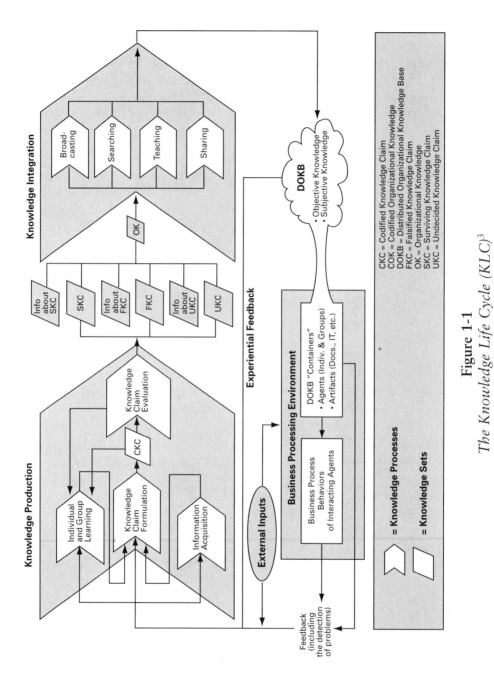

Figure 1-1

The Knowledge Life Cycle (KLC)[3]

KLC is actually *not* a "model" but is, instead, a "framework." What we mean by this is that the KLC can be thought of as a *framework for placing models in context*, in which many different competing views of how knowledge is produced and integrated in organizations can be organized and positioned relative to one another in a coherent way. Moreover, management strategies and programs for enhancing knowledge production, diffusion, and use can be seen in context when viewed against the backdrop of the KLC.

But the KLC is not just a neutral conception or framework of how knowledge is produced and integrated in human social systems. It does reflect a particular point of view. Some of the claims embodied in this view include the following:

- People tend to engage in learning as a result of experiencing gaps in their current and goal states. Detection of these gaps constitutes the emergence of problems, which involve a lack of knowledge of what actions to take in order to achieve desired outcomes.
- The detection of problems by individuals, or *agents*, in a system triggers learning activity that eventually leads to the formulation of "knowledge claims." Knowledge claims are conjectures, assertions, arguments, or theories about which potential actions might lead to desired outcomes, in ways that will close the gap between current and goal states.
- As they engage in learning and the development of new knowledge claims, individual agents sometimes co-attract one another and form groups in which they collectively, and often informally, share ideas and subject them to peer review, in the broadest sense of this term. In these and other ways, they vet and evaluate their claims to their own satisfaction. At an individual and group level, this may be as far as things need go before being placed into practice, but at an organizational level, validation must also occur in the eyes of a wider audience, if not in the minds of a controlling group or authority structure (e.g., management). These processes of *knowledge claim formulation* and *evaluation* can be thought of as "knowledge production."
- Not all knowledge claims formulated by individuals and groups succeed at an organizational level. Those that do can be thought of as surviving knowledge claims; those that don't fall into

either of two categories: undecided knowledge claims, or falsified knowledge claims. Informational accounts about these outcomes are also produced as a consequence of the *knowledge production* process. These additional records themselves are knowledge claims—or *metaclaims*, if you like (i.e., claims about claims).

- As knowledge claims are evaluated and validated at different levels of organizational scale, attempts may be made afterwards by managers and others to share their content and value with other members of the group or organization, in which case efforts are made to *integrate* them into the operations of a wider population of people. This process of managed knowledge sharing and diffusion can be thought of as "knowledge integration."

- As knowledge is successfully integrated throughout an organization, it manifests itself generally in two forms: *mentally held knowledge* by individual or group agents (i.e., knowledge held by people in their minds), or objectively held in the form of explicit linguistic expressions in artifacts (i.e., spoken claims; or claims in documents, computer files, etc.). Here, we find the ideas of the great twentieth-century philosopher Karl Popper[4] to be useful, according to which he distinguished between "world 2" knowledge (knowledge in minds) and "world 3" knowledge (knowledge encoded in linguistic expressions or works of art). Popper also referred to these two forms of knowledge as "subjective knowledge" and "objective knowledge," respectively. The combination of subjective and objective knowledge in an organization may be thought of as an organization's distributed organizational knowledge base, or DOKB (term coined by Joseph M. Firestone and used in KMCI's KLC).

- In discrete form, the components of a DOKB manifest themselves in what we can think of as two kinds of containers: *agents* and *artifacts*. More specifically, they may take the form of beliefs or belief predispositions held in the minds of agents (individuals, teams, groups, communities, departments, divisions, etc.)—these are *subjective* forms of knowledge. But knowledge may also be held in the form of linguistic expressions and/or encodings in speech or in objects, such as files, documents, computer systems, microfilm, disks, videos, tapes, books, articles, papers, essays, lectures, music, other works of art, and so on—these are *objective* forms of knowledge, which we can also refer to as knowledge claims.

■ The knowledge life cycle, strictly speaking, begins with the detection of problems by agents in the context of business processing (i.e., while they are engaged in the practice of instrumental behavior, such as business processes, and as they experience gaps in their knowledge of how to move from current states to goal states), and ends with the choice of newly validated knowledge claims, beliefs, and belief predispositions in the DOKB and its containers. Knowledge *use*, which later follows, occurs within the context of business processing, not knowledge processing, and it is in the midst of knowledge use in business processing, in turn, that new problems arise and are detected. In Figure 1-2 we show the relationships between the KLC (also known as the *knowledge processing environment*) and the *business processing environment*—the two realms of processing do indeed connect and interact with one another.

These and other claims, discussed variously below, comprise the theoretical foundations of second-generation KM. Of particular importance is the view that valuable knowledge does *not* simply exist. In fact, we produce it, and we produce it as a consequence of engaging in knowledge processes that have regularity to them. Once we learn to recognize and expect this regularity, we can then have impact on an organization's capacity to produce and integrate knowledge by making a range of interventions aimed at supporting, strengthening, and reinforcing related patterns of behavior. This, then, is the fundamental outlook held by practitioners of second-generation KM, and the KLC is their most important touchstone.

Knowledge Management versus Knowledge Processing

Armed with an understanding of the knowledge life cycle, we can now make the very important distinction between knowledge pro-

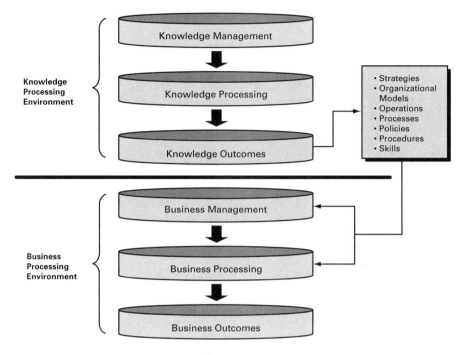

Figure 1-2

The Relationship Between Knowledge Processing and
Business Processing

cessing and knowledge management. At an organizational level, people and groups engage in the kinds of activities encompassed by the KLC. We call this knowledge processing. Knowledge processing includes *knowledge production* and *knowledge integration*, the two major areas of activity within the KLC, as well as their subprocesses. In fact, we can also think of knowledge processing as occurring within the lower levels of scale encompassed by the KLC, namely *individual and group learning*. Individuals and groups also engage in knowledge processing and experience their own knowledge life cycles, accordingly. In this sense, their KLCs are nested within the organizational KLC (a concept that will be discussed further below).

Knowledge management, then, is a management discipline that seeks to have impact on knowledge processing (see Figure 1-3). While the distinction between KM and knowledge processing is a critically important one, the two are constantly being confused with one

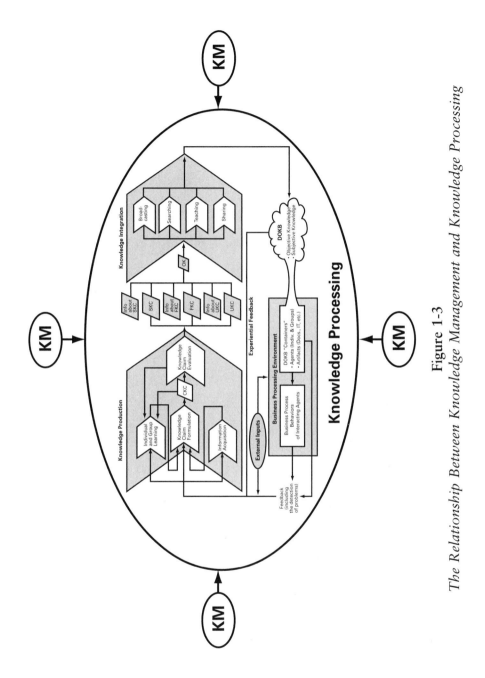

Figure 1-3

The Relationship Between Knowledge Management and Knowledge Processing

another in the marketplace. Designing a portal to enhance knowledge sharing is an act of knowledge management, because it seeks to have impact on an aspect of knowledge processing as defined by the KLC, namely *knowledge integration*. But knowledge sharing is not the same thing as knowledge management. Nor is engaging with others in, say, a community of practice a form of knowledge management. Rather, engaging in a community of practice is a form of *individual and group learning*, a subprocess of *knowledge production*, which, in turn, is a form of knowledge processing.

This distinction between KM and knowledge processing is crucial to understanding the meaning and perspective of second-generation KM because without it, there really is no differentiation between first- and second-generation thinking. In first-generation thinking, there is no KLC, no foundational view of knowledge processing, no social process with regularity to it that accounts for *knowledge production* and *integration* in firms, and no conception, therefore, of KM as something which *has an impact on* knowledge processing. What there is, by contrast, is an assumption that valuable knowledge already exists, and the sooner we get it into the hands of the people who need it, the better.

Ironically, when viewed from the perspective of the KLC, first-generation thinkers are essentially focusing only on the *knowledge integration* side of the cycle, although they might not think of their work in these terms. Moreover, they tend to think of the problem as one of how best to capture, codify, and deploy valuable organizational knowledge. Victory is seen as that pivotal moment in the performance of a business process when a worker suddenly develops a need for information and is quickly able to find it, thanks to the quality of the "KM system." It's all about making the delivery of information successful in support of individual business decisions. First-generation KM is very transactional, in this sense.

Unfortunately, this interpretation of KM has done nothing but confuse the business world for years now, since what's really going on in the scenario above is just information integration (i.e., information or knowledge capture, deployment, and retrieval) and not knowledge management, much less knowledge processing. As discussed earlier, knowledge differs from information by virtue of the strength contained in the claims about claims (metaclaims). If a knowledge processing system lacks metaclaims of a sort that can tell us what the value, performance history, or veracity of its information or knowledge claims are, even as it purports to be a knowledge management system, it really is no more than an information-processing system. And all efforts to build and deploy it, therefore, are merely acts of information management, not knowledge management.

If, on the other hand, a system is developed in such a way that the information or claims contained in it are accompanied by evaluative metaclaims, the presence of such information can give users access to the arguments *behind* the claims, in which case we're now dealing with a knowledge processing system. All efforts to build systems of that kind could, therefore, be fairly described as knowledge management efforts, but the systems themselves are knowledge processing systems, not knowledge management systems, except in the case where they also support knowledge processing by knowledge managers.

Does this mean that information processing and information management have no role to play in knowledge processing? Of course not. Researching and accessing information (i.e., *information acquisition*) plays a significant role in *knowledge production*, as clearly shown in the KLC in Figure 1-1. But we should not confuse knowledge processing and information processing with each other, and we should certainly not view the knowledge manager's work as done simply because we've made information more generally accessible through technology interventions and otherwise. All of that in the absence of validation information (metaclaims) is nothing more than information management and information processing. Knowledge managers should never forget this.

SUPPLY-SIDE VERSUS DEMAND-SIDE KNOWLEDGE MANAGEMENT

As I have explained, the hallmark of first-generation KM is its overwhelming emphasis on the capture, codification, and distribution of existing knowledge throughout an organization. This accounts for the heavy use of technology in most first-generation initiatives. Groupware, information indexing and retrieval systems, repositories, data warehousing, document management, and imaging systems are all classic answers to the prevailing ailments that first-generation KM strategies are designed to address: *inadequate knowledge sharing*.

All of these measures are seen as superior to serendipity or manual efforts when it comes to propagating knowledge from one part of the organization to another. Enhance the transfer of knowledge, first-generation KM practitioners argue, and better organizational performance will follow.

KM interventions aimed solely at the enhancement of knowledge sharing, or integration, can be thought of as "supply-side" in their orientation because of their focus on enhancing the supply of existing knowledge to people who need it. In other words, supply-side KM focuses only on the *knowledge integration* side of the KLC (see Figure 1-4).

"Demand-side KM" takes a distinctly different point of view. Rather than place its bets on the downstream effects of codifying and sharing *existing* knowledge, demand-side advocates suggest, instead, that accelerating the production of *new* knowledge is a far more valuable proposition. Practitioners of demand-side KM are, therefore, mainly interested in enhancing an organization's capacity to satisfy its *demands* for new knowledge. As a result, demand-side KM initiatives focus on enhancing the conditions in which innovation and creativity naturally occur—they focus, that is, on the *knowledge production* side of the KLC (see Figure 1-4).

Helping organizations to create new knowledge faster (i.e., to accelerate their rate of innovation) is seen by demand-side thinkers as a powerful new way of increasing a firm's competitive stance in the marketplace. This message has not been lost on practitioners of second-generation KM. In fact, whereas first-generation KM can be thought of as equivalent to supply-side thinking only, practitioners of second-generation KM embrace *both* supply-and demand-side KM, thereby bringing a considerably more balanced view to the table (see Figure 1-5).

NESTED KNOWLEDGE DOMAINS

The knowledge life cycle shown in Figure 1-1 is "expressed" at the level of an organization. In other words, it depicts the dynamics of knowledge production, integration, and use at a *whole enterprise* level. Embedded within the organizational process, however, are individuals and groups who also learn, and whose patterns of learning may also be described as a KLC. Indeed, *individual and group learning*, per se, is explicitly shown as a subprocess in *knowledge pro-*

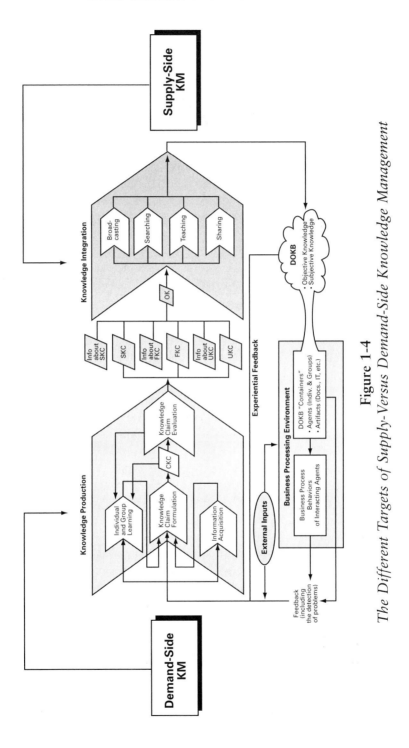

Figure 1-4

The Different Targets of Supply-Versus Demand-Side Knowledge Management

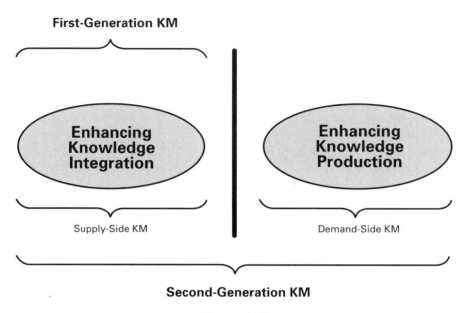

Figure 1-5
First-Versus Second-Generation Knowledge Management

duction since *their* learning contributes in material and often determinative ways to the direction of organizational learning.

What this means is that there are really three levels of learning or *knowledge domains* in an organization: the top-level organization or enterprise; subgroups within the organization; and individuals, some of whom may be members of groups while others are not. Individuals are nested in groups, and groups are nested in organizations (see Figure 1-6). As a result, the *individual and group learning* subprocess in *knowledge production* actually contains many lower-level KLCs, which in some organizations may number in the thousands, if not more. Still, second-generation KM is primarily concerned with the KLC operating at the level of the enterprise, but it recognizes the presence of lower-level KLCs and explicitly takes them into account in the formulation of its strategies and interventions.

It is also not only true that each knowledge domain in a system has its own KLC, but also its own independent outcomes. In other words, what's true for me (my validated knowledge claims) may not be true for you, because we each have our own separate KLCs,

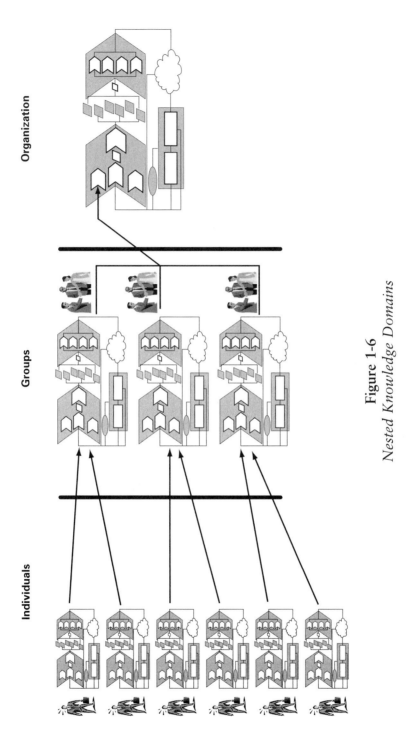

Figure 1-6
Nested Knowledge Domains

and my validation criteria may differ from yours. Savvy knowledge managers know this. When crafting KM strategies at an organizational level, it is often helpful to begin by acknowledging the presence of multiple KLCs, each of which may have its own *knowledge claim evaluation* criteria. How can we expect people and groups in organizations to agree with one another without at least attempting to rationalize our KLCs and the potentially conflicting criteria we use in evaluating knowledge claims—even when we're dealing with the *same* knowledge claims? Here again, use of the KLC as a reference model for planning KM interventions can really pay off, since if it were not for the presence of the *knowledge claim evaluation* subprocess in the context of nested knowledge domains, we might fail to even acknowledge the issue as one that we should be focusing on.

Containers of Knowledge

As noted above, the DOKB shown in Figure 1-1 manifests itself in the *business processing environment* in the form of what we can think of as "containers" of knowledge. These containers are made up of agents (individuals and groups) and artifacts (documents, books, computer systems, etc.). Knowledge held by agents is subjectively held in minds, whereas knowledge held in artifacts is objectively held in the form of explicit, encoded linguistic expressions. When we view knowledge in this way, we can think of everyday expressions of knowledge in organizations in the ways shown in Table 1-1.

The significance of *containers of knowledge*, when viewed from this perspective, is that they hold and reflect the knowledge claims we produce in our KLCs. In addition, they can be seen as the interface between knowledge processing outcomes (the DOKB) and the business processing environment in which decisions and actions are taken by people in their work. The containers perspective is also important because it can serve as a basis for discovering and mapping knowledge.

Organizational Learning

Perhaps the most striking distinction between first- and second-generation KM is the explicit connection now being drawn between

Table 1-1
Containers of Knowledge

Instantiations of Knowledge	Examples	Objective	Subjective
1. Personally-held beliefs in an individual (mind)	An opinion		•
2. Mutually-held beliefs in a group (of minds)	A business process		•
3. Mutually-held beliefs in an organization (of minds)	A business strategy		•
4. Claims expressed in written form	A report	•	
5. Claims expressed in computers	An e-mail	•	
6. Claims expressed in audio-visual form	A documentary	•	
7. Claims expressed orally in person	A speech	•	

second-generation thinking and organizational learning (OL). Popularized by Peter Senge in his hugely influential book, *The Fifth Discipline* (1990),[5] OL has attracted an enormous following and is widely regarded as a reference to the only sustainable advantage in business: *the ability to learn faster than your competitors*. OL, therefore, focuses on how to create and foster effective *knowledge processing environments* in human social systems. Second-generation KM, in turn, is all about beefing up an organization's ability to do just that—to learn, and to learn effectively in sustainable ways.

I like to think of second-generation KM, then, as a management discipline that focuses on enhancing organizational learning. In other words, second-generation KM is an *implementation strategy for organizational learning*. Knowledge management and Senge's OL movement have much to gain by embracing this convergence of thinking, the combination of which is much greater than the sum of its parts. What a fitting tribute to Senge's OL ideas—which after all, highlight holistic *systems thinking* as the *fifth* discipline. Aiming our interventions at the entire KLC, not just some of its parts, is nothing if not systems thinking in the finest tradition. But rather than using systems thinking *for* learning in the Sengian sense, second-generation KM uses it to describe a vision *of* learning. *The KLC is a systems-thinking representation of how learning happens in human social systems!*

The Open Enterprise

To the extent that the KLC, or knowledge processing, comprises a social system, it will invariably have a political dimension to it. For example, in contemplating the execution of knowledge processing in a firm, we could reasonably ask the following questions:

- Who's responsible for the detection of problems and opportunities in the business processing environment?
- Who gets to engage in *knowledge claim formulation* on behalf of the organization? Everyone? Senior management only?
- Whose opinions matter in *knowledge claim evaluation*?
- What responsibility does management have to reveal its knowledge claims and the reasoning behind them before adopting them into practice?
- What rights do nonmanagement workers have in a firm to participate in, or at least have visibility within, management's deliberations over competing knowledge claims?

With these kinds of questions in mind, we can easily imagine knowledge processing environments that might be more or less open to including the broader population of a firm when it comes to *knowledge claim formulation, evaluation,* and adoption by management. The more restrictive management is in the conduct of its knowledge processing affairs, the more "closed" a firm would be; the more inclusive management is, the more "open" a firm would be. Moreover, we could further surmise that *openness* is a better policy, since it tends to result in the adoption of stronger, more rigorously tested knowledge claims, even as it engages the knowledge processing power of *whole firms.* I like to think of this in terms of the difference between *enterprise-wide innovation* and *management-wide innovation.* Enterprise-wide is better.

In their fully elaborated, native, self-organizing form, knowledge processing systems, or KLCs, are politically open—utterly so. Here, democratic approaches where everyone has a say in what gets done is the norm. In business organizations, however, we tend to see less open knowledge processing going on, with knowledge-making being relegated to the hands of managers, who also hold power over decision-making. But political control over decision-making need not restrict access to knowledge making to only the hands of decision-makers. Rather, we can envision organizations in which knowledge processing is more open to the populace, so to speak, even as decision-making authority is not.

Some of us in the field of second-generation KM are beginning to refer to this vision of openness in the KLC as the "open enterprise," or OE, for short. In particular, I and several members of KMCI, including Joseph M. Firestone and Mark A. Notturno, have started to formulate this idea in further detail. To be sure, the idea of the OE is firmly rooted in the philosophy of Karl Popper,[6] whose notion of the "open society" followed from his adherence to what he called "critical rationalism," an approach to learning and knowledge production that stresses the fallibility of knowledge. Since all knowledge is fallible, Popper felt that we should be *rationally open* to criticism of the views that we hold dear and never constrain inquiry. As another great early twentieth-century philosopher, Charles Sanders Peirce, put it, "Do not block the way of inquiry."[7] Think of this as the motto of the open enterprise.

In his very fine book, *Science and the Open Society*,[8] Mark Notturno explains the ethic of *openness* in this way:

We are rational to the extent that we are open to criticism, including self criticism; and to the extent to which we are willing to change our beliefs when confronted with what we judge to be good criticism.[9]

Turning back to organizations or businesses, we can ask ourselves what openness would look like in the conduct of commercial affairs—knowledge processing affairs, that is. As I write this essay, the United States is still reeling from the largest bankruptcy in American history: the collapse of the Enron Corporation. Although time will tell what really happened there, early indications suggest that far from being a surprise, Enron's overreliance on dubious accounting practices was known by several members in the firm, but was suppressed by others in higher positions of power. "What if the broader population of Enron's executives, workers, and stockholders had been privy to its shenanigans?" one might ask. Would things have gotten as far as they did? Or would the behaviors that ultimately cost the company its survival, and its employees and stockholders their nest eggs, have been nipped in the bud early on?

In the wake of Enron's demise, talk of new regulatory interventions aimed at preventing this sort of thing from happening again is boiling in the press. Most of the ideas being considered will in all likelihood lead to constructive outcomes, but at the same time they arguably fail to address the core problem that led to Enron's collapse—a restricted KLC! Again, as Mark Notturno put it, "We are rational to the extent that we are open to criticism." And so we might speculate that Enron, from a cultural point of view, was irrational to the extent that it failed to allow itself to benefit from the well-meaning criticisms of its own people. Indeed, accusations have been made that management there went so far as to deprive its *own people* of access to information concerning its management decisions, even within the ranks of management itself.

In response to the Enrons of the world, KMCI has started working on a policy specification that would seek to ensure openness, not in the *decision-making* process of a firm, for that would unduly interfere with its operation, but in its *knowledge-making* process. In other words, we are starting to formulate *a normative model for openness in the KLC*. Of particular interest to us are steps that could be taken by management and the board of directors in a corporation to ensure that there is sufficient openness in the *knowledge claim formulation* and *knowledge claim evaluation* subprocesses of the KLC. Openness, in this sense, would not in any way undermine the authority of a management regime, but would merely subject its ideas and plans to the bright light of day. Workers, stockholders, and other stakeholders in a firm would have access not only to the knowledge claims held by managers, but also to the knowledge processes through which management knowledge is produced.

Examples of concrete steps that companies could take in pursuit of the open enterprise, or OE, might include the implementation of what I call "free employee presses," or FEPs. An FEP would be a publication in which employees' views on opinions held and decisions made by managers could be constructively aired in an open way. Access to the FEP would be possible for all employees, as well as by board members and stockholders, whose vested interests in the quality of management thinking and decision-making would be well served by such institutions. Of course, this kind of visibility of management should help to prevent the suppression of information and the temptations of unscrupulous managers to keep illicit or dubious behaviors secret in the first place.

But then there's the problem of retribution. How would we prevent managers from taking retaliatory actions against their subordinates who openly disagree with or criticize them in print? In a recent exchange on this very question, Joseph M. Firestone made the following very interesting proposal:[10]

The Managers, the Board, and the stockholders must all agree to accept and support the defining specifications of the OE. Among the defining characteristics will be agreement on the part of Managers, the Board, and stockholders, that they will maintain and support a hands-off policy toward interference with, or punishment of, peer-group-directed communications in any venue (Communities of Practice, FEP, List Serve, Chat Room, etc.) designated as an OE venue when it first receives management approval. Management should specifically be denied the authority to manage such venues once they are formed, and a specific institution reporting directly to the Board and the stockholders, the Ombudsman's office, should be established with enough resources to study the pattern of punishments and rewards given to participants in the knowledge-making venues, as compared with the pattern of punishments and rewards given to nonparticipants.

The CKO [Chief Knowledge Officer]/Ombudsman should also have the duty of, as well as the resources for, hearing complaints for retributive actions performed by managers, and for binding arbitration of such disputes. The Ombudsman, who would have the authority to recommend dismissal of Managers for violation of the non-retribution policies to higher management, to the Board, and even to the stockholders, would not be responsible to Management in any way for his or her employment, but would serve only at the pleasure of the stockholders, as the Board does.

One of the elements of this proposal that I particularly like is its implication that the KM function might report to the board in a corporation and not to its management hierarchy. I have been making this point myself in recent years, and have pointed out that a management hierarchy, along with all of its strategies, operating models, and policies, is nothing more than a collection of knowledge claims that are temporal—and fallible—in scope. To subject knowledge management to the control of a current management regime is a little bit like putting the Pope in charge of enforcing religious openness. Management and strategy *follow* from knowledge processing, not the reverse. The KM function should be positioned accordingly.

Another aspect of an OE, one that is already practiced by many companies around the world in the form of "co-determination" programs (i.e., management schemes in which employees play a role in their own supervision), might be to populate the board with one or more employee representatives elected by their peers. Here again, the objective is openness in *knowledge production*, and by permitting employee representatives to sit on its board, a company can avail itself of the knowledge claim contributions of its entire population—a population that is often disenfranchised from the knowledge production process altogether.

It will be interesting to see where KMCI's conception of the OE ends up in its final form. Again, it is still very much in its formative stages. Nonetheless, it does point to the potential for a very real value that second-generation KM can bring to the table, but which first-generation thinking cannot: *higher quality knowledge processing in commercial firms, and a reduction in management malpractice, errors, and deceit.*

SOCIAL INNOVATION CAPITAL

Even as the professions of knowledge management and organizational learning have been evolving along their own parallel, and sometimes intersecting, paths over the past ten years, so was the exploding new field of intellectual capital (IC) finding its own way into the world. What initially caused interest in this important new field of management was the sudden appearance of widening disparities in company values, as measured by the gaps between their market capitalizations and their book values. Starting roughly in the late 1950s, the gap between these values, as displayed by the Dow Jones Industrials, started to widen significantly (see Figure 1-7). The difference between them is now generally attributed to the

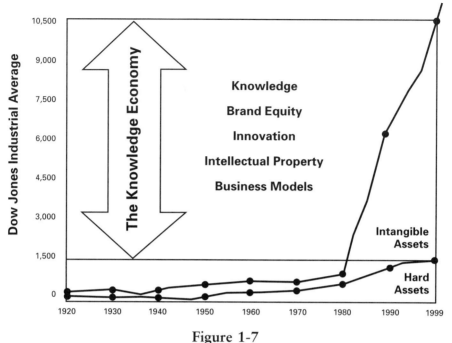

Figure 1-7
New Economic Models: Book Value and Market Value[11]

value of so-called "intangibles," which is at least inclusive of intellectual capital, depending on whose definition of the term you subscribe to.

Since today's generally accepted accounting principles (GAAP) do not provide for the measurement and reporting of intellectual or intangible capital, what most of the discussion in the IC arena has been all about is how to do just that: *measure and report on the value of intellectual capital.* Suffice it to say that the accounting profession's failure to, well, *account* for the value of what many publicly-traded firms are, in fact, worth has been seen by many as untenable. And so the work continues to try and find a standardized way of solving this problem.

Like many others in the fields of KM and OL, I am quite content to defer to the accounting profession to work this out, but according to my own review of the literature in this area, something of enormous importance has been missing: the KLC! In other words, what most, if not all, of the competing views on how to measure and report intellectual capital have failed to do is to reflect the enormous value of a firm's capacity to produce and integrate its knowledge. To my mind, this is a kind of *social capital*. It refers to an organization's social capacity to innovate (i.e., to produce and integrate new knowledge) as a component of its value. I call this form of social capital "social innovation capital," or SIC.

Since first-generation KM always begins with the view that valuable knowledge exists, there is no social process in first-generation thinking that we can put our fingers on and point to as a source of value in a firm. There is only the value of knowledge outcomes (or *knowledge*), which when properly codified and deployed to a worker confers value to the organization by virtue of his or her successful performance. Only second-generation KM, with its view of knowledge processing as a social process unto itself, can speak in coherent terms about the value of *knowledge production* and *integration* as important considerations in computing the IC value of a firm. After all, the only thing more valuable than valuable intellectual capital is the organizational capacity to produce it!

IC measurement and reporting schemes that fail to take SIC into account (i.e., by failing to explicitly reflect the economic value of the KLC in their taxonomies) are arguably incomplete, and are just another vestige of first-generation thinking spilling over into the field of corporate accounting. It is encouraging to note, however, that many in the field of IC have come to regard ignoring SIC as a serious oversight, thanks to the lessons learned from second-generation KM.

SELF-ORGANIZATION AND COMPLEXITY THEORY

Most of the ideas expressed in this paper are firmly rooted in complexity theory. Now seen as a valuable source of insight in understanding how living systems function—including human organizations—the science of complexity has a great deal to say about the nature and role of learning in the conduct of human affairs. Indeed, second-generation KM owes much of its thinking to complexity theory.

Complex Adaptive System (CAS) Model

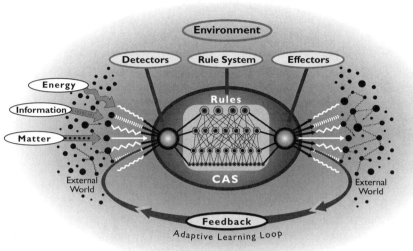

Figure 1-8
Complex Adaptive System (CAS) Model[14]

Of particular relevance in the *science* of complexity is a body of thought known as *complex adaptive systems theory*, or CAS theory.[12] CAS theory holds that living systems (i.e., organizations made up of living, independent agents, such as people) self-organize and continuously fit themselves, individually and collectively, to ever-changing conditions in their environment.[13] They do this, the theory says, by (in our terms) formulating and testing their beliefs and belief predispositions (theories and "mental models") as a way of solving their problems and getting on in life (see Figure 1-8).

Knowledge (in the form of theories and "mental models"), according to CAS theory, can be represented by "rules" that agents (or *people*, in our case) follow in their ongoing attempts to adapt themselves successfully to their environment. Rules, in this sense, are roughly equivalent to our notions of beliefs and belief predispositions. CAS theory, then, is one of the important theoretical foundations behind second-generation KM and its concepts of the *knowledge life cycle, knowledge processing, knowledge claims, knowledge in the mind* (*beliefs and belief predispositions*), and *containers of knowledge*. Moreover, living systems are *nothing* if not *learning organizations*. Understanding how knowledge forms at the level of individual agents and then influences knowledge processing at the level of *the collective* to produce shared organizational knowledge is a lesson taken directly from complexity theory. So, too, is the notion of *nested knowledge domains*, which CAS theory sees as organisms or groups within groups, each of which is capable of evolving its own sets of rules through its own KLC. Indeed, KLCs are fractals.

The application of complexity theory to a broad range of business and organizational development issues is widening in practice. Examples include the New England Complex Systems Institute in Cambridge, MA, whose members have been actively studying the application of complexity and CAS theory to the management of human organizations for years now. Major corporations have also risen to the occasion by investing in dedicated resources, such as Citibank's Complexity and Organizational Behavior Project, to explore and embrace ways of applying complexity's lessons to the management of their affairs. Even the *Wall Street Journal*, thanks to the pioneering efforts of journalist Tom Petzinger, has closely followed the trajectory of complexity theory as practiced by business since the mid-1990s.[15]

But it wasn't until 1997, when the Knowledge Management Consortium International (KMCI) was formed that the profound connections between complexity theory and knowledge management were agressively fleshed out. By simply agreeing to treat human organizations as living systems—consistent with CAS theory's definition of *complex adaptive systems*—all of the theory's insights on how knowledge *happens* in such systems were suddenly seen as entirely applicable to business and industry. Readers of this book should make no mistake about it: *practitioners of second-generation KM believe that people in organizations tend to self-organize around the production, diffusion, and use of knowledge*, and the KLC is the pattern of organizational behavior that follows. It's an emergent property of human social systems. This insight, coupled with the influence of organizational learning on KM, accounts for the strikingly new and different brand of *second-generation knowledge management* that we now see before us—a practitioner's framework firmly rooted in the study of *complex adaptive behaviors* in living systems.

Sustainable Innovation

In my discussion of social innovation capital above, I stated that "the only thing more valuable than valuable intellectual capital is the organizational capacity to produce it!" In truth, however, there is one other thing more valuable to an organization than its social capacity to innovate, and that is *its social capacity to innovate sustainably.* What do I mean by this? Again, we can turn to the KLC for guidance.

According to second-generation thinking, not only is knowledge processing a social process, it is a *self-organizing* one. In other words, people in organizations tend to self-organize around the production, integration, and use of new knowledge. Further, I have argued that patterns form between people at an enterprise-wide level as they do so. Individuals engage in *information acquisition*; groups or communities form; knowledge claims are produced; some claims are validated and others are not; validated claims go on to become integrated within the organization via a variety of means; and so on. These and other aspects of the KLC are self-organizing in their ontogeny, but they are no less predictable in terms of their emergence. People engaged in problem-solving and learning at an organizational level invariably tend toward the behaviors portrayed by the KLC.

One of second-generation KM's fundamental precepts is the claim that because knowledge processing is a self-organizing social process with patterned regularity—of a sort that people in organizations involved in problem-solving and learning ineluctably *tend toward*—KM interventions aimed at supporting such patterns will always lead to more sustainable innovation than those that do not. Why? Because their intended outcomes are consistent with what the predispositional tendencies of the target system already happen to be. This is a simple matter of either *working with the system or against it.*

Fortunately, but not surprisingly, the behavioral tendency of interest here is a desirable one. We *want* people in organizations to focus on solving problems when they occur, and to collaborate with one another in the search for solutions. This is consistent with the pattern displayed by the KLC. KM interventions designed to enhance the pattern, therefore, are arguably more sustainable than those that do not. And they are certainly more sustainable than KM schemes that result in *conflicts* with the KLC. Conflicts of what sort, you may ask?

Let us turn again to Enron. What managers at most companies fail to do—and especially at Enron, it seems—is to distinguish between decision-making and knowledge-making. We explored this issue above in the discussion of the open enterprise, but it has everything to do with the sustainability of knowledge processing or innovation as well. Decision-making on behalf of a firm is the province of managers; there's no question about that. To challenge that premise would be to compromise the stability and effectiveness of private firms, and that is certainly not my intent. But to restrict knowledge processing, or knowledge making, to the hands of managers is sheer folly. More important, it is utterly unsustainable because it conflicts with the knowledge processing tendencies of whole firms and the people who inhabit them.

This is arguably what happened at Enron, although time will tell. The initial record, however, suggests that knowledge of Enron's dubious accounting practices was held close to the vest by its senior managers, and was therefore not open to scrutiny by such interested stakeholders as its board, employees, and stockholders. In other words, Enron was practicing knowledge produced by a small band of leaders, whose claims had not been subjected to anything close to the openness specified by an open enterprise model, much less the bright light of day. And even when objections were raised concerning the validity of such practices, *that* part of the KLC was closed—decision- *and* knowledge-making authority were together confined to a small band of leaders, and the rest, of course, is history.

Successfully managing for sustainable innovation, then, begins with recognition of the distinction between *decision-making* (the province of management) and *knowledge-making* (everyone's job). Next is acknowledging the self-organizing nature of knowledge processing systems, a pattern-like social process that we can describe by the KLC. And finally, we can achieve sustainable innovation by choosing learning-related policies and programs that serve only to support, strengthen, and reinforce the KLC. Anything less than this is ultimately unsustainable because it conflicts with the intrinsic tendency of organizations to innovate in their own particular ways.

This is what we mean by sustainable innovation, an insight unique to second-generation KM whose lineage, however, is deeply rooted in organizational learning and complex adaptive systems theory.

Endnotes

1. This chapter was originally published in October, 1999, as an article under the same title, but has been substantially edited since then to reflect changes in the industry. M. W. McElroy, "The Second Generation of Knowledge Management," *Knowledge Management* (October, 1999), pp. 86–88.

2. M. W. McElroy, "The Second Generation of Knowledge Management," *Knowledge Management* (October, 1999), pp. 86–88.

3. The KLC was developed by members of the Knowledge Management Consortium International (KMCI), a U.S.-based nonprofit association of knowledge and innovation management professionals from around the world (www.kmci.org).

4. K. R. Popper, *Objective Knowledge* (Oxford: Oxford University Press, 1972), Chapter 3.

5. P. M. Senge, *The Fifth Discipline* (New York: Currency Doubleday, 1990).

6. K. R. Popper, *The Open Society and Its Enemies* (London: Reprinted by Routledge, 1998).

7. C. Hartshorne and P. Weiss, editors, *Collected Papers of Charles Saunders Peirce* (Cambridge, MA: Harvard University Press, 1931–1958), pp. 135–140.

8. M. A. Notturno, *Science and the Open Society* (Budapest: Central European University Press, 2000).

9. Ibid., p. xxv.

10. This proposal was made by Joseph M. Firestone by e-mail in an online discussion group moderated by the Knowledge Management Consortium International (kmci-virtual-chapter@yahoogroups.com) in February, 2002.

11. Adapted from William L. Miller and Langdon Morris, *Fourth Generation R & D: Managing Knowledge, Technology, and Innovation* (New York: John Wiley & Sons, 2000), Figure I.1, page xiii; base data from Value Line Publishing, Inc. Used by permission of Langdon Morris.

12. See, for example, J. H. Holland, *Hidden Order: How Adaptation Builds Complexity* (Reading, MA: Perseus Books, 1995).

13. See, for example, R. D. Stacey, *Complexity and Creativity in Organizations* (San Francisco: Berrett-Koehler Publishers, 1996).

14. This illustration was created by Marshall Clemens of Idiagram Co. in Lincoln, MA (www.idiagram.com).

15. For a collection of Tom Petzinger's articles written on related subjects, see T. Petzinger, Jr., *The New Pioneers* (New York: Simon & Schuster, 1999).

2

INTEGRATING COMPLEXITY THEORY, KNOWLEDGE MANAGEMENT, AND ORGANIZATIONAL LEARNING[1]

In what's shaping up to be an unusual and fascinating case of strange bedfellows, three otherwise separate communities of management practice are about to converge. Without knowing it, all three share an intrinsically codependent view of the hot new field of *knowledge management* (KM), the latest rage in business.

Variously referred to as *intellectual capital, intellectual property, knowledge assets,* or *business intelligence,* corporate knowledge is now being viewed as the last and *only* sustainable untapped source of competitive advantage in business. Unlike other forms of capital—land, equipment, labor, and money—knowledge is theoretically infinite. There's always a new idea waiting to be discovered: new ways of doing things, new products, new strategies, new markets. Getting to the next important discovery *first*, then, is the aim of knowledge management.

The three communities involved in this meeting of the minds are: (1) the burgeoning KM community itself; (2) advocates of organizational learning and systems thinking; and (3) supporters of complexity theory and its application to business. What makes the imminent convergence of these three groups so interesting is that each has much to gain from it, but none of them seems to see it coming. With heads down and blinders attached, each has been wrestling with its own narrow scope of interest, rarely stopping to consider cross-disciplinary possibilities. But this is beginning to change.

In a recent interview in *Knowledge Management Magazine*,[2] Peter Senge, creator of the organizational learning movement and author of the hugely influential book *The Fifth Discipline*,[3] was asked about the emerging connection between two of these three areas: knowledge management and *organizational learning* (OL). Senge had previously viewed knowledge management as little more than information indexing and retrieval, but he now sees a new definition emerging. In its new form, Senge sees knowledge management as attempting to address "some of the same critical issues [that the Society of Organizational Learning] members have been struggling with—the sustainable creation, transfer, and dissipation of organizational knowledge."[4]

When asked to comment on the challenges that lie ahead for both communities (KM and OL), Senge posed the following questions:

What is the nature of organizational knowledge, how is it generated, how is it diffused, what does it mean to develop more knowledge-based strategies? What happens at the interface between acquiring information and generating knowledge? These are issues that are deep and hardly trivial by any stretch.[5]

Enter complexity theory.

In what has only recently become apparent, the issues Senge speaks of are precisely those that scholars and researchers of complexity theory have been dealing with for the past fifteen years. Chief among them have been John H. Holland, Keith J. Holyoak, Richard E. Nisbett, and Paul R. Thagard, whose collaborative work, *Induction*:

Processes of Inference, Learning and Discovery,[6] was not only a towering achievement in the study of complexity, but also contained explicit answers to the kinds of questions more recently posed by Senge.

Complex (living) systems are, by any other definition, *learning organizations*. Complexity theory is, therefore, on the verge of making a huge contribution to both KM and OL. But what in particular makes the impending merger of these three communities so compelling? What could account for the apparent synergy between them? The answer to both questions is that each of the three groups has something that the other two desperately need. There's an idea at stake here that's bigger than any one of them can defend alone, or even two of them together. It takes all three to make it work. Knowledge management and organizational learning each lack a theory of how cognition happens in human social systems—complexity theory provides the missing piece.

Like Ships Passing in the Night

"Complexifiers"

The time was October, 1998. Only a few short blocks from Boston Harbor, in the elegant digs of the Swissotel, members of the COMPLEX-M contingent of the New England Complex Systems Institute (NECSI) gathered for the third time in less than a year to continue their intensive study of complexity theory. This eclectic, three-year-old group of business leaders, consultants, scientists, and academics featured an international cast of "complexifiers," people who share an abiding interest in the new science they simply call "complexity."

What distinguished the COMPLEX-M group from the rest of NECSI was its singular focus on the application of complexity theory to the management of human social systems (the "M" stood for management). From where they sat, human organizations were just another class of complex systems prone to the same kinds of behaviors found in, say, weather patterns or animal populations in the wild. Businesses are living systems, they argued, and should be managed accordingly (see Figure 2-1).

Complex Adaptive System (CAS) Model

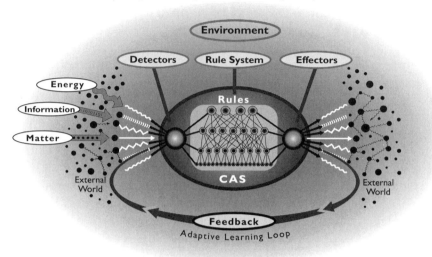

Figure 2-1

Complex Adaptive System (CAS) Model.[7] This model of complex adaptive systems (CAS) was taken from the Internet website of the New England Complex Systems Institute (www.necsi.org). Of particular interest in its representation of complex living systems is the role played by knowledge as portrayed by the "rule system" and the rules it produces. As the system encounters incoming stimuli from its environment (information, energy, or matter), it fashions its response by invoking pertinent knowledge contained in its rule sets. Actions then taken, if any, produce effects within the system itself or externally, the results of which are fed back into the system for immediate and future reference. Rules, or knowledge, are refreshed in the process. Feedback and rules in the science of complexity, then, are strikingly similar to the roles played by "experiential feedback" and "organizational knowledge," as conceived in emerging knowledge management models (see Figure 2-2). Indeed, the subject in both cases is identical: the ontology of learning in living systems.

Complexity theory—or, to be more precise, the *science of complexity*—is the study of emergent order in what are otherwise very disorderly systems. Spirals in whirlpools, funnels in tornadoes, flocks of birds, schools of fish—these are all examples of orderly behavior in systems that are neither centrally planned nor centrally controlled. How and why such coherence emerges in complex systems is a mystery. Nevertheless, understanding its influence on the performance of human organizations could lead to major gains in the conduct of human affairs, especially business.

Complexity studies indicate that the most creative phase of a system, that is, the point at which emergent behaviors inexplicably arise, lies somewhere between order and chaos. Stuart Kauffman of the Santa Fe Institute points out that complex systems produce their most inventive displays in the region of behavior he calls "the edge of chaos."[8] Systems operating in the vicinity of *the edge* exhibit wild bursts of creativity and produce new and novel behaviors at the level of the whole system. Whirlpools spring forth, birds flock in patterns, and whole populations of species ebb and flow accordingly.

In a sense, complex systems *innovate* by producing spontaneous, systemic bouts of novelty out of which new patterns of behavior emerge. Patterns that enhance a system's ability to adapt successfully to its environment are stabilized and repeated; those that do not are rejected in favor of radically new ones, almost as if a cosmic game of trial-and-error were being played. Complexity, therefore, is in part the study of pervasive innovation in the universe.

"KMers"

On a completely different front (again, in the fall of 1998), deep inside the cavernous halls of McCormick Place in Chicago, a business conference devoted to the exciting new field of knowledge management unfolds. This event, KM Expo, has attracted hundreds of visitors who have come to attend dozens of seminars and miles of exhibits. The prospect of leveraging human knowledge for commercial gain is on everyone's mind. To be "knowledge-based" is now all the rage in business—make no mistake, interest in knowledge management is rising fast.

Meanwhile, echoes away from the din of the show, a small group convenes in a remote part of the same building to continue the work of the Knowledge Management Consortium International (KMCI), a think tank made up of KM practitioners. Unlike their peers just a few hundred yards away, members of KMCI hold an utterly unconventional view of the subject—one largely inspired by complexity theory. To those of KMCI, a business is just another class of complex system. Managing knowledge has nothing to do with building computer-based repositories of facts and figures, they argue. Rather, knowledge is the product of natural knowledge processing behaviors (or *innovation*) found in all living systems. Create the conditions in which innovation thrives, they believe, and the evolution of new knowledge will naturally follow (see Figure 2-2).

Launched in December, 1997, KMCI has become one of the most influential think tanks in the field. What KMCI set out to do was to apply insights from complexity theory to the production and integration of knowledge in human social systems, and to develop reference models, tools, and methods that KM practitioners could apply in business as a source of competitive advantage.

"Organolearners"

The scene this time is San Francisco. The setting is the Systems Thinking in Action conference in September, 1998, which by all

---

→

Figure 2-2
The Knowledge Life Cycle (KLC).[9] *This process-based depiction of the knowledge life cycle was created by the KM Modeling Standards Committee of Knowledge Management Consortium International (KMCI), a KM think-tank in Washington, D.C. Embedded within its boundaries are two fundamental stages in the evolution of new organizational knowledge:* knowledge production *and* knowledge integration. *Notice the similarities between the role of feedback in this model and the CAS model taken from complexity theory shown in Figure 2-1. Also common to both models is the representation of knowledge as* rules *and* rule sets, *shown here in the form of organizational knowledge, or OK. A "knowledge claim," as shown in Figure 2-2, is a new belief or rule in its formative stages.*

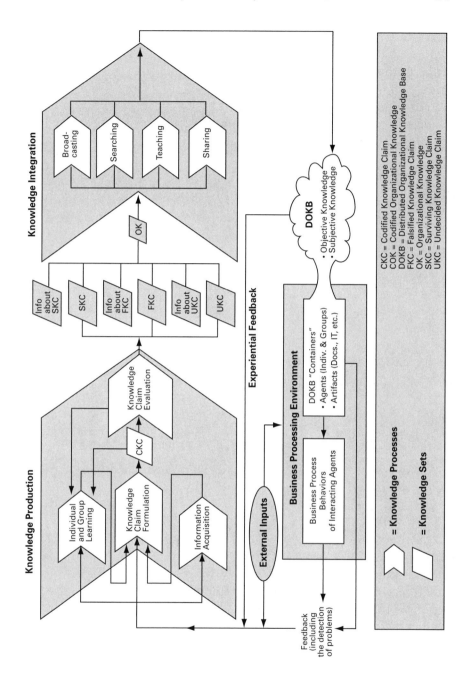

Knowledge Integration

Broad-casting
Searching
Teaching
Sharing

OK

Info about SKC
SKC
Info about FKC
FKC
Info about UKC
UKC

Knowledge Production

Knowledge Claim Evaluation

Individual and Group Learning

CKC

Knowledge Claim Formulation

Information Acquisition

External Inputs

Experiential Feedback

Business Processing Environment

DOKB "Containers"
• Agents (Indiv. & Groups)
• Artifacts (Docs., IT, etc.)

Business Process Behaviors of Interacting Agents

DOKB
• Objective Knowledge
• Subjective Knowledge

Feedback (including the detection of problems)

= Knowledge Processes

= Knowledge Sets

CKC = Codified Knowledge Claim
COK = Codified Organizational Knowledge
DOKB = Distributed Organizational Knowledge Base
FKC = Falsified Knowledge Claim
OK = Organizational Knowledge
SKC = Surviving Knowledge Claim
UKC = Undecided Knowledge Claim

accounts is the industry's premiere annual event in the field of organizational learning. Popularized by Peter Senge, OL has become one of the hottest new fields in business. According to Senge and his disciples, organizations, not just individuals, hold knowledge. We can therefore make the useful distinction, they argue, between *personal learning* and *organizational learning*. Organizations, not just individuals, actually learn (see Figure 2-3).

When compared to the *complex adaptive systems model* (Figure 2-1), the components of Kim's OADI/SMM (Observe-Assess-Design-Implement with Shared Mental Models) model correspond roughly as follows:

OADI/SMM Model	CAS Model (Figure 2-1)
■ Observe (concrete experience)	■ Detectors (sensory perception of feedback)
■ Assess (reflect on observations)	■ Rule system and rules (sense-making)
■ Design (form abstract concepts)	■ Rule system and rules (knowledge creation)
■ Implement (test concepts)	■ Effectors (locomotion, communication, action)
■ Environmental response (feedback)	■ Experiential feedback (feedback)

Although the mapping here is far from precise, the functional similarities between certain elements of Kim's organizational learning model and the complex adaptive systems model shown in Figure 2-1 are striking.

Practitioners of organizational learning, known as "organolearners," therefore see a difference between what *individuals* know and the knowledge held *collectively* by groups of individuals: individual learning leads to individual knowledge; organizational learning leads to collective knowledge. With this in mind, they explain, conflict between the two in most organizations is bound to occur. But the tension between them is actually seen as a stimulant for innovation and creativity. Older established ideas give way to newer, more effective ones as people in business, for example, attempt to resolve their individual and group differences. Organolearners, therefore, see

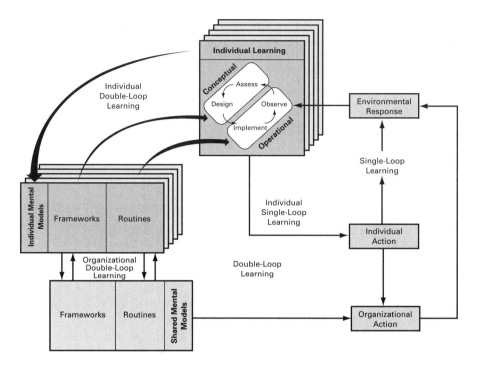

Figure 2-3
Organizational Learning Model (Source: Daniel Kim).[10] *This model is composed of two separate but related learning cycles: individual learning and organizational learning. Kim's model combines the two to convey the importance of interplay between them if learning at either level is to occur: individual learning is informed by organizational knowledge (mental models) and, conversely, organizational knowledge is produced, collectively, by individuals. This idea is similarly expressed in the KM community's view of organizational knowledge processes (see Figure 2-2), which explicitly shows the influence of* individual and group learning *on* knowledge claim formulation *in* knowledge production

constructive nonconformity as a positive force in business. Creative tension, they argue, is a prerequisite for organizational learning and innovation in human social systems.

The implications of organizational learning for business are profound. Managing to outlearn one's competitors, for example, can easily lead to better performance in the marketplace as new ideas translate into lowered costs, higher productivity, or increased revenue. Early in Senge's *The Fifth Discipline*, Arie de Geus, former head of planning for Royal Dutch Shell, eloquently makes the same point: "The ability to learn faster than your competitors may be the only sustainable competitive advantage."[11] Here, de Geus evokes a vision of knowledge as though it were a newly discovered natural resource, as indeed it is. Moreover, his words make it clear to a whole new breed of managers that knowledge and continuous learning are powerful prerequisites for business success.

TWO'S A CROWD, THREE'S COMPANY

Second-Generation Knowledge Management

The genesis of the integration between knowledge management, organizational learning, and complexity theory can be traced to recent events within the KM community alone. Of the three groups involved, only knowledge management has experienced profound changes in how it defines itself, its outlook on the fundamental nature of knowledge, and the value of its prescriptions. In the chain of events leading up to the imminent confluence of the three, this metamorphosis has clearly been the seminal event. Understanding the makeup and significance of these changes, then, is an important first step in appreciating the logic of what is about to happen.

Among the changes now taking place in the practice of knowledge management is a shift in thinking from strategies that stress *dissemination and imitation* to those that promote *problem-solving and innovation*. To date, the goal of KM has been to capture, codify, and distribute organizational knowledge (usually in centrally managed computer systems) so that it can be shared by an organization's knowledge workers in the field. By contrast, the *problem-solve and innovate* strategy, although it places no less importance on sharing and informed decision-making, grants a higher value to learning and knowledge creation. The 3M Company, for example, has a policy called the "Fifteen-Percent Rule," according to which many 3M employees are permitted to spend up to 15 percent of their time dreaming up new products, or new ways of lowering costs or increasing productivity. The result? A remarkable 40 percent of 3M's annual revenues come from products less than five years old—there's that much innovation going on there.[12]

To satisfy this shift in thinking, many practitioners of knowledge management are now turning to the organizational learning community as a source for what it means for an *organization*, not just individuals, to learn. This is a fundamentally new brand of KM, one that has shed its former preoccupation with information technology as the stock response to all knowledge management needs. Knowledge management now regards organizational learning as its new best friend, and in light of its improved, more enlightened outlook, has given itself a new name: "second-generation KM"—not to be confused with its *first-generation*, technocentric ancestry.

But while the logical combination of knowledge management and organizational learning is rapidly gaining favor in both camps, many people believe the new brand of KM has a tough row to hoe. KM efforts to date, they complain, have amounted to little more than a rehash of yesterday's information management schemes. As such, they've had little to do, if anything, with *knowledge*, per se, by any conventional definition of the term. The fact that a great many so-called knowledge management solutions have amounted to nothing more than repackaged *information retrieval systems* has provoked a discernible backlash in the marketplace. The resulting damage that first-generation KM has done to its own credibility could very well slow market acceptance of even the new, more enlightened second-generation style of practice.

Peter Senge, in expressing his own misgivings with *first-generation* KM, explained that "the first wave of knowledge management hasn't been about knowledge at all. It's about information—how to capture it, store it, retrieve it, access it and all that stuff. . . . [little more than] a great excuse to sell a lot of information technology under the guise of managing knowledge."[13] Indeed, much of current KM is merely yesterday's information technologies trotted out in today's more fashionable clothes: data warehousing, document management, imaging, and data mining. Even corporate intranets have been dragged into the fray and are now being referred to by some first-generation practitioners as "knowledge portals."

In practice, first-generation KM schemes have been solely devoted to enhancing the performance of day-to-day business processes by workers. They start by asking two very revealing questions: *What knowledge do people need to do their work? And how can we help them get it?* Both questions expose first-generation KM's narrow pre-occupation with business operations and the role of knowledge in supporting them. First-generation KM, then, can be seen as a management discipline that focuses on *knowledge operations*, or *knowledge deployment and use*. And although this focus is in no way inappropriate or of little value to the organization, it completely side-steps the question of where organizational knowledge comes from to begin with—it fails to address *how knowledge is produced.*

If a first-generation KM practitioner were asked to characterize the role of knowledge management in business, an example of the following sort might be used:

A knowledge worker is sitting at her desk performing a task, then suddenly develops a need for information to complete her work. Where does she turn? Is the knowledge readily available? How long does it take to get it? Does she tap her relationships with other workers? Has technology been effectively placed at her disposal? Is her knowledge source current? Is it complete? Was the task successfully carried out? These are the kinds of questions we wrestle with in knowledge management—it's all about *getting the right information to the right people at the right time* so they can do their jobs more effectively.

This is vintage first-generation KM thinking in action. It's all about delivering information to support a task. And it's all about individual performance in the field. The target of all investments in first-generation KM, then, is the individual worker and the extent to which he or she has access to, and can leverage, information needed to get the job done—where and when it occurs. Nowhere in this proposition is *organizational learning* mentioned, and not once is there any discussion of *knowledge production* or rule-making. Only with the arrival of *second-generation* thinking do we see an application of knowledge management to these issues. What second-generation KM offers, then, is an implementation strategy for *organizational knowledge production and learning.*

Second-generation thinking begins with the assumption that knowledge is something we produce and that innovation is a social process, not an administrative one. Understanding how knowledge is created, how it is shared and diffused throughout an organization—

and not just how to codify and record it in artificial form, or map it into business processes—lies at the very heart of the profound movement from first- to second-generation thinking. Second-generation theory subscribes to the existence of *knowledge processes* and *knowledge life cycles* in human social systems. First-generation thinking has no such foundation. Thus, second-generation practitioners have come to recognize and respect the concept of *organizational learning* and the collectively held knowledge it produces.

This dramatically revamped brand of KM points to another important distinction between first- and second-generation thinking—*supply-side* versus *demand-side* interventions.[14] Although first-generation schemes have concentrated on enhancing the "supply" of *existing* knowledge (and information) throughout the organization, second-generation strategies focus as well on helping organizations to satisfy their "demand" for *new* knowledge. One can think of this as involving an *imitate* versus *innovate* dichotomy. Supply-side schemes take the best organizational thinking (both *practiced knowledge* and *supporting information*), codify it in various forms, and then distribute it through databases, documents, training, or other methods—all of this with intentional imitation in mind. Demand-side schemes focus instead on creating and maintaining the conditions required for optimum production of new knowledge (i.e., innovation). Increasingly, both sides are coming to see the importance of a balanced approach, in which the healthy production of new knowledge *and* its effective distribution and use throughout the organization are regarded as two parts of the same cycle. Second-generation KM has been crafted accordingly.

Complexity's Killer App

Complexity theory is nothing if not *systems thinking* in practice (i.e., Senge's "fifth" discipline). Its insights into the ontogeny of knowledge in living systems, in particular, are germane to both knowledge management and organizational learning. Not surprisingly, then, telltale signs of complexity theory are beginning to appear in both disciplines. For instance, thanks to the influence of complexity theory, practitioners of second-generation KM now believe that all organizational knowledge consists of formally held *know-what knowledge* and formally held *know-how knowledge*— expressed either linguistically or behaviorally. An organization, for example, expresses its know-what knowledge by basing all of its strategies—business, market, product, distribution, sales, and other- wise—on what it believes to be true and valid about itself and the markets in which it operates. Even an organization's structure is a reflection of its know-what knowledge about how best to arrange itself. Know-what organizational knowledge, therefore, amounts to collectively-held knowledge claims on a broad range of subjects.

Similarly, business processes can be seen as nothing more than behavioral expressions of know-how knowledge: *we do WHAT we do THE WAY we do it because of our BELIEF in its VALUE com- pared to other alternatives.* But like all knowledge, procedural knowl- edge is ephemeral. Business processes are constantly being revised as new information about changing conditions in the marketplace continuously evolves. Whenever procedural knowledge is revised or refreshed, behavior and practice are modified in response. In sum, organizations do not practice information, they practice knowledge. And knowledge is forever changing.

It is precisely at this point that the importance of the impending three-way convergence presents itself in final form. The knowledge management and organizational learning communities have discov- ered each other's value. As stated earlier, second-generation KM is emerging as a kind of *implementation strategy for OL*—a tool kit for how to get there from here if what you want to be is a learning organization. But in order for this new partnership to survive the test of time, both sides must have an epistemology that they can agree on—a theory of *how* learning "happens" in human organizations, not just a shared belief in the *value of learning*. This is where com- plexity theory comes into play. Complexity offers one of the most robust and widely-subscribed-to theories on the nature and role of learning in living systems, including the manner in which knowledge evolves in human organizations. This is just the kind of paradigm that second-generation KM and OL need—an executable model that both can hang their hats on.

Complexity theory is systems thinking applied to the behavior of natural systems. Within its bounds is a framework that defines how knowledge evolves in *living* systems, a conceptual model developed more than fifteen years ago by John Holland and others, and now closely studied at the highly-acclaimed Santa Fe Institute. Complex-

ity's theory of knowledge in living systems is specifically known as *complex adaptive systems theory*, or CAS theory (pronounced, "KASS"). In discussing the similarities of adaptive behavior between, say, a metropolis, mammalian central nervous systems, ecologies, businesses, economies, and other CASs, Holland writes:[15]

Even though these complex systems differ in detail, the question of coherence under change is the central enigma for each. This common factor is so important that at the Santa Fe Institute we collect these systems under a common heading, referring to them as complex adaptive systems (CAS). This is more than terminology. It signals our intuition that general principles rule CAS behavior, principles that point to ways of solving the attendant problems.

Inside the workings of CAS theory is the key to understanding how knowledge naturally unfolds in living systems, be they human organizations or otherwise. Complexity's explication of this process, therefore, offers a solid foundation upon which practitioners of second-generation KM can build tools and techniques for use in the real world. By embracing its perspective on how learning happens in living systems, methods employed by practitioners of *both* KM and OL can be measurably improved.

For example, KMCI's knowledge life cycle, Figure 2-2, was largely inspired by the process-based view of rule-making as defined in CAS theory (see Figure 2-1). The similarity between these two models is far from coincidental. Both rely heavily on the presence of feedback loops in the formation of new knowledge, and both interpret *knowledge* as describable by *rules* and *rule sets* (shown as the *distributed organizational knowledge base*, or DOKB, in Figure 2-2). Practitioners of KM and OL have much to gain by incorporating these principles of complexity in their work. Learning to see knowledge as *rules, or claims, produced by natural knowledge processes* is an important first step. Helping businesses to enhance these processes and to measure their downstream effects on organizational learning (measured as *changes in rule, or claim, sets*) is where CAS theory can really pay off in practice.

While CAS theory was originally developed in the early 1980s, it wasn't until KMCI came along in 1997 that the connections between complexity theory and knowledge management formally gelled into the second-generation brand of KM that we now see before us. It was KMCI that first put John Holland's CAS theory and knowledge management together, recognizing that human organizations are, in the Holland sense, *complex adaptive systems*—that is, groups of independent, autonomous agents, all of whom share certain goals and operate in accordance with individually and collectively held claims.

Claims held at both levels, however, are not necessarily in harmony with one another, and the tension between them over time gives rise to the emergence of new ideas to replace old ones. Every new *idea* (or claim) that replaces an old one can be thought of as an *innovation*. Innovation outcomes that lead to changes in knowledge and practice can be thought of as *learning events*. All told, then, CAS theory offers a very clear explanation of how learning and innovation happen in living systems, in terms that both the KM and OL communities can relate to.

Several years after his ideas on complex adaptive systems first appeared in print,[16] Holland published *Hidden Order: How Adaptation Builds Complexity*.[17] Written mainly for the general reader, *Hidden Order* provided a clear and compelling explanation of how learning happens in terms that included consideration of human organizations. Holland described the complexion of CASs, how agents operate within them, and how knowledge, or rule sets, are created. Separately, Holland categorized rules held by a CAS as either declarative or procedural in form (i.e., *know-what* versus *know-how* knowledge, respectively, as discussed earlier).[18] And all knowledge, he explained, is employed by CASs in the pursuit of perpetually adaptive behavior:[19] "Adaptation, in biological usage is the process whereby an organism fits itself to its environment. Here," he continued, "we expand the term's range to include learning and related processes."

Bingo! The last shoe has been dropped.

Holland explicitly links complexity theory to knowledge management and organizational learning by pointing to "learning and related processes" in complex adaptive systems. Like KM and OL, complexity theory concerns itself with the nature and role of *knowledge and learning* in human social systems, which, Holland's work tells us, are CASs. Unlike KM and OL, however, complexity theory provides an explicit model for how learning occurs in living systems. To the discussion of knowledge management and OL, then, complexity adds a way of modeling the *form* that knowledge takes (i.e., *rules*, or what we call claims) and the *means* by which they are produced (knowledge processes). When combined with second-generation KM, a powerfully new executable model emerges that practitioners and users alike can take to the bank—a real prescription for *what to do about it on Monday*. Knowledge management, according to this view, is all about knowledge *process* management.

The life cycle of knowledge evolution in living systems is *a natural process*, and human organizations are by no means excluded from its reach. By incorporating Holland's ideas within the theory and practice of second-generation KM, knowledge management could well turn out to be *complexity's killer app*—a breakthrough of major proportions, and a powerful new tool for helping businesses become the high-performance learning organizations they desperately want to be.

ENDNOTES

1. This chapter was originally published in 2000 as an article under the same title: M. W. McElroy, "Integrating Complexity Theory, Knowledge Management, and Organizational Learning," *Journal of Knowledge Management* Vol. 4 No. 3 (2000), pp. 195–203.
2. W. Karlenzig, "Senge on Knowledge," *Knowledge Management* (July, 1999), pp. 22–24.
3. P. M. Senge, *The Fifth Discipline* (New York: Currency Doubleday, 1990).
4. Karlenzig, p. 24.
5. Ibid.
6. J. H. Holland, Keith J. Holyoak, Richard E. Nisbett, and Paul R. Thagard, *Induction: Processes of Inference, Learning, and Discovery* (Cambridge, MA: MIT Press, 1986).
7. This illustration was created by Marshall Clemens of Idiagram Co. in Lincoln, MA (www.idiagram.com).
8. S. Kauffman, *At Home in the Universe: The Search for the Laws of Self-Organization and Complexity* (New York: Oxford University Press, 1995), p. 26.
9. The KLC was developed by members of Knowledge Management Consortium International (KMCI), a U.S.-based nonprofit association of knowledge and innovation management professionals from around the world (www.kmci.org).

10. Daniel Kim's model contains elements developed by other scholars, especially P. Kofman's individual learning loop (observe, assess, design, implement) and C. Argyris's and D. Schon's notion of single- and double-loop learning. To Kofman's OADI individual learning cycle, Kim added shared mental models, hence the SMM acronym.
11. Senge, p. 4.
12. For a discussion of the 3M experience, see K. Baskin, *Corporate DNA: Learning from Life* (Boston: Butterworth-Heinemann, 1998), pp. 81–83.
13. Karlenzig, p. 24.
14. M. W. McElroy, "The Second Generation of Knowledge Management," *Knowledge Management* (October, 1999), pp. 86–88.
15. J. H. Holland, *Hidden Order: How Adaptation Builds Complexity* (Reading, MA: Perseus Books, 1995), p. 4.
16. J. H. Holland, *Adaptation in Natural and Artificial Systems* (Cambridge, MA: MIT Press, 1975).
17. Holland, 1995.
18. Holland, et al., 1996, pp. 41–42. (Note: Holland and his coauthors actually referred to declarative rules as "synchronic" rules and procedural rules as "diachronic" rules.)
19. Holland, 1995, p. 9.

Part II

PRACTICE IMPLICATIONS

"Knowledge companies need an organizational design that converts insight—knowledge, smarts, invention—into institutional behavior. They need, in other words, knowledge processes. Products embody knowledge and the value of knowledge: They are how it is sold. Projects are the mechanisms by which companies create or invest in intellectual capital, rejigger the way they use knowledge, or experiment: They produce change. Knowledge and intellectual capital fully flower, however, by means of knowledge processes: They institutionalize them. Products die and projects end; processes last."

—Thomas A. Stewart

3

A Framework for Knowledge Management[1]

Starting Points

Knowledge management (KM) has attracted considerable attention in recent years. Nonetheless, there are few widely shared views according to which the term itself is defined, much less a consensus on how best to apply it in business. Nevertheless, advances have been made in recent years to help define the field. One such effort has been that of a nonprofit professional association of KM practitioners, known as the Knowledge Management Consortium International, or KMCI.

Beginning in 1997, KMCI undertook the task of developing industry-standard reference models for KM that practitioners around the world could use as a basis for making valuable interventions in their own organizations. Central to KMCI's thinking was—and still is—two important distinctions. First is the presence of two distinctly different operating modes in every organization: the *knowledge processing environment (KPE)* and the *business processing environment (BPE)*. Second is the related distinction between *knowledge processing* and *knowledge management*. Understanding the meaning of these important distinctions is crucial to appreciating the role that KM can play in business, as well as in avoiding confusion around what KM really is and isn't. Let's explore these ideas further.

First, according to the KM standard developed by KMCI, *knowledge processing* is a social process found in every organization to one degree or another, although the quality and effectiveness of *knowledge production* and *integration* (the two components of knowledge processing) can vary widely from one company to another. This cycle—*knowledge production* and *integration*—has been codified by KMCI in the form of what it calls the "knowledge life cycle," or KLC (see Figure 3-1). The KLC has become the central organizing framework around which a powerful new branch of KM theory and practice has been defined. The purpose of KM, according to this model, is to enhance an organization's capacity to produce and integrate its knowledge, thereby enhancing the quality of, and access to, valuable organizational knowledge.

Out of the knowledge *processing* versus *management* distinction comes the following key definitions (see Figure 3-2):

- *Knowledge processing* is a set of social processes through which people in organizations create and integrate their knowledge.
- *Knowledge management* is a management activity that seeks to enhance *knowledge processing*.

Knowledge use, according to the KMCI framework, is found in the *business processing environment* (BPE), not the KLC. Here, we can make the distinction between the KLC as the *knowledge processing environment* where knowledge is produced and shared (integrated) in organizations, versus the *business processing environment* where knowledge is actually used. People in organizations tend to operate in both domains, but never at the same time. During the normal course of business affairs, we sometimes encounter problems or opportunities, the proper response to which is unclear to us. When this happens, we must effectively "exit" the business processing mode and "enter" the learning, or knowledge processing, mode. This triggers an iteration of the KLC. Once our learning has been concluded, we "return" to the BPE and promptly put our new knowledge to use.

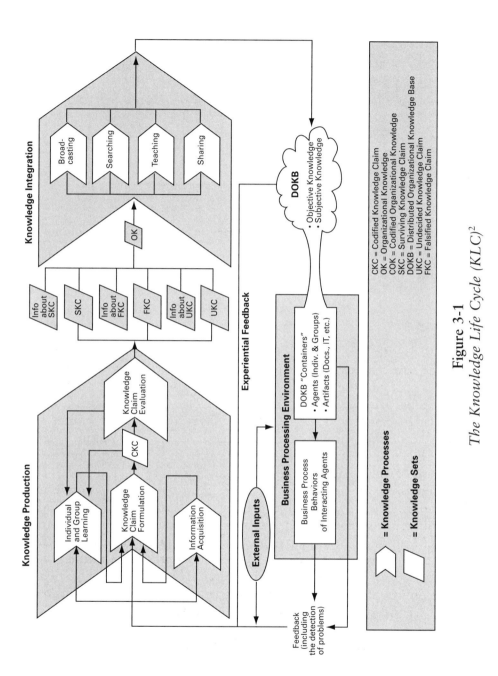

Figure 3-1
The Knowledge Life Cycle (KLC)[2]

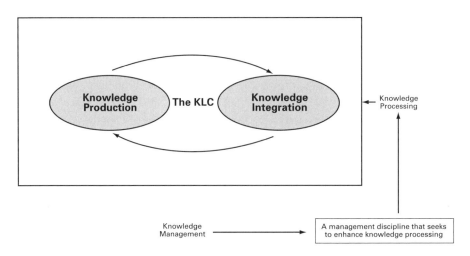

Figure 3-2
Knowledge Processing versus Knowledge Management

Armed with this theoretical foundation, knowledge managers—and the strategies they make for themselves—have an unambiguous, unequivocal purpose, as well as a clearly defined target of attention: *knowledge processing, and the improvement of it.* Success to a knowledge manager is, by definition, determined by the extent to which he or she, through various organizational interventions, has been able to enhance knowledge production and integration in a company. Firms that become more innovative as a result of such interventions, or in which valuable information or knowledge becomes more easily accessible, are testaments to the success of KM. According to this conception, the bottom-line measure of success for any KM strategy or initiative must be expressed in terms of the impact it has had on a business's capacity to produce and integrate its knowledge. This is KM's fundamental value proposition, as well as the philosophical foundation beneath what is now being referred to as "second-generation," or "the new" KM.[3]

METHODOLOGY IMPLICATIONS

Using the *knowledge life cycle* (KLC) as a starting point, second-generation thinking begins with an attempt to characterize an organization's *current knowledge processing environment*. In this way, we can begin to form some opinions and insights as to how well the current cycle is serving the needs of the enterprise, and what its current strengths and weaknesses are. We can then shift our attention to the development of a *target knowledge processing environment*, which would attempt to express an organization's views on how its knowledge processing capabilities could be improved or in any way changed. We can then perform a gap analysis between the current and target environments, and specify the kinds of interventions we think we should use to close the gaps.

In our attempts to characterize current and target knowledge processing environments, we can use a shorthand method of referring to the knowledge life cycle, which reduces it to its supply- versus demand-side dimensions[4] (see Figure 3-3). Supply-side knowledge processing is that part of the KLC that accounts for the capture and distribution of *existing* knowledge to workers who need it (i.e., knowledge diffusion). In other words, supply-side knowledge processing is that part of the KLC that enables the *supply* of knowledge to workers. Demand-side knowledge processing focuses, instead, on those aspects of the KLC that relate to knowledge *making*, or innovation (i.e., knowledge production). Here, the focus is on satisfying an organization's *demand* for new knowledge. Using this terminology, when we make KM interventions aimed at enhancing *knowledge production*, we can refer to them as demand-side KM

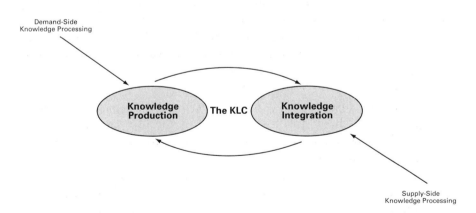

Figure 3-3
Supply- and Demand-Side Knowledge Processing

interventions; interventions aimed at *knowledge integration* can be referred to as supply-side KM. We will use this language shortly.

Next in our methodology is the distinction we make between knowledge management interventions that are *technology*-based versus those that are *socially* oriented. This distinction stems from a principle of enormous importance to the development of a KM strategy: *it's not always about technology*. Knowledge processing is fundamentally a social process that can be *supported* by technology, but that is also susceptible to improvements in its operating dynamics *independent* of technology.

What must come first in the improvement of knowledge production and integration are improvements in the ways people work together to create and share knowledge. After all, these individual and collective behaviors are the targets of technology applications, so we must first be comfortable with their dynamics before we can expect technology to have its intended effects. Armed with this perspective, then, our approach to KM relies on the further distinction we can make between *KM technology interventions* and *KM social interventions* (see Figure 3-4).

The result of our focus on social versus technological interventions and on the supply- versus demand-side of the KLC is a *KM strategy framework* that is expressed in terms of a corresponding two-by-two matrix (see Figure 3-5). This matrix is the central organizing model for the development of KM strategy. Accordingly, all of the information gathered and reported regarding an organization's current and target knowledge processing environments, as well as the specific KM recommendations made thereafter, can be expressed in terms of this two-by-two model. Indeed, many KM strategies will contain elements that fall into more than one of the four quadrants, as perhaps all *comprehensive* strategies should, since unless they do, important needs of the KLC might be neglected.

Next in this discussion of methodology is the question of how management can have an impact in any of the four areas shown in Figure 3-5. In response, I hold the view that management can have a direct impact on the quality and performance of an organization's knowledge processing by making interventions of only two types: *policy interventions* and *program interventions*. Interventions of these kinds can have a determinative or causal effect on behavior, and so it is very important that KM strategies for any of the four

Two Different Targets for KM Interventions

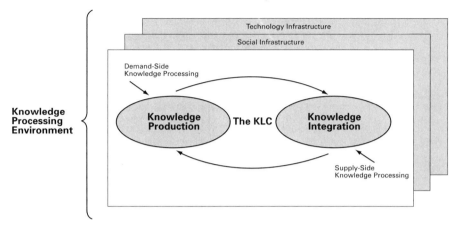

Figure 3-4
*KM Interventions Aimed at Technology versus Social
Infrastructures*

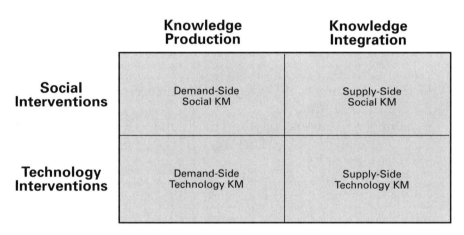

Figure 3-5
Knowledge Management Strategy Framework

areas identified in Figure 3-5 be expressed in terms of specific policy
and program initiatives (see Figure 3-6).

Policy interventions are important to KM strategy because they
reflect management's intentions and desires about how knowledge
production and integration should occur in an organization. Policies

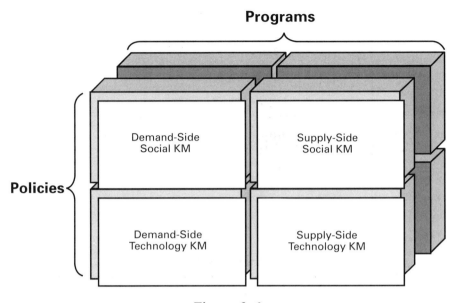

Figure 3-6

Policy versus Program Interventions in Knowledge Management

also sometimes reflect the culture of an organization, and can be seen as the *voice of culture* to the extent that they reflect an organization's deepest beliefs and principles.

Program interventions, on the other hand, are action-oriented attempts to fulfill policies. They represent an organization's best efforts to live up to its principles as reflected in policy, but that can be fulfilled by a variety of concrete actions. Programs are, as well, very often uncertain in their outcomes; whether or not they actually manage to fulfill a policy can only be determined after the fact—that is, after experimentation and trial-and-error, the results of which may lead to new programs or program modifications.

It is also critically important that policies and programs be aligned and synchronized with one another—they must be mutually reinforcing. And since programs are operationally downstream from policies, it is particularly important that before rushing to implement a new KM program or initiative, we stop to determine whether or not the backdrop of existing policies—even unspoken ones—are, in fact, supportive of what we're about to do. For all of these reasons, KM strategies should be expressed in terms of specific policy and

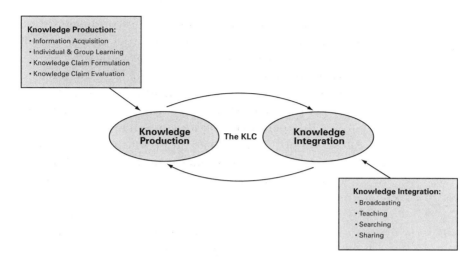

Figure 3-7
Elements of the Knowledge Life Cycle

program initiatives that we believe will help an organization meet its knowledge processing goals.

The particular *kinds* of policies and programs of interest to us in this context are, of course, only those that can have impact on an organization's *practices* in knowledge production and integration. Here, we need to take the two stages of the KLC and break them down into more detail, so as to expose the dimensions of each of them on which managers can actually have a direct impact (see Figure 3-7). We must then identify the particular kinds of policies and programs that will arguably have an impact on knowledge processing behaviors in a firm, both individually and collectively.

But before we can do any of that, we must have a solid basis for knowing what policy and program areas to focus on, and why. Earlier, we acknowledged two fundamental premises behind an approach to KM formulated by the KMCI. The first was as follows:

■ *Knowledge processing* is a set of social processes through which people in organizations create and integrate their knowledge.

This is an important principle central to the practice of what has come to be known as second-generation KM, or the new KM. But the principle here goes much deeper: supporters of second-generation thinking not only see knowledge processing as a social process, but as a *self-organizing* one as well. The patterns of behavior we see expressed by the KLC in Figure 3-1 are *emergent*; they take shape under their own steam—that is, no management is required! Left to their own devices, people in organizations will naturally tend to engage in the pattern-like behaviors depicted by the KLC.

We can, of course, support, strengthen, and reinforce those behaviors. And this is precisely what second-generation KM is all about. But since the behaviors of interest to us are already *in there*, so to speak, conventional management thinking, according to which we try to make things happen in deterministic ways, won't work here— the best we can hope for when using such approaches is temporary compliance. But that kind of strategy is ultimately unsustainable, because it fails to acknowledge the autonomous nature of the target system. When it comes to knowledge processing, social systems have a strategy of their own. The most fruitful course of action from a KM standpoint, therefore, is to (1) accept the system for what it is (a self-organizing social system with pattern-like regularity to it), and (2) choose policies and programs that will have the effect of supporting, strengthening, and reinforcing the pattern.

This approach to KM is, in fact, the basis of my own Policy Synchronization Method, or PSM. Rather than attempt to determine or *prescribe* knowledge processing behaviors through conventional management interventions, such as imposing incentives and rewards programs, I advocate a style of second-generation practice that takes a more *deferential* approach. First, we must learn the patterns endemic to the system; then we must choose policies and programs that support the pattern. This is the exact opposite of traditional management dogma, which says that first we must choose policies and programs, and then command people to behave in accordance with our dictates. In the PSM method, policies and programs follow from knowledge of behaviors (endemic ones), not the reverse.

This all amounts to an approach that strives to *set the conditions* for emergent knowledge processing, as opposed to one that attempts to design it (knowledge processing). Setting the conditions for self-organizing systems has two sides to it. First, we should attempt to favor policies and programs that make it possible for the systems of interest to us (social knowledge processing systems, in this case) to be ideally constituted—structurally, that is. In the case of human social systems, we know from the literature on adaptive systems theory that high rates of diversity in membership, extensive interactions between agents, and the presence of groups or communities are structurally ideal when it comes to creativity and adaptivity.[5] These insights, therefore, should be—and are—reflected in the policy and program areas set forth below under the "Structural Dimensions" heading.

Next is the operational side of the system. Again, a snapshot of the dynamics of interest to us here is depicted in the KLC shown in Figure 3-1. The KLC is a kind of circulatory system through which problems and solutions are processed. People populate this system and engage in the activities described by it. Their capacity to do so, freely and without constraint, is therefore essential to an organization's ability to detect and solve problems. We must, therefore, have policies and programs that set the conditions for these behaviors, and which support, strengthen, and reinforce them. Equally important, we must *not* have policies and programs that *conflict* with them; for if we do, our ability to learn and innovate will be unsustainable over the long run. On the basis of the dynamics reflected in the KLC, then, we can specify a second set of knowledge processing policies and programs in an "Operational Dimension," as indicated under the heading of that name below.

In total, then, I recommend in my PSM method that practitioners of KM focus on managing the content of eight areas of knowledge-related policies and programs, organized into two categories. These are the policy and program areas that knowledge managers can use to set the conditions for knowledge processing. In each of the definitions set forth below, the KM issue discussed deals with questions of what policies and programs, if any, are (1) *currently* in use, or (2) *could* be in use, in order to enhance knowledge processing.

Structural Dimensions

These are policy and program areas that relate to the organizational complexion of knowledge processing, in terms of the social and political makeup of the system as well as its support of interpersonal communications and information flow.

■ **Ethodiversity**—Policies and programs that attempt to determine the degree of diversity in values and worldviews held by members of an organization (i.e., their ethos diversity). Impacts the range of perspectives and experiences available to an organization as it searches for solutions to problems and opportunities.[6]

■ **Connectedness**—Policies and programs that attempt to determine the density of opportunities for interpersonal communications between people and groups in organizations. Impacts the degree of interactions between people and the velocity of information flow.[7]

■ **Community Formation**—Policies and programs that determine the extent to which an organization encourages and supports the self-organized formation of learning-related groups or communities of learning, practice, and so forth.[8]

Operational Dimensions

These are policy and program areas that relate to the manner in which people and groups in organizations actually interact with one another in the course of producing and integrating knowledge. Here, we are not so much concerned with the *structure* of knowledge processing as we are with its *dynamics*.

■ **Individual Learning**—Policies and programs that permit different degrees of freedom for individuals to pursue learning agendas of their own choosing. Impacts *knowledge claim formulation* activity.[9]

■ **Group Learning**—Policies and programs that permit different degrees of freedom for groups or communities to pursue learning agendas of their own choosing. Impacts *knowledge claim formulation* activity.[10]

■ **Knowledge Production**—Policies and programs that permit different degrees of openness and enterprise-wide participation in the *knowledge claim formulation* and *evaluation* stages of the organization's formal *knowledge processing environment*. Impacts *knowledge production* activities and outcomes at the organizational level.[11]

■ **Knowledge Sharing**—Policies and programs that permit different degrees of openness relative to decisions made by a management regime, as well as the depth and effectiveness of knowledge diffusion throughout an organization. Impacts *information acquisition* and the scope and quality of *knowledge integration.*[12]

■ **Knowledge Entitlement**—Policies and programs that permit different degrees of employee entitlement to the knowledge claim outcomes they co-create (e.g., patents, trademarks, copyrights, etc.). Acknowledges intrinsic motivation to innovate and has impact on *individual and group learning*, as well as *knowledge claim formulation* and *evaluation* activities.

These eight areas of policies and programs are *leverage points* for knowledge managers interested in improving knowledge processing in organizations. There is no right answer for any one of them. Rather, it is the combination of these variables in customized and local ways that drives the quality of knowledge processing performance in a firm. In most cases, getting the most appropriate mix of policies and programs right for a given company will require some trial and error over time, with successive refinements being made along the way. Indeed, this is a fairly good description of what knowledge managers do: *they seek to improve knowledge processing in organizations by managing policies and programs that have impact on behaviors in the knowledge life cycle.*

As an example of how this framework comes to life in actual practice, consider a case from the 3M Company.[13] At 3M, a policy exists in the "Individual Learning" category of the KLC that essentially states: *Employees shall have meaningful opportunities to engage in self-inspired, self-directed learning.* What this means, in effect, is that 3M has adopted the view that company *management* is not always in the best position to know what learnings today will have impact on performance tomorrow. Nor are today's strategies, products, and processes necessarily the right ones for the future. Rather than rely on only the imaginations and passions of senior management or the R&D function, 3M has opted to effectively engage the creative power of its *broader* population by making the freedom to pursue individually motivated research and learning a matter of enforced corporate policy.

At the program level, 3M's individual learning policies are being fulfilled by several programs, including one known as the "Fifteen-Percent Rule." The Fifteen-Percent Rule specifies that employees will be permitted to spend up to 15 percent of their time engaging in self-inspired, self-directed learning, and that 3M's budget will pay for them to do so. Moreover, employees who subsequently develop promising new ideas—whether they be for new products, better business processes, or cost-reduction schemes—are subsequently supported though development budgets set aside to help cultivate the fruit of its Fifteen-Percent Rule program. We can see that 3M is also making creative interventions in the "Knowledge Production" category, because much of the organizational knowledge it adopts (product knowledge) comes directly from employees throughout the company who are not, otherwise, members of the management hierarchy.

The business impact? 3M enjoys one of the highest rates of innovation in American industry, with fully 40 percent of its annual product revenues consistently coming in from products less than four years old; and 10 percent coming in from products less than one year old. By making deliberate interventions at the levels of policies and programs in the several areas identified above, 3M has been able to have direct impact on the performance of its *knowledge processing systems*, which, in turn, has led to significant commercial gains in the marketplace.

CONCLUSION

The practice of knowledge management has evolved into a second-generation form that rests heavily on the distinction now being made between knowledge processing and knowledge management. According to this new conception of KM, organizations are seen as collectives that produce and integrate their knowledge through a social process known as the knowledge life cycle, or KLC. The purpose of KM, then, is to enhance the performance of the KLC, which will, in turn, improve the business performance of the firm.

Knowledge managers can plan and carry out their interventions by differentiating between social versus technological interventions, and they can also make the distinction between interventions aimed at improving *knowledge making* (production) versus *knowledge sharing* (integration). Moreover, by casting some of their interventions in the form of *policies* and others in the form of *programs*, knowledge managers can have an impact on the extent to which a firm's KM initiatives are aligned with its culture, and vice versa.

These are the hallmarks of second-generation KM, also known as the new knowledge management.

ENDNOTES

1. This chapter was originally published in March, 2002 as an article under the same title: M. W. McElroy, "A Framework for Knowledge Management," *Cutter IT Journal* Vol. 15, No. 3 (March, 2002) pp. 12–17.

2. The KLC was developed by members of the Knowledge Management Consortium International (KMCI), a U.S.-based nonprofit association of knowledge and innovation management professionals from around the world (www.kmci.org).

3. M. W. McElroy, "The Second Generation of Knowledge Management," *Knowledge Management* (October, 1999), pp. 86–88.

4. Ibid.

5. See, for example, R. W. Ashby, *Introduction to Cybernetics* (New York: John Wiley & Sons, 1956); J. H. Holland, *Hidden Order* (Reading MA: Perseus Books, 1995); R. D. Stacy, *Complexity and Creativity in Organizations* (San Francisco: Berrett-Koehler, 1996).

6. See, for example, Ross Ashby's "Law of Requisite Variety" (Ashby, 1956), as well as discussions on the importance of diversity to adaptive behaviors in "complex adaptive systems" (Holland, 1995; Stacey, 1996).

7. See, for example, Holland, 1995; Stacy, 1996.

8. E. Wenger, *Communities of Practice* (Cambridge: Cambridge University Press, 1998).

9. See, for example, studies conducted on the impact of intrinsic versus extrinsic motivation on learning and self-actualization: L. D. Kamada, "Intrinsic and Extrinsic Motivation Learning Processes: Why Japanese Can't Speak English," a paper presented at the Japan Association of Language Teachers' International Conference on Language Teaching and Learning, November 22–24, 1986; E. L. Deci and R. M. Ryan, "Curiosity and Self-directed Learning: The Role of Motivation in Education," in L. Katz, editor, *Current Topics in Early Childhood Education*, Vol. 4 (Norwood, NJ: Ablex Publishing Company, 1982); A. Maslow, "Self-Actualization and Beyond," from Proceedings of the Conference on the Training of Counselors of Adults, sponsored by the New England Board of Higher Education, and the Center for the Study of Liberal Education for Adults, held May 22–28, 1965; R. A. Zbrzezny, "Effects of Extrinsic Rewards on Intrinsic Motivation: Improving

Learning in the Elementary Classroom," a dissertation submitted by its author in partial fulfillment of the requirements of a course (E591) at Indiana University of South Bend, April 10, 1989.

10. Wenger, pp. 250–253.
11. See, for example, K. R. Popper, *The Open Society and Its Enemies* (London: Reprinted by Routledge, 1998); M. A. Notturno, *Science and the Open Society* (Budapest: Central European University Press, 2000).
12. See, for example, discussions on the importance of information flow to adaptive systems: Stacey, pp. 179–180.
13. For a discussion of the 3M experience, see K. Baskin, *Corporate DNA: Learning from Life* (Boston: Butterworth-Heinemann, 1998), pp. 81–83.

4

DOUBLE-LOOP
KNOWLEDGE
MANAGEMENT[1]

These are trying times for the field of knowledge management. Shunned by many as little more than yesterday's information technology trotted out in today's more fashionable clothes, KM has responded by evolving itself into two distinct, if not competing, schools of thought. Accordingly, many of us have begun to differentiate between *first-* and *second-generation KM*.[2] Second-generation KM emphasizes knowledge production in addition to the information codification and sharing emphasized by first-generation schemes. This emergent focus on knowledge *creation* points to a much higher value proposition for KM than has been proffered to date: *the prospect of increasing an organization's rate of learning, and hence, its rate of innovation.*

The advent of second-generation KM, then, can be seen as a convergence in thinking between the organizational learning and knowledge management communities. In effect, second-generation KM has emerged as an implementation strategy for organizational learning—a practitioner's model for how to help organizations increase their capacity to learn, innovate, and adapt to change. Unlike its first-generation ancestry, second-generation thinking is more concerned

69

with the *emergence* of knowledge, not just its *mechanical application* in practice.

TWO LEVELS OF LEARNING

In his well-known article entitled *Teaching Smart People How to Learn*,[3] Harvard Business School professor Chris Argyris described the difference between what he called *single-loop* and *double-loop* learning in the following way:

To give a simple analogy: a thermostat that automatically turns on the heat whenever the temperature in the room drops below 68 degrees is a good example of single-loop learning. A thermostat that could ask, "Why am I set at 68 degrees?" and then explore whether or not some other temperature might more economically achieve the goal of heating the room would be engaging in double-loop learning.

During the course of normal experience, we invoke internally held rules as we respond to events. When the traffic light turns green, we go; when it's red, we stop. In this context, the term *rules* means *knowledge*, in that much of our knowledge can be expressed in the form of if/then statements.[4] Conditions that satisfy the *if* side of a rule trigger the *then* side (*if* the traffic light turns green, *then* release the brake, depress the accelerator, and proceed carefully ahead). Organizational knowledge can be similarly expressed. Rules can inform workers of what to do in defined situations, such as, *if* the customer wants x, *then* do y followed by a, b, and c.

By contrast, in double-loop learning, people not only reference such rules but constructively challenge them. In the Argyris example above, the double-loop response to the below-68-degrees condition was to reflect on the value of the prescribed single-loop response by considering whether an alternative to simply turning the heat on might fetch better results. In the human mind, this kind of double-loop thinking leads us to construct alternative scenarios in which we play out likely outcomes. We can then test promising new ideas and potentially choose to override or replace the rote response. Depending on how well the new rule fares in practice, we either reinstate the old one or replace it with the new, more successful innovation. Our *knowledge* (i.e., the rules that produce successful outcomes in practice) evolves accordingly.

The extent to which an organism engages in healthy rule-making and learning will, to a large degree, determine its outcomes in life. An agent (e.g., person, animal, community, business, economy, etc.) that rarely tests its rules will tend to perform more poorly in practice than one that constantly challenges, upgrades, and refreshes them. Agents include organizations. A business that rarely revises its approach to the marketplace or its operating routines will tend to ossify and atrophy. On the other hand, companies that engage in healthy levels of rule-making and revision are inherently more capable of adjusting to changes in their environment. Indeed, organizational agility depends, to a large extent, on just how well an organization's *learning system* works.

That, then, is the principal aim of second-generation KM—to enhance an organization's ability to engage in constructive levels of double-loop learning and, therefore, its capacity to adapt. In a sense, what we're talking about here is *double-loop KM*, an OL practitioner's method for helping organizations, not just individuals, learn.

Double-Loop Knowledge Management

Understanding Argyris's notion of single- versus double-loop learning is an important first step in appreciating the fundamental differences between first- and second-generation KM. For example, only first-generation KM assumes that current knowledge is valid. The goal of such approaches is to optimize the delivery of existing organizational rules to workers, so that they can function successfully in a business processing mode.

This is why technology has played such a dominant role in knowledge management to date. After all, computers and telecommunications networks are unparalleled in their ability to deliver information to people, where and when it's needed. Thus, conventional knowledge management practice boils down to little more than *getting the right information to the right people at the right time*, using tools such as document management, imaging, data warehousing, data mining, and information-retrieval systems. Although useful, this approach tends to support *single*-loop learning alone and is less concerned with supporting the production of new knowledge.

Even corporate intranets, including the new, KM-spun variety of "information portals," are nothing more than first-generation KM, single-loop learning tools—very useful in supporting the performance of tasks, but of little value when it comes to real organizational double-loop learning. Therefore, although knowledge-sharing strategies are of indisputable value to an organization, they completely side-step the question of where valuable organizational knowledge comes from in the first place—that is, they fail to ask, "how is organizational knowledge created?" In response, second-generation knowledge management integrates the first-generation's emphasis on *integrating* knowledge while adding a new focus on *producing* it. To fully appreciate this, however, we need to understand where knowledge resides within an organization and how it gets there.

Knowledge Containers and Rules

One of the fundamentals of second-generation KM is the concept of *knowledge containers*—that is, codifications of various kinds through, and in which, shared knowledge is held and expressed.[5] For millennia, human civilizations have been embedding knowledge in "containers" such as myths, rituals, dance, and other cultural artifacts. Indeed, these containers, along with our societies' institutions, reveal much about our cultural values, beliefs, rules, and the ways in which they have evolved over time. Moreover, the codification of collective knowledge facilitates knowledge transfer from one generation to the next without individuals having to rely on the frailties of human memory. Cultural artifacts can thus be seen both as a record of organizational knowledge and an environmental factor motivating behavior. Thus, although we might have thought that knowledge management was new, as far as second-generation practitioners are concerned, it is as old as the hills.

How does the concept of knowledge containers apply to the corporate world? Well, business processes, such as how to handle a mortgage application, are really nothing more than codified expressions of *procedural knowledge—know-how* knowledge. Business strategies, such as whether a brokerage should be in the mortgage business or not, are codified expressions of *declarative knowledge—know-what* knowledge (see Table 4-1). Much of a firm's organizational knowledge, then, is expressed in the form of procedural and declarative rules held in various container types.[6] Some knowledge is

Table 4-1
Containers of Knowledge

	Declarative Knowledge (Know-What)	Procedural Knowledge (Know-How)
Business Strategies	•	
Products and Services	•	•
Business Processes		•
Organizational Structures	•	
Policies and Procedures	•	•
Culture and Values	•	•
Information Systems	•	•
Individuals and Teams	•	•

Note: Includes automated, hard-copy, and other knowledge artifacts.

expressed in literal linguistic forms, such as business plans and procedures manuals, while other knowledge is performed in the business processes or organizational structures that we enact.

Although many modern-day knowledge containers take the form of information systems, documentation, videos, and other recorded representations, they are just as commonly found in corporate stories, repeated patterns of behavior, and leadership styles. Regardless of where knowledge is held, the distinction between procedural and declarative knowledge is important for two reasons. First, in order to double-loop learn, an organization must *know what it knows*, as well as see and recognize its own knowledge as such. Understanding that knowledge is often expressed in the form of rules contained in such places as culture, business strategies, processes, and organizational schemes makes it easier for practitioners to help discover and articulate what their organizations know.

Second, recognizing that declarative knowledge *drives* procedural knowledge can dramatically increase an organization's rate of learning and innovation. For example, IBM's declarative knowledge of *what* the market for e-business solutions consists of will partly determine its approach for *how* to engage customers and competitors in the marketplace. Ultimately, every process that employees follow in practice (i.e., their procedural knowledge) can be traced to their collectively held knowledge about the e-business market (i.e., their declarative knowledge). The slightest error in any underlying declarative assumptions can render whole operating divisions obsolete or entire value chains irrelevant in the blink of an eye. Therefore, it is important to know that the leverage for making lasting, profound change is in altering declarative knowledge rather than in tinkering with procedural knowledge.

Having established second-generation KM's view of procedural versus declarative knowledge rules, and the *containers* in which they are held, the next concept of fundamental importance to this discussion is the process by which new rules come into existence.

THE KNOWLEDGE LIFE CYCLE

To address the shortcomings of the earlier phase of knowledge management, experts in the field have developed a two-phase model of the *knowledge life cycle:* knowledge production and knowledge integration (see Figure 4-1). It is here in particular that the influence of organizational learning theory has had its strongest effects on knowledge management. Until recently, KM's basic assumption has been that "valuable knowledge exists"—one need only capture, codify, and share it. Learning, or knowledge creation, never really entered into the conversation. By embracing the OL community's notion of collectively-held knowledge and group learning, a more complete life-cycle view of the subject has emerged. Knowledge exists only *after* it has been produced, and *then* we capture, codify, and share it.

In this view of knowledge creation, during the *knowledge production* phase organizations generate new knowledge through mostly spontaneous interactions among individuals and groups, during which new "knowledge claims" (i.e., procedural or declarative rules in their seminal stages) are formed. Once they have been formulated, new knowledge claims are subjected to testing or validation processes of various kinds. We can refer to this as "knowledge claim evaluation." Exactly how this happens, and with what degree of formality, varies widely from one organization to another. Nonetheless, the satisfaction of validation criteria typically leads to the formal adoption of new knowledge at the organizational level in the form of new procedural and declarative rules, which are expressed by, or held, in the form of one or more knowledge containers.

The second phase, *knowledge integration*, involves distributing and sharing new knowledge, including first-generation-style attempts to codify and share it (see Figure 4-2). A new business process, for

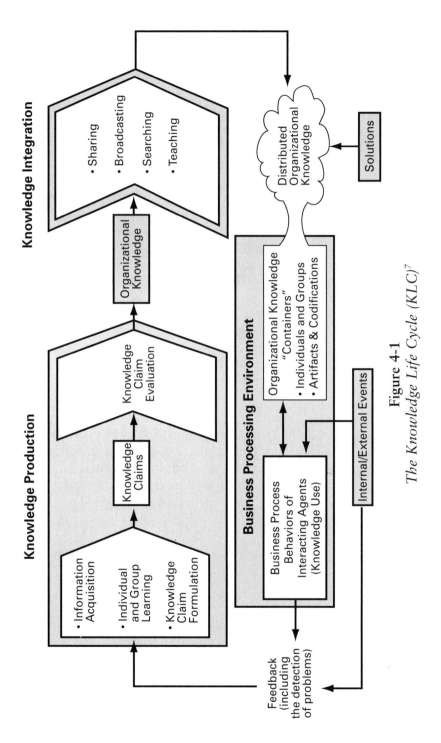

Figure 4-1
The Knowledge Life Cycle (KLC)[7]

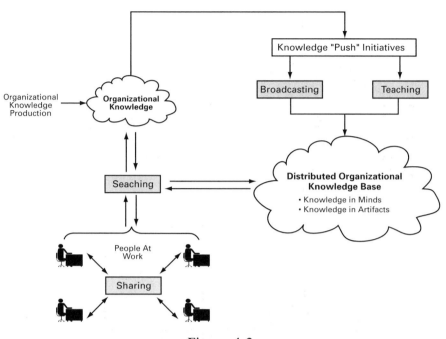

Figure 4-2
Knowledge Integration (Single-Loop Learning)

example, doesn't instantaneously supplant yesterday's standard operating procedures. Getting large numbers of workers to follow newly devised processes calls for an act of willful transformation, both by the sponsor of the new process as well as by the workforce that the changes affect. Integrating new procedural knowledge therefore entails the deliberate abandonment of one set of operating rules in favor of another.

To help illustrate how this cycle works, think of your own organization and try to isolate a well-defined business process in your own department or business unit. It might be the mortgage application process in a bank, or the order fulfillment process in a manufacturer, or some other workflow that you can clearly envision from start to finish. What you've conjured up in your mind is a chunk of procedural organizational knowledge that is expressed in practice by the patterns of work that people collectively follow. This knowledge may also be expressed in other knowledge containers, such as written procedures manuals or training programs.

Now, think back to how long this process has been practiced in its current form—has it been weeks, months, or years? Next, try to visualize the pattern of practice that preceded it. More important, see if you can reconstruct the circumstances by which the preceding knowledge was discarded and the new knowledge embraced. Where did the new workflow idea come from? How was it developed? What process accompanied its formulation and how was that process staffed? What shape did it take as it moved toward the evaluation phase? Your answers to these questions will characterize your own organization's *knowledge production* process and the people, processes, and technologies that made it work.

Next, ask yourself, how was the new process evaluated? What criteria were used to measure its value against then-current operating procedures? Who performed the evaluation? Was it a special-case effort, or are new knowledge claims systematically formed in similar ways? Here again, your answers will characterize your organization's approach to *knowledge claim evaluation*. And finally, trace the circumstances by which the new business process was formally shared and propagated throughout the firm. This is the *knowledge integration* process. You have now traced the development of current procedural knowledge across all stages of the life cycle in your own company.

The value of this exercise is that it can not only assist you in understanding the two-phase life cycle, but can also help you make the crucial distinction between knowledge "content" management (first-generation KM) and knowledge "process" management (second-generation KM). By focusing on improving the fundamental knowledge processes at work behind all of an organization's knowledge containers, second-generation KM helps make the best practices in knowledge *creation*, not just codification and sharing, available to everyone in the firm.

With this life-cycle framework in mind, most of what constituted first-generation KM boiled down to a focus on *knowledge integration*, with little or no focus on *knowledge production*, much less validation. But even the best knowledge integration work produces little meaningful organizational learning. And because the production of new knowledge lies at the heart of organizational learning, it's easy to understand why KM and OL have evolved on such separate paths over the years.

The secret of successful double-loop organizational learning can be found in the combination of *knowledge claim formulation* and *evaluation.* Of particular importance are the processes by which new ideas are formed and subjected to group or social scrutiny for open criticism and potential adoption. Indeed, the greatest challenge we face as practitioners of double-loop KM and organizational learning is to help foster the conditions in which new ideas can be freely expressed and objectively critiqued at an organizational level.

Implications for Practice

What are some of the tactical dimensions of this new approach to organizational learning? What specific steps can practitioners take— *on Monday morning*—to improve the learning performance of their collective constituents?

As presented above, a well-managed knowledge and learning environment consists of two basic components: clearly expressed knowledge containers, and healthy life cycles through which organizational knowledge is created and shared. Below are some examples of initiatives that practitioners can take to put double-loop knowledge management to work.

Taking Stock of Knowledge Containers

Revealing an organization's knowledge by documenting where procedural and declarative knowledge lies (i.e., its knowledge containers and content) is among the first steps in the practice of double-loop knowledge management. Unlike first-generation KM, which only focuses on the creation of artificial knowledge-integration systems (e.g., IT-based repositories, enterprise information portals, etc.), second-generation practice seeks, first and foremost, to understand and enhance existing knowledge containers in all of their forms, both natural and artificial. The result is an end-to-end view of organizational knowledge and where it resides (see Table 4-1 for examples).

Profiling Knowledge Processes

Using the two-phase life cycle as a guide, practitioners can survey existing knowledge processes as a baseline indicator of how well the organization is currently learning. For example, businesses that relegate most of their knowledge production and validation functions to the ranks of management might be characterized as sub-optimal learners—too little emphasis is placed on enterprise-wide learning or innovation. This categorization might lead the company to recognize the need for bottom-up innovation programs, thereby increasing the rate of organizational learning and innovation. The organization could, in turn, take remedial steps to establish critical knowledge processes in places where they might be missing or incomplete. In manufacturing, for example, the implementation of continuous improvement programs such as *Kaizen* has led to widespread advances in productivity at companies throughout the world.[8] Unlike conventional top-down management programs, *Kaizen* initiatives tap directly into the workforce, are bottom-up in their orientation, and continuously produce innovations at a rate that exceeds that of even the most talented management teams.

Publishing current procedural knowledge, and the declarative knowledge that supports it, might be all that it takes to involve an organization's workers in systematically challenging existing organizational knowledge and developing new "best" practices.

Another fundamental tool in every practitioner's toolkit is a technique for converting organizational knowledge expressed in different ways into a standard form. For example, a business strategy is reducible to all of the underlying declarative knowledge an organization regards as true and valid about itself and the marketplace. This might include how the market is structured, what trends are in play, and knowledge of how competitors are approaching the same opportunities. Why not make these rules explicit? More important, why not subject them to constant scrutiny by making them plainly visible and, therefore, open to improvement? How many organizations, for example, actually publish their prevailing organizational knowledge for the benefit of their own workers? Although most organizations do make organizational knowledge accessible to their employees to some extent, rarely is it for the purpose of encouraging constructive criticism from the grassroots. Yet this is precisely the kind of visibility, and process, organizational knowledge needs if it's ever going to receive the benefit of omnidirectional scrutiny.

Tools and techniques for expressing implicit and explicit organizational knowledge exist in commercial form. One such tool, *Knowledge Harvester*[9] provides a technique and a language that practitioners can use to express organizational knowledge in a standardized way. Knowledge Harvesting, Inc., takes commonly expressed organizational knowledge and converts it into procedural and declarative statements. Over time, tools of this sort will be seen as fundamental to the practice of second-generation KM. As such, they will be used not only to catalogue existing organizational knowledge, but also to determine the extent to which an organization is actually learning. Dysfunctional learning organizations, for example, would exhibit relatively stagnant rule sets; highly adaptive firms, by contrast, would display rapid *turnover* in rules and, hence, higher rates of innovation.

MEASURING RETURN ON KNOWLEDGE MANAGEMENT INVESTMENT

As organizational knowledge changes or evolves, evidence of this learning can be seen in the form of new rules, retired rules, more rules, fewer rules, or different combinations of new and old rules, all of which can be detected by examining changes in the content of knowledge containers. By tracking the evolution of knowledge held by an organization at different points in time, practitioners can quite literally measure rates of learning and innovation. Indeed, returns on investments made in KM will increasingly be measured by their effects on *rule-making* and *rule-set refresh rates*, in addition to their downstream effects on business performance.

Measuring returns on investment from KM and OL initiatives, then, should occur in two ways: (1) by tracking the evolution of rules held in knowledge containers, and (2) by measuring related changes in the performance of the organization (i.e., in correlated business outcomes). Knowledge management investments should be weighed accordingly. First, is the impact of investments on the knowledge processing capacity of a firm, and second, is the downstream impact of enhancements in knowledge processing on business performance.

Second-generation knowledge management explicitly links organizational *learning* with the concept of organizational *knowledge*. In particular, it offers fresh perspectives on how knowledge is created and diffused in organizations (by way of *knowledge processes*) and also on how it is practiced and expressed (through *rules* and *knowledge containers*). These perspectives are therefore germane to *both* disciplines. Indeed, in the new field of second-generation KM, double-loop knowledge management not only embraces organizational learning as an important part of its foundation, but also offers practical tools and techniques for what to do about it on Monday morning.

ENDNOTES

1. This chapter was originally published as an article under the same title in October, 1999: M. W. McElroy, "Double-Loop Knowledge Management," *The Systems Thinker* Vol. 10, No. 8 (October, 1999), pp. 1–5.
2. M. W. McElroy, "The Second Generation of Knowledge Management," *Knowledge Management* (October, 1999), pp. 86–88.
3. C. Argyris, "Teaching Smart People How to Learn," *Harvard Business Review* (May-June, 1991), pp. 99–109.
4. J. H. Holland, *Hidden Order: How Adaptation Builds Complexity* (Reading, MA: Perseus Books, 1995), pp. 45–50.
5. This idea is taken from the knowledge life cycle framework created by members of the Knowledge Management Consortium International (KMCI), a nonprofit association of knowledge and innovation management professionals (www.kmci.org.). The knowledge life cycle is shown in Figure 4-1.
6. J. H. Holland, Keith J. Holyoak, R. E. Nisbett, and P. R. Tagard, *Induction: Processes of Inference, Learning, and Discovery* (Cambridge, MA: MIT Press, 1986), pp. 41–42. (Note: Holland and his co-authors actually referred to declarative rules as "synchronic" rules and procedural rules as "diachronic" rules.)
7. The KLC was developed by members of the Knowledge Management Consortium International (KMCI), a U.S.-based nonprofit association of knowledge and innovation management professionals from around the world (www.kmci.org).
8. See, for example, M. Imai, *Kaizen: The Key to Japan's Competitive Success* (New York: McGraw-Hill, 1986); A. C. Laraia, P. E. Moody, and R. W. Hall, *The Kaizen Blitz* (New York: John Wiley & Sons, 1999).
9. Developed by Larry Wilson at Knowledge Harvesting, Inc., Birmingham, AL (www.knowledgeharvesting.com).

5

WHERE DOES KNOWLEDGE MANAGEMENT BELONG?[1]

One of the clear indicators of knowledge management's youth as a discipline is the extent to which its position in corporate structures can vary wildly from one firm to another. Indeed, one of the more vexing problems for would-be knowledge managers is determining where to position themselves in the corporate hierarchy. Let's consider the options.

Perhaps the most common—and knee-jerk—reaction to the question of where to put KM is to lodge it somewhere on the IT side of the house. The logic here, of course, is that KM is just another application of IT, and so it rightfully belongs in the hands of the CIO (chief information officer). This approach accounts for the fact that many IT trade publications, such as *CIO* magazine, have embraced KM as *one of their own*, and now routinely treat it as though KM is nothing more than the latest rage in IT. But is it?

From here, the field of play gets increasingly fuzzier. Even in cases where knowledge management is presided over by a *Chief Knowledge Officer*, or CKO, oversight of this function can still vary widely, from

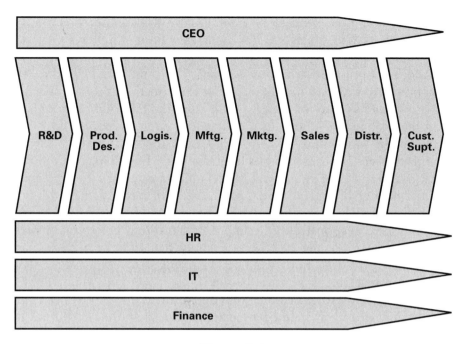

Figure 5-1
The Value Chain[2]

IT functions on the one hand, to R&D, finance, or HR on the other. Unfortunately, the mere act of establishing a CKO title does little to resolve the central question of where KM logically belongs in a firm. Let's continue looking at the options beyond IT, all of which typically begin by making reference to the value chain (see Figure 5-1).

The R&D option has much to recommend it, since R&D is, after all, the knowledge-making arm of a firm. In practice, however, KM functions situated within R&D tend to focus *only* on the needs of R&D. As far as improving the performance of R&D is concerned, there's nothing wrong with this. But it does precious little to serve the knowledge-related needs of the rest of the firm. Moreover, there's a great deal more knowledge to concern ourselves with in business than simply product or technology knowledge (the province of R&D). Strategy-related knowledge, knowledge of markets, customers, business processes, business models, marketing, finance, HR, IT, and every other dimension of business are also subject to quality knowledge-making and use. Although peripherally related to R&D,

none of these areas tend to be *managed* by R&D, and so the positioning of KM inside R&D for their benefit would have little to recommend it.

Another option for the positioning of KM in a firm is the HR function. After all, we're talking about the effective creation and use of knowledge *by* and *for* people. With all of the talk of *human capital* now being bandied about in management circles, one would think that the HR function would rise to the occasion and embrace KM as one if its own. But this has not been the case. HR managers tend to stick to the basics of managing HR-related transactions (benefits programs, hiring, firing, etc.) and rarely venture beyond the limits of their historical charter. On the other hand, the HR function has historically held responsibility for managing training programs, which in the broader scheme of KM absolutely fits into the picture. But there's more to KM than training. Learning also comes into play. Understanding the difference between the two, and that training often interferes with learning, sometimes runs counter to the traditional view of HR as held by its managers, a view that continues to keep KM outside of the HR function.

Another option is the finance function. After all, many people believe that the dramatic spread between the market and book values of companies is attributable to the *value added* by knowledge, or intellectual capital. We now commonly see titles such as *Director of Intellectual Capital (DIC)* or *Director of Intellectual Property* in such firms as KPMG in the United States, Skandia SFS in Europe, and others. At Skandia, the DIC position is closely aligned with the finance function, which every year publishes an intellectual capital report in tandem with its annual financial report. And so for the most part, DIC functions tend to focus mostly on descriptive measurement, and rarely on management or process modeling. Instead, they tend to defer to other functions within the firm for the production and management of IC, whose works, they hope, will favorably affect the growth and value of IC from one year to the next.

FRAMING THE QUESTION

What the entire discussion of KM placement options thus far has failed to consider is the very important question of *what the question is*. In other words, if KM is the answer, what was the question?

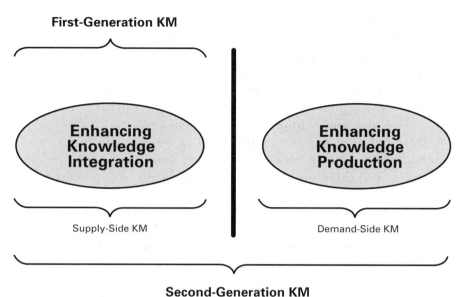

Figure 5-2
First- versus Second-Generation Knowledge Management

Resolving this issue can go a long way toward determining where KM belongs in a firm. Consider the following.

I have often found it useful to make the distinction between *first-* and *second-generation KM*[3] (see Figure 5-2). In first-generation KM, the central question of interest is *how to more effectively share valuable knowledge.* The emphasis here is on sharing; therefore, IT-based solutions usually come quickly to mind. Vintage first-generation practitioners can usually be heard preaching their favorite mantra: *getting the right information to the right people at the right time!* When it comes to doing that, there's no comparison to the role that IT can play in supporting the capture, codification, and distribution of valuable knowledge. According to that logic, KM belongs in the IT function.

Second-generation KM takes a slightly different view, however. Instead of focusing only on the *distribution* of valuable knowledge (i.e., supply-side KM), it focuses as well on the *creation* of such knowledge (demand-side KM).[4] KM, when practiced in this fashion, has an entirely different value proposition in mind. Although second-generation thinkers are no less interested in effective knowledge sharing, their real passion lies in helping organizations to become better knowledge *producers*. Here lies the basis for the overlap in second-generation KM and the related field of *innovation management*. What practitioners of both disciplines have in mind is the competitive advantage gained by increasing the rate and quality of innovation in a firm. Although IT may have a role to play in achieving this goal, it is *not* the central issue of interest. Rather, second-generation knowledge managers are more interested in people and processes, and therefore tend to position themselves anywhere *but* inside the IT function.

Next is the human capital proposition. If the question is, *how can we increase the value of our human capital*, solutions that emphasize training rise quickly to the surface. Not surprisingly, the HR function then emerges as the most logical locus of KM. This, too, is an expression of first-generation KM, since it places its primary emphasis on knowledge sharing, this time in the form of institutional training programs. As the source of institutional training programs in most firms, HR winds up taking responsibility for KM. But here, as in all first-generation schemes, the logic of the *question* is faulty and so, therefore, is the answer.

The problem with all first-generation mindsets is that they begin with the convenient assumption that *valuable organizational knowledge already exists; all we need to do is focus on its effective capture, distribution, and use*. In the process, first-generation thinkers carelessly sweep aside the question of where such valuable organizational knowledge comes from in the first place. It is the "stork theory" of knowledge management (i.e., valuable knowledge just mysteriously "arrives"). Not so with second-generation conceptions. This is why all KM placement decisions rooted in first-generation models should be rejected out of hand. Why? *Because there's no meaningful place for innovation in any of them!*

A BETTER SOLUTION

One of the other fatal flaws in first-generation KM is its excessively transactional and hierarchical foundation. Not only are such conceptions of KM concerned with *getting the right information to the right people at the right time* (i.e., one business or decision transaction at a time), but they also proceed on the assumption that determining what the "right information" happens to be is the inalienable right of management. Hence, most first-generation KM methodologies begin with the step of identifying an organization's existing business strategy, and from there they go on to infer the informational needs of workers required to *fulfill the strategy*. Even some second-generation schemes suffer from this mistake, which is to overlook the fact that strategy, itself, is a product of knowledge production. Although most see KM as something that is subject to, and determined by, strategy, it is actually the reverse that is true. Strategy follows from KM, since strategy is a product of knowledge processing in a firm (i.e., knowledge production and integration), and the purpose of KM is to enhance knowledge processing.

This issue is a politically charged one. As a principal in IBM's knowledge management consulting practice in 1999, I ran into it headlong with colorful results. As an artifact of first-generation thinking, IBM's KM methodology suffered from a severe case of supply-side bias (and maybe still does), a condition I fingered and objected to at the time. As I said then, and do now, the problem with such approaches to KM is that they begin by assuming the strategy in use at a particular time is valid. In other words, an organization's business strategy is always assumed to be valid, thereby reducing the KM function to merely serving up *the right information to the right workers at the right time* in accordance with the strategy du jour. If strategy should change, so should the KM solution.

This didn't sit well with me. As a principal developer of second-generation thinking in the field, I knew that strategy, too, was subject to knowledge processing in a firm, and not the reverse. Knowledge management strategy should transcend business strategy, I argued, and KM interventions and methodologies should be crafted accordingly. By doing so, business strategy itself would also benefit, since, after all, the formulation of strategy is a knowledge production affair. Well-conceived *knowledge strategies* serve and support *all* forms of organizational knowledge, not just the ones that happen to *follow* or revolve *around* strategy. And strategy-makers themselves, I argued, should not be viewed as immune to the effects of knowledge processing, or as somehow above or exempt from the social processes that the rest of us rely on for learning. But this was not to be at IBM. To treat business strategy as anything less than the privileged domain of senior managers was anathema to my colleagues. Strategy was seen as sacrosanct, untouchable, and irrelevant to the scope of knowledge management. Other people's knowledge may be subject to KM, but not senior managers, not CEOs, not the executive elite in a firm. Suffice it to say that my stay at IBM was a brief one.

Since then, in contemplating the most appropriate role for KM in a firm, I have found it useful to ask the question raised earlier above: *if KM is the answer, what was the question?* My own reply is as follows: *How can we improve knowledge processing in the firm?*

As a staunch practitioner of second-generation thinking, I like this question because it places an equal emphasis on knowledge making and sharing in a firm. *Knowledge doesn't simply exist, people in organizations create it.* Knowledge then diffuses across an organization and is gradually placed into practice by its members. Meanwhile, more new knowledge percolates in the production process and eventually diffuses across the firm and is later put into practice. There are always many overlapping knowledge cycles at various stages of their ontogeny in a firm, the central model for which is shown in Figure 5-3. This particular model was developed by the Knowledge Management Consortium International (KMCI), a nonprofit association of KM practitioners who banded together in 1997 to create such models as a common basis for practice.

Turning back to the question of where KM logically belongs in a firm, the answer, in my view, is that it transcends the value chain in all respects (see Figure 5-4). In practice, what this means is that KM should not, like other elements of the value chain, be compartmentalized. The "chain" metaphor here is not at all appropriate. Knowledge processing in a firm is not a step in the production process, is not a transaction that takes place between a firm and its customer, and is not, like HR, IT, and finance, merely a corporate support function. Knowledge life cycles pervade the operation of a firm at all levels, all of the time. We're either *processing knowledge* or *processing business*, usually with some of each going on intermittently all the time. And the quality with which we do these things makes all the difference from a competitive standpoint in determining our standing in the marketplace—performance-wise and value-wise.

The twofold positioning of KM as shown in Figure 5-4 is meant to depict the need for KM leadership at a transcendent level, as well as KM *practice* at a local, operating level. At a leadership level, I believe there should be some independence behind the KM function so as to avoid the risk of it becoming too deeply rooted in, or beholden to, the strategy or management regime du jour in place at

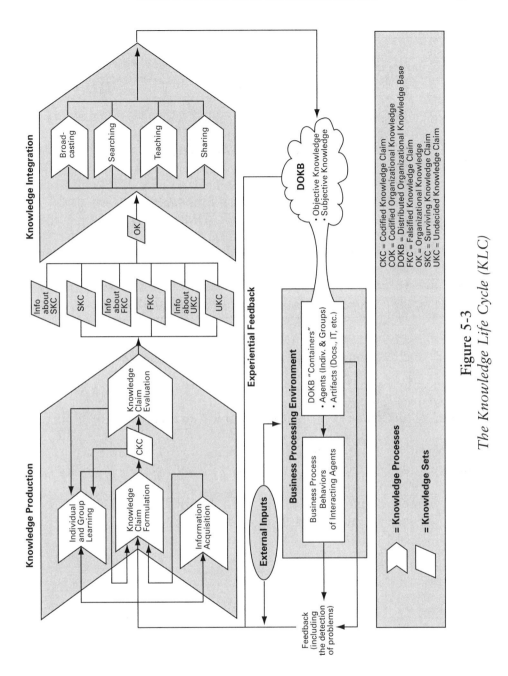

Figure 5-3
The Knowledge Life Cycle (KLC)

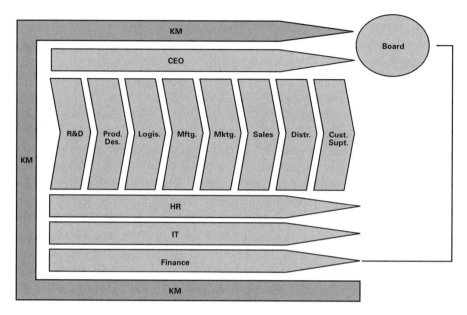

Figure 5-4
Positioning Knowledge Management in a Firm

a given point in time. This can be achieved with an appropriate degree of detachment from the in-power management of a firm, perhaps by having the KM function report directly to the board of directors or to an equivalent oversight function, in the same way that finance and the officers of a firm have a fiduciary responsibility to stockholders that transcends their duty to management.

So as not to conflict, or interfere, with the authority of a chief executive, the implementation of this idea might merely take the form of requiring that the management regime of a firm always includes a KM function that has oversight and management responsibility for knowledge processing, including the processes through which strategy itself is developed and integrated. That way, the CEO's strategy- and decision-making authority remains untouched, while the organization as a whole and its stakeholders benefit at the same time from a more neutral and constructive knowledge processing environment. Accordingly, any KM strategy in effect should demonstrably address the care and feeding of knowledge processing to the board's satisfaction, much as the board exercises its oversight of the finance function.

Finally, the diagram shown in Figure 5-4 illustrates the role of KM as a backdrop to the entire operations of a firm. Strategies developed by the KM function to improve the production, diffusion, and use of valuable organizational knowledge should be implemented and practiced at all levels. Much like the consistent practice of generally accepted accounting principles (GAAP) by all members of a firm, generally accepted knowledge principles (GAKP) should also be embraced. And both should be coordinated with the executive function but governed by the board. Only in these ways will it be possible to avoid subjugating the knowledge processing interests of a firm to the vicissitudes of temporal management regimes or parochial— and sometimes unscrupulous—leaders. In a time when the value of firms has at least as much to do with the quality of its knowledge as with its financial assets, both sources of value should be managed and protected in equivalent ways. The days of treating knowledge as anything less than a major corporate asset, deserving of its own degree of fiduciary oversight, are clearly numbered. KM strategies developed from now on should be crafted with this important principle in mind.

Endnotes

1. This chapter was originally published as an article in 2001: M. W. McElroy, "Where Does KM Belong? A Better Solution," *Knowmap: The Knowledge Management, Auditing and Mapping Magazine* Vol. 1, No. 4 (2001) (www.knowmap.com).
2. Adapted from the value chain concept introduced by Michael Porter: M. E. Porter, *Competitive Advantage: Creating and Sustaining Superior Performance* (New York: The Free Press, 1985).
3. M. W. McElroy, "The Second Generation of Knowledge Management," *Knowledge Management* (October, 1999), pp. 86–88.
4. Ibid.

6

THE POLICY
SYNCHRONIZATION
METHOD[1,2]

Quick, what's the definition of knowledge management? Don't know? Join the crowd. Welcome to the most successful fuzzy idea in the history of management. KM has been successful in the sense that everybody seems to be doing it, and fuzzy in the sense that nobody seems to agree on what it is. Definitions of knowledge management generally range from data warehousing or data mining on the one hand, to vague notions of communities of practice as comprising the salvation of business and humankind, on the other. Would the real knowledge management please stand up!

Despite all the confusion in the marketplace, there apparently has been some agreement for many on one common theme: knowledge management is all about *getting the right information to the right people at the right time*. Practicing knowledge management has therefore been mostly about *information* capture, indexing, storage, and retrieval—which means that it should come as no surprise to anyone that the conventional practice of KM has been utterly technocentric. If KM is all about delivering information to people on a timely basis, what better way to do so than to arm them with technology and the data du jour of their choosing? *Have it your way*, as it were.

These delivery-oriented approaches to knowledge management amount to what I like to think of as "supply-side" KM schemes.[3] The practice of supply-side KM begins with the assumption that valuable organizational knowledge exists, and that the primary task of the knowledge manager is to find it, codify it, and deliver it to the working masses. The unspoken model here is significant. Someone— an authority structure of some kind—is doing the finding, codifying, and delivering. The recipients of this largesse, on the other hand, are on the receiving end only. Knowledge is handed down from heaven, as if from God to the people—hence, the supply-side metaphor.

The opposite of supply-side KM is demand-side KM. Unlike supply-side schemes, which tend to begin with the assumption that knowledge exists and must only be found, codified, and delivered, demand-side practitioners make no such starting assumption. Instead, they first ponder the question of where valuable organizational knowledge comes from in the first place. Sure, sharing valuable organizational knowledge is important, they argue, but shouldn't we also be focusing on the production of new knowledge, and not just on the management of the old? Shouldn't we also be looking into how can we increase the capacity of an organization to satisfy its demand for *new* knowledge, as it strives for competitive advantage and improved performance? These are the central questions posed by practitioners of the new KM.

THE STORK THEORY OF KNOWLEDGE

The general failure of the knowledge management profession to focus, in earnest, on the question of knowledge production amounts to a kind of hysteria or denial—an unspoken, unacknowledged, but universally shared aversion to "going there," in favor of accepting a kind of modern-day myth of the stork as an explanation for where *knowledge babies* come from. Indeed, knowledge management has opted for the convenience of not having to worry about how we make knowledge. That's too scary a problem to tackle: too fuzzy, too controversial, too theoretical. Or as the King of Austria reportedly once said to Mozart, it has "too many notes."

Here is a quiz: Two knowledge managers are working for two similar companies. One decides to practice supply-side knowledge management and focuses only on the capture, codification, and distribution of existing organizational knowledge. The other decides to practice both demand-side and supply-side KM together, and sets about the task of enhancing her firm's ability to generate new knowledge, as well as to manage the old. Assuming both are equally successful at their jobs, which company is better off in the end?

Answer: The second company is better off in the end, of course, because not only is it managing the integration of existing knowledge as effectively as the first, but unlike the first, it is also accelerating its rate of organizational learning and knowledge production. As a result, it is outlearning its rival by discovering and creating new knowledge on a regular basis. Knowledge babies don't come from storks, you see; organizations actually make them.

Two or more people collaborate to solve a problem. They engage in a kind of dialectical foreplay, and together they hatch new knowledge babies. What's more, this process (presented in more detail below) is understandable to us. We know how it works, or at least how it's supposed to work. The implications of this knowledge cannot be overstated.

We now know not only how knowledge production works, but also how to recognize cases in which knowledge-baby production is *not* working and what to do about it. Most of these insights can be traced to the influence of complex adaptive systems theory (CAS theory), which provides a powerful view of how knowledge is produced in living systems. According to CAS theory, knowledge evolves in the minds of individual learners who sometimes go on to co-attract one another on the basis of their shared interests.[4] Communities of interest or practice then sometimes form, through which groups of many individuals collaborate in the production of new knowledge of a mutually held kind. Some of this knowledge may later escalate into adoption by an entire organization, after which an innovation, or an episode of organizational learning, can be said to have occurred.

Familiarity with the pattern of knowledge-making set forth in CAS theory is key to determining whether or not "natural" knowledge production is happening in an organization. Social patterns of behavior that conform to the characteristic dynamics of complex adaptive systems signal health in learning and knowledge production, and social patterns to the contrary do not. Still, the conventional practice of knowledge management has largely ignored these insights, choosing instead to hide behind the myth of the stork—because *the new knowledge management* has too many notes, is too scary, and is too theoretical. Enough, already.

For shorthand purposes, let us refer to the old practice of supply-side KM as "first-generation KM," and the practice of balance between supply- and demand-side KM as "second-generation KM."[5] It is the practice of second-generation KM, then, that I am referring to when I say "the new KM."

In the new KM, the myth of the stork is dead. People in organizational settings create new knowledge, we argue, and they do so by following certain regular and predictable patterns of knowledge-making behavior. We believe that by focusing our investments and management efforts on supporting and strengthening these behaviors, we can enhance the production of organizational knowledge—even accelerate the rate of organizational learning and innovation. In the new KM, knowledge management, organizational learning, and business innovation converge into a single body of practice.

A LIFE CYCLE VIEW

In the late 1990s, a small band of devoted *"new KM thinkers,"* myself included, got together to develop a body of second-generation practice under the auspices of the Knowledge Management Consortium International (KMCI). Out of that effort came a theoretical model that attempts to portray the process by which organizations produce and integrate new knowledge. We called this vision of knowledge processing *the knowledge life cycle,* or KLC (see Figure 6-1). Here's a rough narrative of the organizational knowledge processing story embodied by the KLC:

1. All knowledge begins in the minds of individuals. "Organizations learn only through individuals who learn."[6] An important early step in the production of new, shared knowledge, then, is the individual learning experience. Individual learning, of course, also leads to learning by groups and communities; and they, too, contribute to organizational learning.

2. As individuals learn, they begin to sense continuities and discontinuities with their experience. In other words, their experience

either agrees with what they think they know, or it doesn't. In cases where it doesn't, tension arises that must be resolved. This might be in the minds of individuals who see their employers heading in directions that they firmly believe are mistaken. These people then turn to each other for relief, as it were. They seek each other out; they co-attract one another; and they engage in a process of commiseration and constructive dialogue. They create their own knowledge, or rules. As Ralph Stacey puts it, "Some of those rules come to be shared in small groups, or even across the whole system: in other words, group and organizational cultures develop that are not part of the officially sanctioned culture or ideology."[7] It is in this way that communities of knowledge, interest, or practice spring forth.

3. These communities or groups then engage in a process of knowledge making and evaluation. Each member brings his or her "knowledge claims" to the table, and together they are scrutinized, discussed, modified, and refined. New knowledge is shaped in this way, and out of this process comes community-made knowledge claims of a highly refined and tested form. In cases where these community-validated knowledge claims are at odds with the prevailing wisdom or practice of the day, tension builds again, but this time not at the level of the individual, but at the level of the organization.

4. Community-made knowledge claims, in cases where they conflict with the status quo of knowledge-in-practice, often escalate to the level of an organization's authority structure or senior management. Here again, the same community knowledge-making process unfolds, and in the end, new knowledge may or may not emerge at the level of the authority structure. An authority structure is, after all, just another group or community, one that differs from the rest, however, given the power it holds.

In cases where authority-structure communities embrace and create new knowledge, attempts to diffuse such knowledge into practice, or to "integrate" it organizationally, generally follow. This is the *knowledge integration* phase of the KLC. In the first stage of this phase, new knowledge propagates across the organization either informally or by directly managed attempts to do so. On the managed side, we call this "training" or "broadcasting." On the informal side, we call it "searching" or "sharing."

As new knowledge becomes integrated within the organization, its embodiment in practice becomes more apparent. If so, we can say that it has become adopted in practice in the *business processing environment*. Here we can also say that an episode, or cycle, of organizational learning has occurred. Behaviors change, accordingly. As Chris Argyris and Donald Schon put it in their book, *Organization Learning II*, "The output of organizational inquiry may take the form of a change in thinking and acting that yields a change in the design of organizational practices."[8] Each occurrence of organizational learning can, in turn, be regarded as an innovation. The means by which new knowledge is produced and integrated into widespread organizational practice is what we mean by the term "innovation." Innovation and organizational learning are largely synonymous terms.

5. Once new knowledge has progressed to the point of widespread dominant practice, its application by individuals in business processes begins to produce experience in the field. The effects of practicing new knowledge feed back to its practitioners, who in turn learn from these effects and form judgments and opinions on the *value* of the new knowledge, accordingly.

Not only do these value assessments lead to alterations in practice, but they also serve to stimulate the production of new ideas and new problems in the minds of individuals, who then go on to imagine the next generation of the same idea, or better ones yet. In other words, feedback from knowledge in practice engenders new problems, new learning, and inventive tendencies in the minds of individuals, which takes us back to the beginning of the cycle set forth in step 1 above. And so the whole process then repeats itself, continuously and recursively.

The knowledge life cycle, as described above, was created using a blend of complexity theory, organizational learning, epistemology, sociology, and system dynamics. As such, it has an unmistakable multidisciplinary *systems thinking* spin to it, thanks mainly to the influence of the science of complexity. What many people may find surprising, then, is that most of the ideas expressed in this paper are firmly rooted in complexity theory. Now seen as a valuable source of insight in understanding how living systems function—including human organizations—the science of complexity has a great deal to say about the nature and role of cognition in the conduct of human affairs.[9]

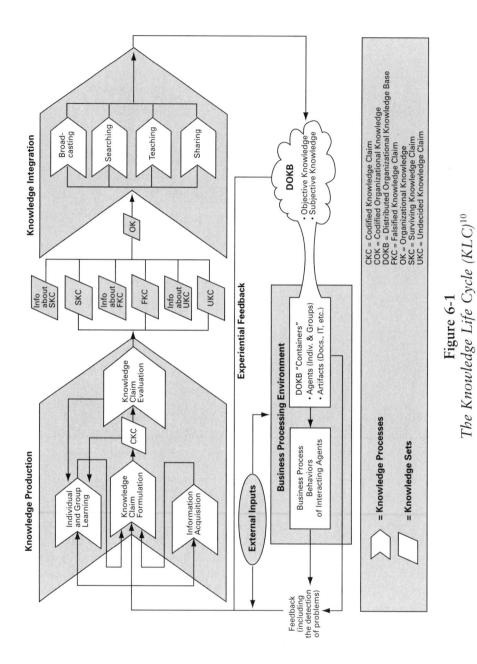

Figure 6-1
The Knowledge Life Cycle (KLC)[10]

Indeed, as noted earlier, second-generation KM owes much of its thinking to complex adaptive systems theory, or CAS theory, which holds that living systems (i.e., organizations made up of living, independent agents, such as people) self-organize and continuously fit themselves, individually and collectively, to ever-changing conditions in their environment. They do this, the theory says, by modifying their knowledge *of fact* and *of practice* (i.e., their *know-what* and their *know-how* knowledge) as a consequence of their interaction with their environment and the effects of their own and others' actions.[11]

Knowledge in the mind, according to CAS theory, can be represented by rules that agents follow in their perpetual quest to successfully adapt themselves to their environment. According to this view, living systems are nothing if not learning organizations. Understanding how knowledge forms at the level of individual agents, and rises to the level of *the collective* to become shared organizational knowledge, is a lesson in process taken directly from complexity theory.

The application of complexity theory to a broad range of business and organizational development issues is widening in practice. Examples include the New England Complex Systems Institute,[12] and the Institute for the Study of Coherence and Emergence,[13] whose respective members have been actively studying the application of complexity and CAS theory to the management of human affairs for years.

Major corporations have also risen to the occasion by investing in dedicated resources, such as Citibank's Complexity and Organizational Behavior Project,[14] to explore and embrace ways of applying complexity's lessons to the management of their own affairs. Even the *Wall Street Journal*, thanks to the pioneering efforts of journalist Tom Petzinger, has been closely following the trajectory of complexity theory as practiced by business since the mid-1990s.[15]

But it wasn't until 1997, when the Knowledge Management Consortium International (KMCI) was formed—a think-tank in Washington, D.C.—that the profound connection between complexity theory and knowledge management was formally embraced.[16] By simply recognizing human organizations as living systems—consistent with CAS theory's definition of *complex adaptive systems*—all of the theory's insights on how knowledge *happens* in such systems were suddenly seen as applicable to business and industry. This insight, coupled with the influence of organizational learning on KM, accounts for the strikingly new and different brand of *second-generation knowledge management* that we now see before us—a practitioner's framework firmly rooted in the study of living systems, also known as *the new knowledge management*.

TOO THEORETICAL?

Unfortunately, new ideas all too often provoke the kinds of complaints mentioned above as being "too vague," "too scary," or "too theoretical" to be of any use on a purely "practical" basis. Detractors of the new knowledge management might already be saying to themselves, "Come on, who's kidding whom? This business of '*a practitioner's framework firmly rooted in the study of living systems*' may sound good in the classroom, but it's dead-on-arrival in the boardroom. We need executable models that we can deploy '*on Monday morning*,' that come with clearly defined value propositions and measurable benefits—*economic* benefits, that is. Nothing less will do."

Fair enough. Let's take a crack at it.

First, let's tighten the scope of our opening hypothesis a bit. That is, that businesses, which are human social systems, are subject to the implications of complex adaptive systems theory (CAS theory). We can say this, we believe, because human social systems are living systems, and comprise "exactly the kind of system that the science of complexity deals with."[17] Still, this is decidedly different from conventional thinking, which has tended to regard businesses as collections of objects that in this instance we call *people*. When it comes to conventional thinking on matters related to knowledge production, sharing, and human performance, the most commonly held first principle might read like this: *People in organizations can be manipulated to form social systems that create new ideas and new products*. Rarely are business plans expressed in these terms, but this assumption is at least implicitly contained in most of them.

The new knowledge management begins with a different first principle: *Knowledge production in organizations is an emergent social process*. Human social systems, by their intrinsic nature, give rise to collective knowledge-making by their members as a byproduct of their individual learning and interpersonal interactions. What invariably bubbles up from all of this is new knowledge. In other words, no manipulation or management is required to get people to innovate in organizations; human social systems are already endowed with predispositions to do so.[18]

Let me put it in more business-friendly terms: Organizations innovate by their very nature (see knowledge life cycle discussion above). *You don't manage innovation, you either get out of its way or you engage it on its own terms, not yours.* Better yet, you acknowledge its primacy in human social systems, and you support, strengthen, and reinforce it.

Now, here's where the hardcore inspiration of *take it to work and put it to use on Monday* comes in. If organizations are already fundamentally predisposed to create new knowledge—and that's what they do and always have done, and if we think we have some inkling of how they do this, which can only be described as attributable to self-organization—then rather than think in terms of trying to manage or manipulate organizations toward some desired outcome (e.g., better knowledge making or sharing), why don't we begin by declaring victory at the outset and celebrate the fact that what we want is already *in there*?

Wait! You say it's *not* there? Or it's not there to the desired *extent*? You agree, of course, that people learn without being told to do so. And that people affiliate with one another in communities of interest without being told to do so; and of course people engage in co-invention and all of the other things described above in the knowledge life cycle without being told to do so to some degree. What you want, however, is for them to do it more often? Or more intensively? Or more effectively? Or more collaboratively? Or more prolifically? Is that what you want? Is that what you mean?

Or do you still cling to the notion that you can manage or manipulate people into following certain other knowledge-making or -sharing regimes of a manager's making? This issue requires resolution of the central question implied above, which is *do you agree with "first principle number one" or "first principle number two"?* Because you can't have it both ways. And if you are a first-principle-number-one believer, I challenge you to explain how throughout all of human history men and women have been making shared knowledge at the planetary level without once being subjected to knowledge-making management schemes of an administered kind. I'm talking about knowledge-making at the level of whole social systems such as science, religion, philosophy, politics, medicine, and education.

These are all knowledge-making social systems (self-organized communities) operating on a planetary scale that have never been subjected to any form of centralized planning, control, or management, and yet they have all somehow managed to create mutually held new knowledge throughout time. The philosopher of science Thomas Kuhn observed that evolutions in science, in particular, have been anything but managed. "Competition between segments of the scientific community is the only historical process that ever actually results in the rejection of one previously accepted theory or in the adoption of another."[19] CAS theory applies to all levels of scale, whether all of humanity at one extreme or Acme Widgets, Inc. at the other.

That all said, surely it is possible to create artificial knowledge-making systems that can produce new knowledge by following *prescribed* patterns of behavior, rather than relying on patterns that *emerge*, such as the life cycle described above. After all, we do this all the time in the form of R&D departments, market research functions, product planning and development, steering committees, task forces, and so on.[20] Even our predominant form of management in most businesses is arguably artificial and patently oligarchical (management by the privileged few). But are these approaches to knowledge-making sufficient and, ultimately, sustainable? Probably not.

Oligarchical businesses systematically fail to take the full creative power of their human inhabitants into account, and they regularly make knowledge that has a long history of leading to unsustainable behaviors over the long term. If you have any doubt of that, then I'm sure you wouldn't mind volunteering your basement at home to serve as a repository for the millions of tons of spent nuclear fuel produced by the energy industry in the United States, for which there are no suitable places of long-term storage on Earth. Or perhaps the asbestos industry's attempts to go on pushing their products despite their knowledge of the attendant risks to human health will convince you. Or the tobacco industry's equally reprehensible behavior. Or the chemical industry's unbridled release of synthetic products into the atmosphere every day. Or the life sciences industry's reckless experiments in genetic engineering. Or Firestone/Bridgestone's cover-up of

its faulty tire products. Or Enron's overreliance on dubious accounting practices. Does anyone really think that left to their employees'
devices, as opposed to only those of their management teams, any
one of these companies or industries would have made the same mis-
takes or gotten as far as they did with them? I doubt it.

After a few hundred years of practicing unsustainable business on
Earth, one starts to get the impression that the cause of our ills may
not be so much a matter of bad decisions being made by bad people
as, perhaps, it is that our knowledge processing systems themselves
are dysfunctional. Oligarchies are sub-optimal when it comes to
knowledge making for the masses. Top-down knowledge making
always is. Bottom-up knowledge making, however—of the self-
organizing kind described in the life cycle narrative above—always
does a much better job over the long-term, and is therefore inherently more sustainable and more prolific. Just look at the ants!

Human social systems—businesses included—are endowed with
certain knowledge processing behaviors that can best be described as
*the tendency to self-organize around the production and integration
of knowledge.*[21] Practicing the new knowledge management therefore
begins with this insight, and continues with the belief that these
behaviors should be acknowledged, embraced, supported, and reinforced. Anything less than that is patently unsustainable. The new
knowledge management is all about *sustainable innovation*!

AN EXECUTABLE PROCESS MODEL FOR CREATING SUSTAINABLE INNOVATION

Here follows, courtesy of the new knowledge management perspective, a creation process for a knowledge life cycle that will
sustain innovation metaphorically condensed into a seven-day
period. Central to the approach advocated below is CAS theory's
perspective on how knowledge production and integration happen in
human social systems. In addition, I invoke concepts taken from the
literature in organizational learning to repair CAS theory's failure to
adequately address the origin and role of self-organized communities
in human social systems as a precursor for collective knowledge
making.[22]

Although CAS theory does a superior job of describing the role of
genetic algorithms in the unfolding of individual learning, with few
exceptions,[23] it leaves much to be desired on matters related to com-

munity formation and group learning. Here, organizational learning theory (OL) steps handily into the breach. By combining the two fields of thought, we arrive at a place in which both individual and organizational learning are accounted for using principles that both camps seem eager to embrace, especially the principles of self-organization and emergence in complex systems.

A third pillar in our theoretical platform stands in the form of the theory of autopoiesis as developed in the late 1970s by Maturana and Varela.[24] Autopoiesis, which roughly means *self-making*, is a specific account of the principle of self-organization so commonly evoked in complexity theory, and therefore offers more than we find in CAS theory in terms of understanding how self-organization happens in living systems.

By appealing to various aspects of these three mutually-enriching bodies of thought (CAS theory, OL, and autopoiesis) in the discussion below, I argue that practitioners of second-generation knowledge management can improve both the rate and quality of organizational innovation by strengthening and reinforcing related social processes. Above all, however, I stress that these processes are naturally emergent as opposed to engineered. It would therefore make no sense at all to attempt to build, much less engineer, them. Human social systems are already endowed with all of the processes needed to engage in knowledge production and integration. Instead, I argue for the implementation of policies that are aligned, or synchronized, with organizational tendencies to self-organize around the production and integration of shared knowledge.

To achieve my ends, I advocate the management of knowledge processing policies. Although in most instances policies are used as management tools for guiding behavior, I promote the reverse. Instead of behavior following from policy, I argue that in the case of organizational innovation, policy should follow from behavior. Knowledge processing behaviors in human social systems are antecedent to interventions of any kind. They're already *in there*. Policies, therefore, should be crafted in such a way that they do not conflict with such behaviors; rather, they should support them. Knowledge managers should take their cue from behaviors already embedded in human social systems and plan their strategies accordingly. In this regard, my method takes an utterly deferential approach to managing innovation, not a prescriptive one.

Monday Morning

On Monday morning, the organization practicing the new knowledge management will do the following things. First, it will organize an effort to discover and document its current practices in four knowledge processing areas of interest:

- *Embryology (of knowledge):* The embryology of knowledge refers to the extent to which individuals in an organization are free to pursue their own learning agendas, as well as the degree to which they are free to self-organize into knowledge-making groups, or communities of knowledge, interest, or practice.

  Self-managed, self-inspired learning by individuals is a hallmark of complex adaptive systems. Indeed, most of what CAS theory deals with is self-motivated individual learning as the mainspring of adaptive behavior in living systems. According to Holland, "A major part of the modeling effort for any CAS, then, goes into selecting and representing stimuli and responses, because the behaviors and strategies of the component agents are determined thereby."[25] Indeed, not only are organizations self-organized in their *collective* learning regimes, but so, too, are *individuals*, upon whom organizations rely heavily for their inspiration and leadership. To attempt to manage such important sources of innovation through prescribed learning agendas is to subdue the very source of energy that leads to adaptive behavior in human social systems.

  Individuals whose passions and interests cause them to engage in creative thinking and innovation tend to seek dialogue and feedback from others who might share their views. This is especially true in cases where the views and opinions involved are contrary to those held by the status quo in an organization. The anxiety that follows serves as a profound source of innovation, both in the minds of individuals and in the collectivities of groups. In discussing the role of groups in rule-making and innovation, Ralph Stacey says, "This means we cannot view creativity purely as an attribute of an individual. An individual is creative only if he or she is a member of groups that are capable of assisting in the containment of anxiety, although the degree to which individuals rely on groups for this purpose varies enormously." He goes on to say, "Ultimately, creativity, and thus innovation, lie in interaction within a group."[26]

Current practices in this area are commonly found in terms of where companies invest in their employees' learning, and how much of these investments are made in the form of formal training programs versus employee-managed informal learning. Self-organized communities, on the other hand, can be measured, in a sense, through the use of social network analyses, as well as by gauging the extent to which self-organized communities are formally supported by management in the form of time, infrastructure, and other corporate resources.

■ *Politics (of knowledge):* The politics of knowledge processing in an organization can have a dramatic impact on the overall rate of business innovation and the quality of ideas produced. Most organizations tend to be organized oligarchically around these functions. Management teams and their administrative designates, including R&D functions, product planning, and so forth, tend to monopolize innovation while the rest of the organization is relegated to knowledge-following and a regimen of obedience.

In a complex adaptive system, politics are no less important, or prevalent, in the development of shared knowledge and as a determinant of group behavior. Moreover, the principle of self-organization in such systems tends to result in pure anarchies, or in the case of human social systems, democracies and parliamentary systems. In Erich Jantsch's words, "The natural dynamics of simple dissipative structures [in which CASs are included] teaches the optimistic principle of which we tend to despair in the human world: The more freedom in self-organization, the more order!"[27]

Of course, oligarchies, dictatorships, and all sorts of other repressive regimes can be found in the realm of human affairs, but these systems tend to die out sooner and are rarely sustained. According to the present method, this is attributable to the degree of misalignment between the natural wont of human social systems and the policies imposed on them by misinformed politicians.

Discovering current practices in this area is best accomplished by starting with the identification of significant organizational knowledge currently in practice (business strategies, organizational models, business processes, products, and services, etc.), and then tracing their evolution to the formal processes by which they were created. Next, determining how these legacy processes have been—and are now—populated with, and performed by, people will reveal the core complexion of who gets to make new knowledge in the organization today, and under what political constitution their power to do so is enforced.

■ *Intellectual Diversity:* The degree to which a business supports a plurality of ideas, even dissident ones, will also have a material impact on its overall performance in innovation. Firms that seek diversified intellectual "ethographies" (diversities of values, worldviews, and ethos) will tend to be more innovative than those that don't. Here it is useful to begin the search for practices related to intellectual diversity by looking at the HR recruiting and hiring process. The extent to which intellectual diversity is considered at all can be very revealing.

On the importance of diversity among agents in a system, intellectual diversity and otherwise, CAS theory is unequivocal. Among the commonalities held by CASs, according to Holland, is their dependence upon the "aggregation of diverse elements."[28] Similarly, Ralph Stacey, another scholar of complexity theory, puts it this way: "Complex adaptive systems are driven by three control parameters: the rate of information flow through the system, the richness of connectivity between agents in the system, and the level of diversity within and between the schemas [i.e., knowledge bases] of the agents."[29] It is my contention that Stacey's third parameter, diversity of knowledge held by agents, is entirely manageable, if only in the form of how organizations can take very deliberate steps to recruit and retain members who bring divergent views, experiences, and interests to the table. Too often, however, organizations do precisely the opposite.

One organization that I regard as particularly enlightened on this subject recently put it to me this way: "Here, we are more interested in becoming *a well-rounded organization of individuals*, than we are in becoming *an organization of well-rounded individuals*."[30] This credo routinely leads to the admission of very different people into the organization when compared to one another, thereby leading to a highly diverse enterprise with an arguably impressive and equally diverse pool of knowledge potentialities, as opposed to a monoculture in which everyone is alike in the same "well-rounded" way. This diverse pool of potentialities may be seen as an adaptive toolbox providing an organization with a deep and flexible capacity to fit itself to its environment. The more diverse an organization's ethography is, the more likely it will survive and prosper.

■ *Connectedness:* The density of communications or connectivity in a firm is also important to business innovation. The degree to which a culture enables and supports effective communications and connectivity between individuals and groups will materially affect the rate and quality of its innovation.

Turning back to Ralph Stacey, we see that two of his three fundamental "control parameters" for complex adaptive systems consist of: "the rate of information flow through the system," and "the richness of connectivity between agents in the system."[31] In other words, what Stacey is referring to is the rate and quality of communications in a CAS as enabled by its connectivity scheme. Holland, echoing a similar theme, stresses the importance of "extensive interactions" between agents in a CAS as a primary factor in determining the coherence and persistence of the system.[32]

Mapping current technology infrastructures and the connectivity they provide is certainly important here. But it is also important to characterize the density and makeup of social networks, as well. In some firms, it is taboo for employees to speak with their supervisors' peers without first "going through" their supervisor to do so. Even more taboo would be "going around" their supervisor to speak with their boss's boss. The presence of communications networks, technological or social ones, and the protocols according to which they function play pivotal roles in the knowledge-making affairs of businesses and should be assessed, accordingly.

These four areas of organizational life are the most important variables in human social systems when it comes to how well an organization learns and produces new knowledge. Together, they reflect certain principles that form the foundation of practice in the new KM.

Tuesday Morning

Having documented current practices in each of the four areas discussed above, the organization practicing the new knowledge management will now set about the task of inferring from these practices (or by further direct discovery) what their precipitating and underlying rules and polices are. Here, I invoke the following model:

$$\text{Principles} \rightarrow \text{Policies} \rightarrow \text{Rules} \rightarrow \text{Practices}$$

This model may be stated in the form of an assertion: An organization's principles, or values, give rise to its policies, which in turn give rise to its rules, which influence its practices.

An authority structure can certainly reach agreement on what its principles or values happen to be, but it can hardly manage the application of its principles in the form of detailed practices to such an extent that every worker's behaviors in the field are directly guided, or determined, by management. Short of that, polices are developed that are inspired by principles and that loosely guide behavior. Actual behavior, however, is far more granular, that is, it is only guided by policies indirectly but is not directly determined per se. That requires policy-driven rules, usually formulated at a local level by individuals themselves.

According to this framework, an "Embryology (of Knowledge)" policy might be adopted by management that says, *"All employees shall be encouraged to engage in significant degrees of self-directed learning with the organization's full support and encouragement."* The fulfillment of this policy, however, could be wildly different from one part of the organization to another.

In one case, employees might be granted 5 percent of their company time to engage in self-directed learning, but in others the percentage might be considerably higher. Budgets allocated for such learning might also vary. Their relative size vis-à-vis dollars spent on mandatory training might vary as well. There are many different ways to implement even the simplest policy, and yet all of them might arguably comply with the same governing policy. Rules developed at a local level would vary accordingly. In any case, practices follow from rules, which spring forth from policies. This is why we begin the effort with an understanding of practices and then work our way backwards to our goal.

Just as rules reflect underlying policies, so does the same framework suggest that policies reflect underlying principles, or values. These too, then, should be determined either by inference or by direct discovery. Knowing what ultimately drives an organization's policies, rules, and practices in the four areas of interest will be of tremendous value when it comes to exploring opportunities for change and improvement. If the policies change, but the underlying principles behind them don't, it should come as no surprise to anyone later on that attempts to practice the new policies will ultimately run afoul of the organization's value system. This absolutely applies to knowledge processing policies and practices as well as to any other dimension of organizational life.

Before moving on to Wednesday's work, there is one more task to complete. The organization must baseline its current rate and quality of innovation. There is no one way to do this, and so how it is done is up to the organization. But whichever way is chosen, it must be one that will satisfy an organization's needs and that can be reused later on to determine the effects of KM interventions in the latter stages of the effort.

I will offer two thoughts on how to baseline innovation in the current context, but will leave the question open for organizations to research and pursue later on. In choosing the organizational scope of this process, it will be necessary to narrow the baselining effort to a smaller group, or at least to one that is open and receptive to what the organization is about to do. In addition, it would be helpful if the group of choice has records of knowledge production of some sort going backwards in time—say, two to five years or so. This can be done by focusing *not* on all forms of organizational knowledge, but on a few representative ones only.

For example, in an R&D environment, records on research reports, or even patents, are often held for long periods of time, offering tangible evidence of the authors' rate and quality of innovation. In an HR function, it might be personnel programs; in marketing it might be new ad campaigns; in sales it might be new contract offerings; in manufacturing, it might be new production processes; in finance, it might be new cash flow and investment management schemes. These are all expressions of organizational knowledge that are subject to continuous improvement or outright displacement by new or better ideas. Every such innovation or improvement constitutes an innovation, or an organizational learning event, and can be counted accordingly. Rates of innovation are measured in such ways.

Measuring the quality of an innovation can be accomplished in at least three ways. One would be to correlate the value of the incremental revenue gained, or the cost saved, through the implementation of specific innovations. Again, this can be established through retrospective analysis.

A second technique would be to trace the evolution of new knowledge, in retrospect, to the process that created it, and to grant a higher value, or quality, to innovations that were subjected to, and survived, thoughtful validation. According to this principle, knowledge created through community deliberations will almost always have a higher value in practice than knowledge imposed by oligarchs, if only because knowledge co-created by members of a community has been subjected to more stringent validation. Knowledge produced by communities on a bottom-up basis also tends to be more acceptable in practice than knowledge imposed through top-down measures due to the investments people have made in its creation, validation, and adoption.

A third method would be to focus on the extent to which a knowledge processing system has allowed its hosts to solve their problems. This approach flies in the face of the "rate of innovation" mantra. Who cares what the rate of innovation is if it doesn't include the knowledge of how well a rate—any rate—manages to meet the frequency at which problems arrive? An organization whose rate of innovation is triple what it was the year before, but whose problems have quadrupled in the same period, is not half as admirable as another organization whose rate of innovation is less but has kept pace with its problems.

Wednesday Morning

Now that the firm's current knowledge-related environment, in terms of the four policy areas of interest, is mapped (I call it the organization's *knowledge operating system*, or KOS),[33] the organization is in a position, for the very first time, to contemplate meaningful change and improvement to its rate and quality of learning, innovation, and performance. In our practice of second-generation KM, we have come this far without once turning to the "capture and codify" obsession of supply-side thinking, much less its characteristic knee-jerk resort to technology.

Now today, Wednesday, the new knowledge management organization will engage in the single most powerful kind of intervention available to practitioners of knowledge management—new or old. It will apply a new skill that I will refer to here as the *Policy Synchronization Method*, or PSM.

Let's start off with an analogy. Back in the 1960s and 1970s, and to some extent still today, many people in the teaching profession experimented with and advocated the twin principles of *intrinsic learning* and *intrinsic motivation* as the basis of their methods.[34] The theory behind these principles is that individual students tend to learn better when they're learning what *they* want to know rather than what *you* want them to know. In other words, when they are motivated intrinsically by their own interests as opposed to extrinsically by some third party's, they invariably learn more, learn faster, and retain their knowledge over longer periods of time than when the process is reversed.[35] So, these intrepid teachers argued, stop trying to get them to learn better and more effectively, and recognize that they already do so under the right conditions. Create and maintain those conditions, they suggested, and *high performance learning* will flourish.

Now, let's briefly analyze what happened with intrinsic learning and why it worked. First, the theorists at the time began by acknowledging the predispositional learning behaviors of individual students (children, in this case). Next, they characterized these behaviors and made them explicit. They were then in a position not only to know what these predispositional behaviors were, but to evaluate the effectiveness of their current and past teaching habits against them. In other words, if the learner learns well by doing "X" and we instead systematically make him or her do "Y" as a matter of practice, then what we have before us is a poorly synchronized policy-to-behavior condition that is inherently unsustainable. By synchronizing the policies with the target system's intrinsic pattern of behavior in the behavioral domain of interest, we can not only support the desired behaviors, but we can strengthen and reinforce them as well.

In other words, rather than fighting the system to obtain certain desired results, one could embrace the same system's desirable native practices in the same behavioral area of interest and obtain even better results by strengthening and reinforcing them. With prior knowledge of *how learners learn*, then, one could conceivably craft policies that reciprocate and strengthen such learning behaviors and reinforce them, in the exchange. Or, one could ignore these insights and cram kids in classrooms whether they like it or not, and force-feed them what *we* want them to learn for twelve-plus years.

Among the fascinating results from early studies in intrinsic learning were the following:

- Intrinsic motivation "is based on people's need to be competent and self-determining."[36]
- There appear to be two primary factors that foster the intrinsic motivation to learn:[37]
    1. The first is choice. Not surprisingly, people tend to focus more intently on activities of their own choosing and interests.
    2. The second is "positive competence feedback." "When subjects get feedback indicating that they are quite competent, they seem more interested in the activity and they persist at it longer" than those who do not get the feedback.[38] Perhaps this is one of the reasons why groups and communities form and persist: they serve as sources of positive feedback for individuals engaged in creativity and innovation.
- Next was the discovery that imposed educational agendas can actually undermine learning: "Whenever people's behavior becomes controlled by some extrinsic factor, they seem to be left with less intrinsic motivation." "Apparently, the fact of the rewards or controls undermines their sense of self-determination, for they begin to see their behavior as being determined by the reward contingencies rather than by their own interest in the activity."[39]

As I asked earlier, is it bad decisions being made by bad decision-makers that caused bad learning results, or is it the knowledge-making system itself in which decision-makers are operating that causes bad results? I think it's the latter, and I think the present system is unsustainable precisely because of the false mental models underlying the educational system we have today, *despite* the brilliance of the insights gained from intrinsic learning studies forty years ago that contradicts those models.

I choose to embrace the lessons learned from the intrinsic learning studies. They imply that organizations, like individuals, exhibit certain self-organized learning-related tendencies that are ultimately immutable. With these tendencies in mind, the Policy Synchronization Method offers one simple imperative: *embrace them.*

On Wednesday, then, the new knowledge management organization will begin the process of systematically assessing the degree of alignment or disparity between the current knowledge processing policies held by the firm and a target set of ideal policies, as inspired by an understanding of how learning happens in complex adaptive systems.

Wednesday's work will therefore have amounted to a carefully executed gap analysis of a traditional kind as applied to a new domain: the organization's *knowledge operating system*, or KOS. At the end of the day, the deliverable will consist of a fully developed study of gaps and opportunities to bring the organization's KOS more closely into alignment with the target model. This, in turn, might point to many different areas in which gaps exist, the resolution of which may take the form of just as many, or more, potential interventions. Proposing which of these opportunities to in fact focus on and how to do so will be the organization's next step. But that is Thursday's work.

Thursday Morning

Thus far, the organization has studied and profiled its current practices, rules, and policies in the four areas germane to knowledge processing. In addition, its knowledge managers have established a baseline of how well the organization has performed over time under its present system, expressed in terms of its historical rate and quality of innovation. And finally, the organization has just completed a gap analysis that determined the degree of disparity between current and target knowledge processing policies in the four areas of interest. Thursday, then, will amount to a planning day. It's time for the knowledge managers to plan and prioritize their interventions.

In the Policy Synchronization Method (PSM), not all of the four policy domains are equal when it comes to their influence. Some policies are more important than others, at least in terms of how and when they should be deployed. In the early stages of a PSM intervention, it is the "politics of knowledge" policies that should come first.

In complex adaptive systems, all knowledge-making is bottom-up in origin, in that it involves individual and group learning. There are no chief knowledge makers, dictators, commanders, or autocrats. There are leaders in such systems, but they derive their authority from the fact that they are the "attractor basins" (i.e., surrogate focal points) of self-organized knowledge processing. In other words, they can act on behalf of other agents whose interactions place them at the nexus of the self-organizing process, but only so long as they remain at the center. As soon as their knowledge claims no longer represent the emergent result of the system's knowledge processing interactions, their authority withers.

All knowledge made under such systems is no less bottom-up in construction. This includes knowledge of knowledge processing policies themselves. More to the point, it is the political system that either makes it possible, or not, for the dynamics of self-organized knowledge processing in a social system to unfold. Getting the correct political system in place, then, is the first order of business in any PSM project, because all organizational knowledge, including the remaining knowledge processing policies, are produced by such systems and cannot be prescribed independent of them.

For these reasons, the new knowledge management organization will prioritize plans for the implementation of a new knowledge-making political system that will make it possible for all stakeholders in the organization to participate in not only the knowledge processing system itself, but also in the process that produces the rules that will govern it. What this means is that no longer will all organizational knowledge be created by oligarchies (i.e., management only). Knowledge production will become less oligarchical and more democratic.

At Deere and Company in Moline, IL, knowledge managers are already experimenting with a knowledge processing political system that will make it possible for knowledge claims produced by self-organizing communities of interest to have a voice in the formal planning and decision-making processes of the firm—a seat at the table, as it were. In effect, self-organized communities of knowledge are being recognized as a valuable source of organizational knowledge and they are being formally embraced into the politics of knowledge-making at Deere.[40]

What's so interesting about this experiment is that it in no way threatens or erodes the decision-making authority of senior management at Deere, nor does it oblige management to agree with community input. Rather, it simply opens up innovation in a very formal way to the entire population of the firm, with a particular emphasis on the role that self-organizing communities of interest can play in the process. Deere's planning-related business processes are being redefined accordingly.

Next in the priority of planned interventions comes "embryology" policy interventions. In order for the new political system to have its greatest and most beneficial effects, people should be learning on a self-directed basis as much as possible, and communities of interest practice, knowledge, and so on should be forming and flourishing at a healthy, natural pace. Indeed, organizational policies should make it possible for the organization to evolve into a healthy *community of communities*. Policies related to how people can be free to learn on their own terms, and how communities can freely form, should be defined, implemented, and funded. Planning the initiatives to do so is the organization's second priority.

Third in the list of planning priorities should be a combination of steps required to revamp policies in the diversity ("ethodiversity") and connectedness areas. In the diversity area, targets will most likely be in the HR recruiting and hiring arena. Adopting policies that compel the organization to move toward becoming a "well-rounded organization of individuals," as opposed to an organization of well-rounded individuals, should be the goal. Similarly, policies that improve the internal flow of information and that make external information more readily available can only work to the organization's advantage if they are supported by policies that encourage innovation and the application of new knowledge. Policy interventions in these two remaining areas, then, should be the last planning priority and should be defined accordingly.

Now, by the end of the day on Thursday, the organization should have prepared a comprehensive action plan that is expressed in terms of prioritized policy interventions and transformation efforts. But there's a twist to the actual implementation that will commence on Friday. Thursday's plan is merely a straw man, a proposed set of new policies that cannot simply be rolled out on the basis of a single planner's thinking. There are no czars in complex adaptive systems. Rolling out the plan without subjecting it, first, to the very knowledge processing system that it seeks to create would be an act of hypocrisy. Friday's work must therefore be carried out with this caveat in mind.

Friday Morning

According to the plan created on Thursday, the first order of business is deploying the new "political" knowledge processing system. A comprehensive set of new policies must be created according to which stakeholders from all corners of the organization can play a role in the production of new knowledge. Policy recommendations must be crafted accordingly, and the new political model can then be deployed.

The organization now has a working, more democratic knowledge processing system up and running, all of which unfolds in keeping with a target model, or a vision of how it should work, who should participate in its operations, and how it should interface with individuals, communities, and senior management. All of that is its strength, but also its weakness.

What has been done is to successfully launch a planner's or team's vision of what the optimal knowledge-making political system should consist of, as determined or influenced by the planners' policy prescriptions. An externally-designed model has therefore been imposed on a complex adaptive system under the assumption that it will work well and that its composition is inherently suitable for its intended target: the organization.

But nowhere in the planning process were the stakeholders of the target system themselves involved. How could they have been? They still occupied a system that was anything but democratic. They had no say in the process. Only the planners, operating under the authority of the well-intended oligarchy were in a position to make plans to change the system. And now the planners have deployed the first critical piece, a political system that should have been of its own making, but was not.

Resolving the quandary is a surprisingly simple task. Rather than view the initial fruits of the planners' labor as a permanent solution, distance the organization from it and declare it to be merely a prototype, a straw man—nothing more than a political system that has been bootstrapped by knowledge managers, but which is now in the organization's own hands. The bootstrapped contingent should then take its own constitution into its own hands, and redefine itself more to its own liking. Assuming a culture is in place that abhors illegitimate power grabs, what comes out of this process is a fully initialized political system that is ready to take on the remainder of the week's work.

Having recast itself in accordance with its members' own wishes, the new political system spends the rest of the day taking all of the knowledge manager's other policy-related intervention plans under consideration. It systematically reviews and either accepts, rejects, or modifies the proposed policy interventions in the other three areas (embryology, diversity, and connectedness) and then recasts the plan so that it becomes more to its own liking. The knowledge manager's job is to attend and support this process. By the end of the day on Friday, a self-validated, self-determined political system will exist, and a full slate of validated policy transformation efforts will be ready for Saturday.

Saturday Morning

Saturday's work is simple. It's execution time. The revised and validated policy-transformation efforts prepared on Friday are systematically carried out from dusk to dawn. Individual learning and community formation policies are deployed (embryology), diversity policies are deployed, and the new connectedness policies are rolled out as well. By the end of the day, an entirely new *knowledge operating system* (KOS) has been initialized and is up and running, albeit in its early, seminal stages.

Sunday Morning

Suffice it to say that the "first week" in the implementation of a PSM project offers no rest for the weary. There's one last—actually ongoing—step in the process: perpetual monitoring and adjustment. Even if you, the knowledge manager, believe you can launch a KOS that perfectly meets the needs of the organization, it will only meet the needs of the organization today (Sunday). Tomorrow is another day, as will every other day be from now on. The world is a moving target. Markets change; customers change; your own internal circumstances change. And so it's imperative that the performance of the new KOS be continually measured to determine how well the new operating system is performing.

This is where the baselining methods used earlier on Tuesday come back into play. After a reasonable period of time operating under the influence of the new KOS, you should return to the scene to revisit its current rate and quality of innovation using the same tools and techniques you used earlier to baseline its historical performance in the same areas. Better yet, you should encourage the new political system to devise a set of practices that will make it easier to track organizational innovation as a natural byproduct of its operations. This need not be confined to simply counting widgets or new ideas. Of far greater value would be methods that make it possible for organizations to measure the economic impact of its innovations on a systematic basis. Tools and techniques of this sort are just now beginning to emerge.

Because the process of monitoring and adjusting the KOS will be an ongoing part of your job, Sunday's work, in a sense, will never be done. This aspect of the PSM method comprises a good portion of what practitioners of second-generation knowledge management do: they monitor, modify, and administer knowledge processing policies and associated rules and practices. Knowledge managers are *knowledge policy and program* managers. They don't manage knowledge, per se. According to the new knowledge management, they merely manage the organizational capacity to produce and integrate it.

CONCLUSION

Ralph D. Stacey, in discussing the management and research implications of complexity theory in his very fine book, *Complexity and Creativity in Organizations*, makes the following statement:

What the science of complexity adds is a different theory of causality, one in which creative systems are subject to radical unpredictability, to the loss of the connection between action and long-term outcome. The purpose of the theory and the research is then to indicate how conditions might be established within which spontaneous self-organization might occur to produce emergent outcomes.[41]

I maintain that this, indeed, is precisely what the Policy Synchronization Method makes it possible to do—to establish the conditions "within which spontaneous self-organization might occur to produce emergent outcomes." The conditions, I believe, are policies and programs within the knowledge processing environment of a firm. *That* is the system of relevance here, and policies and programs are its conditions. By managing the policies and programs that comprise the environmental conditions of a firm's *knowledge operating system,* a knowledge manager can have a profound impact on the rate and quality of innovation therein. This is the promise of the Policy Synchronization Method, a direct application of complexity theory to the management of innovation in human social systems.

Endnotes

1. This chapter was originally published in October, 2000, under a different title: M. W. McElroy, "The New Knowledge Management," *Knowledge and Innovation: Journal of the KMCI* Vol. 1, No. 1 (October 15, 2000), pp. 43–67.
2. The "Policy Synchronization Method" is the subject of a U.S. patent application filed with the Patent and Trademark Office in September, 2000 by Macroinnovation Associates, LLC of Windsor, VT (www.macroinnovation.com). It currently holds patent-pending status.
3. M. W. McElroy, "The Second Generation of Knowledge Management," *Knowledge Management* (October, 1999), pp. 86–88.
4. See, for example, J. H. Holland, *Hidden Order: How Adaptation Builds Complexity* (Reading, MA: Perseus Books, 1995); R. D. Stacey, *Complexity and Creativity in Organizations* (San Francisco, CA: Berrett-Koehler, 1996).
5. McElroy (1999), p. 86.
6. P. M. Senge, *The Fifth Discipline* (New York: Doubleday Currency, 1990), p. 139.
7. Stacey, p. 26.
8. C. Argyris and D. A. Schon, *Organizational Learning II* (Reading, MA: Addison-Wesley Publishing Company, 1996), p. 12.
9. M. W. McElroy, "Integrating Complexity Theory, Knowledge Management, and Organizational Learning," *Journal of Knowledge Management* Vol. 4 No. 3 (2000), pp. 195–203.
10. The KLC was developed by members of the Knowledge Management Consortium International (KMCI), a U.S.-based nonprofit association of knowledge and innovation management professionals from around the world (www.kmci.org).

11. J. H. Holland, *Adaptation in Natural and Artificial Systems* (Cambridge, MA: MIT Press, 1992).

12. The website for the New England Complex Systems Institute is www.necsi.org.

13. The website for the Institute for the Study of Coherence and Emergence is www.isce.edu.

14. S. Kelly and M. A. Allison, *The Complexity Advantage* (New York: Business Week Books/McGraw-Hill, 1999).

15. For a collection of Tom Petzinger's articles written on related subjects, see T. Petzinger, Jr., *The New Pioneers* (New York: Simon & Schuster, 1999).

16. Knowledge Management Consortium International, www.kmci.org.

17. Stacey, 1996, p. 24.

18. M. W. McElroy, "Using Knowledge Management to Sustain Innovation," *Knowledge Management Review* Vol. 3, Iss. 4 (Sept./Oct. 2000), pp. 34–37.

19. Thomas S. Kuhn, *The Structure of Scientific Revolutions* (Chicago: University of Chicago Press, 1970 edition), p. 8.

20. W. L. Miller and L. Morris, *Fourth Generation R & D* (New York: John Wiley & Sons, 1999).

21. See, for example, H. R. Maturana and F. J. Varela, *Autopoiesis and Cognition* (Dordrecht, Holland: D. Reidel Publishing Company, 1980); E. Jantsch, *The Self-Organizing Universe* (Oxford: Pergamon Press, 1980).

22. Argyris and Schon.

23. See Stacey (1996), for example, in which CAS theory is explicitly applied to learning and innovation in human social systems.

24. Maturana and Varela.

25. Holland, 1995, p. 8.

26. Stacey, p. 139.

27. Jantsch, p. 40.

28. Holland, 1995, p. 4.

29. Stacey, p. 99.

30. Stated by a college admissions officer from Dartmouth College in 1999 during a high school presentation at Kimball Union Academy in Meriden, New Hampshire.

31. Stacey, p. 99.

32. Holland, 1995, p. 4.

33. The phrase, knowledge operating system, was coined by Mark W. McElroy and is trademarked by Macroinnovation Associates, LLC.

34. See, for example, studies conducted on the impact of intrinsic versus extrinsic motivation on learning and self-actualization: L. D. Kamada, "Intrinsic and Extrinsic Motivation Learning Processes: Why Japanese Can't Speak English," a paper presented at the Japan Association of Language Teachers' International Conference on Language Teaching and Learning, November 22–24, 1986; E. L. Deci and R. M. Ryan entitled, "Curiosity and Self-directed Learning: The Role of Motivation in Education," in L. Katz, editor, *Current Topics in Early Childhood Education*, Vol. 4 (Norwood, NJ: Ablex Publishing Company, 1982); A. Maslow, "Self-Actualization and Beyond," from Proceedings of the Conference on the Training of Counselors of Adults, sponsored by the New England Board of Higher Education, and the Center for the Study of Liberal Education for Adults, held May 22–28, 1965; R. A. Zbrzezny, "Effects of Extrinsic Rewards on Intrinsic Motivation: Improving Learning in the Elementary Classroom," a dissertation submitted by its author in partial fulfillment of the requirements of a course (E591) at Indiana University of South Bend, April 10, 1989.
35. Ibid.
36. Deci and Ryan, p. 9.
37. Ibid., p. 10.
38. Ibid.
39. Ibid., p. 9.
40. From first-hand observations made by the author during visits to Deere and Company in Moline, IL.
41. Stacey, p. 264.

Part III

SUSTAINABLE INNOVATION

".. . [T]he wild animal population does not display its normal behavior except in the presence of its normal environment."

Aldo Leopold

7

The Principle of Sustainable Innovation

I begin this essay with an open confession of my intent to exploit the ambiguity of the term "sustainable innovation" in my title. Indeed, there is an intentional double entendre at work here, one that I feel I should acknowledge and explain before I proceed. On the one hand, there can be sustainable innovation in the sense that the output or business of a firm is sustainable. On the other hand, there can be sustainable innovation in the sense that the *innovation process* employed by a firm is sustainable.

To illustrate my point using an exaggerated example, consider a firm that has devoted all of its human resources to innovating new products or services with, say, environmental ethics in mind. Although the outcomes of innovation in such a firm might be laudable, its innovation routine, per se, would hardly be sustainable. Despite the merits of its enterprise, with everyone engaged in product and service development, there'd be no one left to tend to the work of the firm, such as making products, filling orders, or dealing with customers. Clearly, there is a difference between the notion of sustainable innovation in the enterprise or work *product* sense of the term, versus innovation that is sustainable in the work *process* sense of the term. The former deals with innovations and the enterprises in which they are produced, and the latter deals with the innovation process itself as a component of the value chain, and which is independent of products produced or the sustainability of an enterprise.

With this important distinction in mind, I choose to use the term sustainable innovation in such a way that both of its senses are invoked. In my vision of sustainability in business, the idea not only applies to *outcomes* in the product or enterprise sense of the term, but also to the *process* through which outcomes or innovations are created. In fact, I believe that sustainable practice in business (outcomes) is utterly dependent upon whether or not sustainable innovation *processes* are in play—the former cannot exist without the latter, at least not for long. This is not to say, however, that sustainable innovation programs will always lead to sustainable outcomes, or that firms that practice sustainable innovation will always be sustainable in their commercial affairs. But I do believe that sustainable commerce in business is at least *unlikely* in the absence of sustainable innovation. And I also believe that although sustainability in innovation will not necessarily lead to sustainability in outcomes, sustainability in outcomes cannot occur without sustainability in innovation.

Unsustainable Innovation

Let's turn back the clock of time for a moment and go back to the period during which the company Johns Manville first learned of the disturbing reports on the dangers of its asbestos products to human health. Let's assume that those reports were known to management, as the legal record suggests they were, and let's further assume that instead of concealing that knowledge from its employees and from the public at large, the adverse effects of its products on human health were freely publicized and openly shared by management. How many Johns Manville employees, if given the chance, would have opted to move ahead with the company's products in the face of that knowledge? A majority? I don't think so. Chances are that Manville's patently harmful products would have been stopped dead in their tracks at the first sign of trouble in the marketplace. Why? Because they were unsustainable, *to say the least.*

Now let's take the same trip backwards in time to the tobacco companies and ask the same question of their employees. Next we move on to the workers of NASA prior to the Challenger disaster (O-ring failure) and ask their employees. Then on to the workers of Ford and Firestone (tire failures); Monsanto (biospheric and genetic contamination); Texaco (racism); Royal Dutch Shell (cultural and environmental devastation in Nigeria); DuPont (ozone layer destruction by CFCs); Exxon (the Valdez disaster); and more recently, Enron and others (management malpractice leading to bankruptcy and the loss of retirement funds and savings for thousands).

Instead of deferring to the closed-door policies and decision-making regimes of all these practitioners of questionable commerce, what if the patently unsustainable nature of the practices planned and perpetrated by each of them had first been subjected to critical review by their employees, their shareholders, the communities in which they operate, and society in general? What if instead of confining the innovation process (i.e., knowledge making and adoption) in each case to secluded centralized teams, ideas planned for commercial deployment had been critiqued, as well, by broad coalitions of stakeholders as opposed to only by authority structures operating in the shadows of senior management? Under the close scrutiny of stakeholder review, how many of these offenses would have gotten as far as they did? Not many, I think.

After years of witnessing such travesties in business, not to mention the less disastrous but no less questionable decisions firms make about their own core businesses every day, one starts to get the impression that things may have far less to do with bad decisions being made by bad decision-makers than with bad knowledge being hatched from within bad knowledge processing systems! Is it possible, I've asked myself, that the knowledge-making or innovation routines employed by mainstream businesses are somehow fatally flawed, and that *they*, not managers, are responsible for the poor quality of decisions so commonly made by even the most successful, most experienced firms? My conclusion? Not only possible, but probable. Why? Read on.

THE POLITICS OF KNOWLEDGE

The questions I often ask about how innovation is handled or managed in a firm include queries like: *How is innovation structured in the firm? Who gets to make business strategy here? Who gets to decide on which products or services to offer? Who gets to determine what business processes will be followed? Or what markets to be in? Or whether or not to bribe that dictator in Africa whose forests we plan to rape and whose people we plan to displace? Who gets to decide what we'll do on these and other matters? In short, who gets to participate in making the knowledge here that we will all later be asked to live with and support? How does knowledge processing happen around here?*

I also find it useful to think of knowledge making in political terms. I call this idea the *politics of knowledge.*[1] When viewed from a political perspective, knowledge making in business usually takes the form of oligarchies, or worse yet, authoritarian dictatorships. In any case, knowledge-making power is usually vested in the hands of the privileged few in most firms, those we call senior management. What a waste we make of the creative power of the vast majority of people who work in such firms as Ford, Firestone, DuPont, Exxon, and others, but who happen to lack a seat at the knowledge-making table, as it were. I am convinced that at some point in the hopefully-not-too-distant enlightened future, managers will look back on the politics of knowledge as it existed in the late-twentieth and early-twenty-first centuries and say to themselves, "*What a foolish waste of human capital that was! This business of relegating innovation to the hands of a few while ignoring the power of the many. What could they possibly have been thinking?*"

Under these circumstances, it's no wonder that the outcome of such distorted knowledge-making regimes so often consists of extraordinarily bad ideas. Peer review and the kind of vetting that comes only from transparency in management, and stakeholder and community participation, is fundamentally crucial to knowledge making in human social systems. Knowledge processing is a *whole-social-system affair*—innovation should be enterprise-wide in scope, not just *management-wide*. Sociologists know this.[2] Anthropologists know this.[3] Even the science of complexity has acknowledged this principle as beautifully expressed in its *complex adaptive systems theory*, or CAS theory.[4] CAS theory is, by any other definition, a theory that explains the ontogeny of knowledge processing and organizational learning in living systems—human systems, included.

THE "KNOWLEDGE DRIVE"

Human social systems come preprogrammed with knowledge-making routines that have evolved over the millennia, and which inevitably emerge under their own steam from within the social milieu found in all organizations. Indeed, innovation is a self-organizing, self-propelled process in human social systems.[5] Organizations, societies, communities, and businesses are all *knowledge-making systems* at their most fundamental level. That's what they fundamentally do! Moreover, they require no special management or supervisory direction to engage in innovation. Rather, human social systems tend to self-organize around the production and integration of new knowledge, purely as an emergent consequence of the interplay between individuals and groups engaged in the pursuit of common goals.

It is perhaps important to point out here that the corporate form of business organization, and its attendant management hierarchy, is only a hundred-year-old concept. Somehow, we all managed to get along just fine in the millennia that preceded the corporation when it came to innovation and the advance of human knowledge. It would seem worthwhile, then, that we give some serious thought to the manner in which humanity has managed to produce its knowledge during all those centuries without the benefit of centralized planning and control. Shouldn't today's attempts to improve business innovation be subject to inspiration and enlightenment from such insights? Might not, as the *Wall Street Journal* recently forecasted, *self-organization* be "the next big thing" in business?[6]

Self-organization is not only real, it accounts for how human knowledge has evolved over the millennia, and for how we have, until recently that is, always managed to innovate in sustainable ways. Now, however, we seem content to forget or ignore this hereditary social process and to distort it with the most unnatural and disruptive knowledge-making routines found on earth. We treat innovation as though it were an administrative process, as if we were commanding plants to grow in a garden while foolishly overlooking the fact that plant growth stems from endogenous forces, not human design. Only we humans do this.

To achieve this we create artificial knowledge-making groups and give them names like R&D or product development, and we command them to make new knowledge. Meanwhile, the vast majority of workers in business stand idly by and wait for the next great idea to come flying over the wall with marching orders attached for the masses. We've relegated the bulk of our workforce in business to a regimen of knowledge-followership, even as we systematically ignore their infinite knowledge-making potential. In the process, we infantize the majority of our workers and expose ourselves to the limitations of oligarchical knowledge-making and to the dangers of dubious and unsustainable innovations.

This is our common approach to innovation in most firms, and it is utterly unsustainable because it conflicts with the manner in which human social systems are hereditarily endowed to learn. It should come as no surprise to anyone, then, that the fruits of such systems are themselves unsustainable. How could they be otherwise? They were conjured up by small oligarchies with narrow interests and were rarely subjected to broad stakeholder reviews for testing and evaluation. Indeed, unsustainable innovation regimes routinely beget unsustainable human behaviors and outcomes. The one inevitably leads to the other.

Listen to how Leif Edvinsson puts it in his new book, *Corporate Longitude*:

This is the nub of the problem. We have not developed effective organizational structures to optimize the efforts of knowledge workers. What we have at present are two extremes. Traditional companies have industrial organizational structures, which struggle to cope with the volatility of the knowledge economy. Some new economy companies, meanwhile, have taken away the old structure without putting anything sustainable in its place.[7]

This brings me to my notion of "policy synchronization"[8] as a sound basis for achieving sustainable innovation in *both* senses of the term. I believe that the ways in which we organize for innovation in a firm should be aligned with the endemic patterns of knowledge-making I referred to earlier (see Figure 1-1). Think of it as analogous to the sex drive. You don't legislate sex, you get out of its way and adopt policies that support its natural expression. Or, at the very least, you avoid adopting policies that might conflict with its self-organizing fulfillment. This is not to say that artificial insemination and reproduction are not possible; or that birth control does not have a useful place in society. Of course this is all true, and we practice such methods. But all of them are predicated on a deferential understanding of how reproduction unfolds in its characteristically self-organizing way. In other words, we defer to *its* process, not ours, and we tailor our policies and practices accordingly.

With this principle of self-organization in mind, I ask why our approach to knowledge making should be any less deferential than the one we take toward sex making? If knowledge-making behaviors, like sexual behaviors, are truly intrinsic to human social systems, then the best approach to enhancing innovation is arguably the same one that has worked so well for us in the domain of sexual affairs for time immemorial: *accept the fact that it's a self-organizing process that works best in the absence of meddlesome management!* Innovation-related policies and programs should be crafted, accordingly, especially those conceived with innovation *enhancement* in mind.

What I'm suggesting here is that innovation-related policies in human social systems should be synchronized with the endemic tendency of such systems to self-organize around the production and integration of knowledge. Although the conventional wisdom in most management circles tells us that "behavior follows from policies," in the domain of knowledge making and business innovation, it is precisely the opposite that holds true: *policies should follow from behavior!* By synchronizing innovation-related policies and programs with intrinsically-held patterns of self-organized knowledge-making behavior in human social systems (i.e., the "knowledge drive"), businesses can realize the incomparable advantage of achieving *both* sustainable innovation and sustainable outcomes in commerce.

ENDNOTES

1. M. W. McElroy, "The New Knowledge Management," *Knowledge and Innovation: Journal of the KMCI* Vol. 1, No. 1 (October 15, 2000), pp. 43–67.
2. See, for example, D. Stark, "Heterarchy: Distributing Authority and Organizing Diversity," in J. H. Clippinger, III, editor, *The Biology of Business* (San Francisco: Josey-Bass Publishers, 1999).
3. See, for example, M. Mead, *Continuities in Cultural Evolution* (New Brunswick, NJ: Transaction Publishers, 1999).
4. See, for example, R. D. Stacey, *Complexity and Creativity in Organizations* (San Francisco: Berrett-Koehler Publishers, 1996).

5. Ibid.
6. B. Wysocki, Jr., "Self-Organization: The Next Big Thing?" *Wall Street Journal* (July 10, 2000), p. 1.
7. L. Edvinsson, *Corporate Longitude—Navigating the Knowledge Economy* (Stockholm, Sweden: Bookhouse Publishing, 2002), p. 114.
8. The "Policy Synchronization Method" is the subject of a U.S. patent application filed with the Patent and Trademark Office in September 2000 by Macroinnovation Associates, LLC of Windsor, VT (www.macroinnovation.com). It currently holds patent-pending status.

8

Managing for Sustainable Innovation[1]

Second-Generation Knowledge Management

In Chapter 1 of this book, I chronicled the arrival of second-generation knowledge management. In doing so, I described several of its distinguishing characteristics, including its hallmark recognition of the distinction between supply-side versus demand-side knowledge management. Supply-side strategies tend to focus only on the distribution of existing organizational knowledge, and are usually technocentric in their orientation. Demand-side strategies, by contrast, focus instead on satisfying organizational needs for new knowledge, and therefore tend to be learning- or innovation-oriented. One focuses on *knowledge sharing*, the other on *knowledge making*. Second-generation KM, unlike its first-generation supply-side cousin, attempts to strike a balance between supply- and demand-side thinking by addressing needs on both sides of the line. Only second-generation KM takes a measured approach in this way.

Over the past couple of years, the development of second-generation KM has continued to unfold. In addition to theory, we now have some tangible practice models before us that can be used by developers of knowledge management strategies to help fulfill the promise of second-generation thinking—that is, continuous learning and sustainable innovation. This is the allure to what Arie de Geus, former head of planning for Royal Dutch Shell referred to as, "the only sustainable competitive advantage" in business—"the ability to learn faster than your competitors."[2] Regardless of its other advantages, first-generation, supply-side KM, with its myopic focus on capturing, codifying, and sharing existing information, offers a poor prescription for improving organizational learning and business innovation. In the practice of knowledge management, only second-generation thinking tackles these issues. The question, then, becomes how to practice second-generation KM. What concrete steps can an organization take not only to share knowledge more effectively, but also to *create it* more prolifically?

A Social Process

The answer to the question of how to improve learning and innovation lies in the recognition of knowledge production as a social process.[3] People don't innovate, organizations do! Clearly, individual creativity plays a role in the process, but innovations spring forth from the efforts of groups, not individuals. And how could it be otherwise? In order for an idea to become widely practiced, it must first become widely accepted. Wide acceptance, in turn, implies acceptance by groups and whole social systems. The process by which new knowledge is formulated by individuals, validated by communities, and embraced into practice by organizations is what we call innovation.

Another of the key principles outlined in Chapter 1 was the concept of the knowledge life cycle (see Figure 8-1). According to that idea, organizational knowledge is produced and then integrated within the operating behaviors of a social system. In other words, new knowledge is produced by individuals collaborating in groups, who collectively formulate new ideas, validate them, and then propagate their knowledge across the organization, such that the individual and collective behavior of all of an organization's members changes in accordance with the new knowledge. Not all organizations engage in this pattern of behavior effectively, but according to second-generation thinking, all organizations are no less naturally inclined to do so. Why is this so?

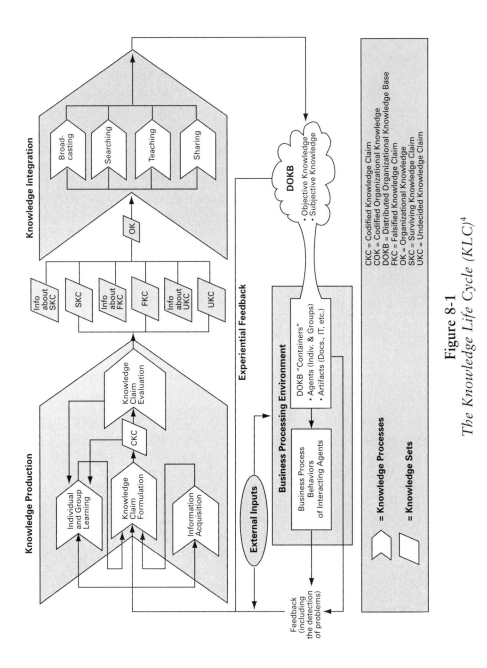

Figure 8-1
The Knowledge Life Cycle (KLC)[4]

What many people may find surprising is that most of the ideas bound up in second-generation KM are firmly rooted in complexity theory. Now seen as a valuable source of insight in understanding how living systems function—including human organizations—the science of complexity has a great deal to say about the nature and role of social cognition in the conduct of human affairs.[5] Indeed, second-generation KM owes much of its seminal thinking to complexity theory.

Of particular relevance to KM in the *science* of complexity is a body of thought known as *complex adaptive systems theory*, or CAS theory.[6] CAS theory holds that living systems (i.e., organizations made up of living, independent agents, such as people) self-organize and continuously fit themselves, individually and collectively, to ever-changing conditions in their environment. They do this, the theory says, by modifying their knowledge, which, in turn, leads to changes in behavior. In short, people and organizations practice their knowledge. If you ever want to determine what an organization knows, all you need to do is observe its practice. Regardless of how else it might be expressed, organizational knowledge is always articulated in the form of organizational behavior and can be deciphered accordingly.

FIRST PRINCIPLES

On the assumption that human organizations are complex adaptive systems, general principles on how CASs make and share their knowledge ought to be of instructional value in our attempts to determine how we can help organizations become better learners and innovators. Many models have been developed for this purpose, mostly by the Santa Fe Institute in New Mexico, which is far and away the citadel of thinking in complexity theory. Having inspected these models and immersed myself in them for the past several years, I have come to the conclusion that not only is CAS theory germane to management in business, but that there are four fundamental areas of knowledge-related behavior in human social systems, which if properly attended to can yield significant gains in learning, innovation, and competitive performance in commerce. It is the care and feeding of these four dimensions of organizational behavior and makeup, then, that practitioners of second-generation KM should be focusing on. Here they are:[7]

- *Embryology (of knowledge)*: The embryology of knowledge refers to the extent to which individuals in an organization are free to pursue their own learning agendas, and the degree to which they are further free to self-organize into knowledge-making communities of interest or practice.
- *Politics (of knowledge)*: The politics of knowledge making, diffusion, and use in an organization can have a dramatic impact on the overall rate of business innovation and the quality of the ideas produced. Most organizations tend to be organized oligarchically around these functions. Management teams and their administrative designates, including R&D functions, product planning, and so forth, tend to monopolize innovation while the rest of the organization is relegated to knowledge-following and a regimen of obedience.
- *Intellectual Diversity*: The degree to which a business supports a plurality of ideas, even dissident ones, will also have a material impact on its overall performance in innovation. Firms that seek diversified intellectual "ethographies" (diversity in ethos) tend to be more innovative than those that don't.
- *Connectedness*: The density of communications networks are also important to business innovation. The degree to which a culture values rich communications and connectivity between individuals and groups will, therefore, materially affect the rate and quality of its innovation.

These four aspects of organizational life are the most important variables in human social systems when it comes to how well an organization learns and produces new knowledge. Together, they reflect certain principles that form the foundation of practice in second-generation thinking. In other words, these are our *first principles*. It is critically important that the practice of second-generation KM—or the practice of anything, for that matter—be predicated on a set of explicitly held principles, since a failure to do so carries the risk of embarking on strategies that might conflict with principles *actually* held, but which have not yet been fully expressed (i.e., they may only be tacitly or implicitly held). Exposing the inconsistencies between what we *say* we stand for, versus the implications of what we actually *do*, can be very illuminating for even the most carefully managed firm.

Policies As Leverage

Once the matter of first principles has been sorted out, practitioners should next focus on how best to get knowledge-related social processes moving in the right direction (again, innovation is a *social* process, not an individual one, and especially not an administrative one). In other words, practitioners must focus on how knowledge-processing behaviors and conditions in the organization can be changed, where needed, such that they become more fully aligned with first principles. There are two ways to do this.

One is to simply order people into complying with a set of new behaviors by declaring new rules. (Incidentally, this rule-based approach is the one typically used by practitioners of first-generation thinking: *If we order people to contribute knowledge to the KM system, they will. If they don't, we'll induce them to do so using incentives and rewards—or punishments. That should do the trick.* Unfortunately, the best we can hope for under this approach is temporary compliance, and a real headache of enforcement.)[8]

The second approach is to permit, but not command, the desired behaviors through policy. In other words, rather than ordering people to form communities of practice, instead adopt a policy that endorses the *self-organization* of workers into communities and that offers assistance to employees who wish to do so, without commanding community formation. Similarly, a policy such as 3M's "Fifteen-Percent Rule," which makes it possible for many employees there to spend up to 15 percent of their time engaging in self-directed learning, encourages people to pursue their passions, but does not command, much less dictate, what their passions should *be.*[9]

I am convinced that because of the temporary compliance problem associated with the rule-based approach, constructive policy-making is the best means of creating an environment where sustainable innovation is possible. The practice of second-generation KM, then, ultimately takes the form of devising, implementing, and enforcing new policies (knowledge-processing policies, that is) that give rise to desired behaviors, but that do not command them.

Practice Implications

Examples of policy choices for implementation in each of the four areas of interest follow below.

■ *Embryology (of knowledge):* My belief in the critical importance of the four factors above as the quintessential determinants of how well an organization can learn and produce new knowledge is based on a fairly simple model of how learning naturally occurs in human social systems. Rooted in CAS theory, this model begins with the assumption that self-organized groups (or communities of interest, practice, etc.) are a fundamental source of new knowledge in any organization.[10] Without a healthy *community of communities*, one should expect to see lower levels of innovation than would otherwise be possible. Therefore, policies that invite and support the formation of communities—but that do not prescribe them—are extraordinarily important to the embryology of knowledge.

Next in the formula should be policies that make it possible for individuals to define their own learning agendas with unflagging organizational and management support. This is also part of the embryology dimension, because as Peter Senge pointed out in his book, *The Fifth Discipline*, "Organizations learn only through individuals who learn."[11]

Just how far to extend this policy for unbridled learning is a subject for experimentation in the field, but suffice it to say that training programs that are rigidly prescribed and enforced from the top of an organization are arguably counterproductive when it comes to eliciting higher rates of business innovation. Strict training regimes, and the certification programs that often accompany them, are little more than knowledge enforcement schemes imposed from above. As such, they tend to reflect a central authority's view of what's important to know, thereby relegating employees and workers to knowledge-followers, never knowledge-makers. I personally prefer an approach that favors individually-determined training programs over prescribed ones, although I recognize the need for a mix of both.

■ *Politics (of knowledge):* The next category of policies is the political one. Given the view of knowledge processing depicted in Figure 8-1, policies in the area of *Politics* generally address the questions of who gets to participate in the process, under what circumstances, and how? Here, most firms tend to operate as oligarchies when it comes to learning. A central authority of some kind, such as a management team or a board, makes the knowledge that everyone else is expected to practice. In addition, they tend to exploit their executive power by monopolizing knowledge production and regulating knowledge integration. This need not be the case. There's no reason why management couldn't be just as effective in running the day-to-day affairs of a business without the attendant monopoly on knowledge-making found in most firms today. After all, this is how most democracies operate—the executive branch is separate from the legislative branch. In return, these governments and the societies they serve are structurally open to their constituents' creativity, not just the people who happen to hold executive power at a given point in time. I see no reason why policies couldn't be adopted in business that would lead to the same structure, behaviors, and benefits in the areas of learning and innovation. In any case, all policies that deal with the distribution of power to create and integrate knowledge fall into the category I refer to as the politics of knowledge.

■ *Intellectual Diversity:* The third area of policy is intellectual diversity, or what I also call "ethodiversity" (i.e., diversity in ethos, values, and worldviews). As an example of this, consider the difference between HR policies aimed at recruiting *well-rounded individuals*, versus alternative policies by which a firm might seek to become a *well-rounded organization of individuals*. In the former case, people are screened and hired in accordance with how well they fit a target profile, so that virtually everybody hired tends to think alike, has a common worldview, and so forth. In the second case, people are screened and hired in accordance with how well they come across as individuals with *unique* interests, *unusual* capabilities, and *different* worldviews. Following the latter strategy leads to *well-rounded organizations*, which places a far greater range of ideas and possibilities at the disposal of its constituents than would otherwise be available. Needless to say, I favor the latter approach.

■ *Connectedness:* Last is the area of connectedness, which is also something that can be controlled or influenced by policy. The frequency and quality of communications between individuals and groups can obviously have an impact on the evolution of ideas in business. Individuals collaborating in groups can hardly be expected to practice knowledge-making as a social process if their ability to communicate with one another is somehow curtailed or restricted by policy, practice, or limited infrastructure.

This not only points to technology as an important element of business innovation, but also to the realm of protocol and hierarchy as issues worthy of attention by second-generation practitioners. Protocols that state that I can only talk directly to my boss but not to his or her boss arguably dampen innovation. The issue here is freedom of communication, not just the density of telecommunications networks. Here again, constructive policies can be embraced that are designed to instill higher levels of dialogue between individuals, regardless of their administrative rank or place in the pecking order.

CONCLUSION

If there has been a breakthrough in thinking in the evolution of second-generation KM—and I believe there has been—it lies in the realization that human social systems engage in certain regular patterns of behavior by which they collectively *produce* and *integrate* knowledge. When taken together, these patterns can be seen as an integrated life cycle model that can serve as a foundation for practice in our efforts to improve organizational learning and business innovation. This is clearly a contribution that can be traced to the influence of complexity theory on knowledge management.

Indeed, the fundamental essence of human social systems is that they fall into the category of *complex adaptive systems*, or CASs, as defined by the science of complexity. As such, they survive over time by continually adapting themselves to changes they encounter in both their internal and external environments. They do this by engaging in collective sensing and responding activities, which manifest themselves in the form of social processes.

On the *responding* side of the pattern is the continual production of new knowledge in response to new experiences and new conditions. New knowledge is then applied at the level of individual and collective practice, and the organization adapts itself to its environment, accordingly. When reality changes, new knowledge is yet again *re*-produced in response. That's what complex adaptive systems do— *they're persistent knowledge-processing systems!*

What is of such fundamental importance in this view of human organizations as *knowledge-making systems* is that no management whatsoever is required for these patterns to unfold. The behavior of interest is utterly emergent and bottom-up in origin. Human social systems come *predisposed* to make knowledge in accordance with the same endemic social patterns found in all complex adaptive systems. Human CASs, on the other hand, are more deliberative in nature and are *social* CASs. We make knowledge through conjecture and refutation, and through argument—innovation in the realm of human affairs is an entirely social and linguistic affair.

That said, in order to improve either the rate or quality of innovation in business, we must ultimately focus on the social patterns of behavior that account for organizational *knowledge production and integration*. All organizations are hereditarily endowed with the same basic patterns in these areas. The most effective approach to take, then, is to adopt policies that are aligned with these innate patterns of behavior, and that support, strengthen, and even amplify them.

Policies that fail to meet this test of alignment are doomed from the start and can only be expected to engender temporary behaviors of a disingenuous kind. Social systems exposed to that kind of stress will invariably return to their natural state, in which knowledge production and integration are carried out in the form of *unmanaged* social processes. It's better to accept and embrace the natural knowledge-making proclivities of human social systems than to ignore or supplant them with managed alternatives of an artificial kind. After all, there's no need to manage or prescribe knowledge-related behaviors, much less *rules*, in human social systems—they're already *in there*. We just come that way. Human social systems are *predisposed* to create new knowledge, even in the complete absence of management. That's what we fundamentally do. But we do it in a particular way—*our way*. Recognizing and acknowledging the characteristic shape of *how we do so* is critical to our success in business and in life.

If we're really serious about wanting to improve organizational learning and business innovation, the smartest thing we can do is to embrace policies that are *in agreement with how we naturally do those things*, such that our management policies and our native tendencies are mutually supportive and resonate with one another.

We're not machines, we're human social systems. Our knowledge management strategies should be crafted accordingly.

ENDNOTES

1. This chapter was originally published in 2000 under a different title: M. W. McElroy, "Using Knowledge Management to Sustain Innovation," *Knowledge Management Review* Vol. 3, Iss. 4 (Sept./Oct. 2000), pp. 34–37.
2. P. M. Senge, *The Fifth Discipline* (New York: Currency Doubleday, 1990), p. 4.
3. R. D. Stacey, *Complexity and Creativity in Organizations* (San Francisco: Berrett-Koehler, 1996).
4. The KLC was developed by members of Knowledge Management Consortium International (KMCI), a U.S.-based nonprofit association of knowledge and innovation management professionals from around the world (www.kmci.org).
5. Stacey.
6. See, for example, J. H. Holland, *Hidden Order: How Adaptation Builds Complexity* (Reading, MA: Perseus Books, 1995).
7. Based on the "Policy Synchronization Method," which is the subject of a U.S. patent application filed with the Patent and Trademark Office in September, 2000, by Macroinnovation Associates, LLC of Windsor, VT (www.macroinnovation.com). It currently holds patent-pending status.
8. A. Kohn, *Punished by Rewards* (Boston: Houghton Mifflin, 1993).
9. For a discussion of the 3M experience, see K. Baskin, *Corporate DNA: Learning from Life* (Boston: Butterworth-Heinemann, 1998), pp. 81–83.
10. See, for example, Senge; Stacey; E. Wenger, *Communitites of Practice* (Cambridge: Cambridge University Press, 1998).
11. Senge, p. 139.

9

SUSTAINABLE INNOVATION AND THE "LEARNING DRIVE"

Historians of late-twentieth- and early-twenty-first-century management practices may very well record the failure of business process reengineering (BPR) as comprising the death knell for reductionist thinking in postmodern times. Indeed, the very idea that people operating in nonlinear social systems could be manipulated with precision like so many belts and pulleys in a grist mill seems in retrospect, even to contemporary Taylorists,[1] like mechanistic thinking run amuck. *"What could they possibly have been thinking?"* historians will ask, as they look back on the crash of reductionism and the rise of systems thinking in its wake. We are arguably on the threshold of a new paradigm in management theory and practice, the effects of which are now being felt in earnest on several important fronts. One of them is in the province of intellectual capital, or knowledge management.

Despite its checkered reputation thus far, knowledge management (KM) is proving resistant to criticism while its practitioners are becoming increasingly more sophisticated. And why shouldn't KM exhibit that kind of resilience? After all, the proportion of economic value now attributed to so-called intangible or intellectual assets in business is higher than ever (75% of market values as reflected in the Dow Jones Industrial Average in 1997).[2] By contrast, as recently as 1980, the same index reflected market values owing to intangible assets at "zero dollars." In other words, the value of the Dow Jones Industrial Average in 1980—only twenty-two years ago—was mainly confined to traditional book values, or hard assets. Since then, the value of intellectual assets as a component of total *market caps* has increased exponentially. No wonder, then, that a whole new breed of professionals has emerged in a field we now call knowledge management.

In my own efforts to characterize the conventional practice of knowledge management, I have found it useful to differentiate between what I call *supply-side* versus *demand-side KM*.[3] In general, supply-side thinking focuses on the *sharing* and *distribution* of *existing* organizational knowledge, while demand-side thinking focuses on the *production* and *adoption* of *new* knowledge. Most of the KM thinking and hype in the marketplace to date has been firmly rooted in supply-side propositions. I call this orientation (i.e., the supply-side-only one), first-generation knowledge management.[4]

More recently, however, a new breed of KM practitioners has embraced the mystery of knowledge production and is beginning to think more in terms of whole knowledge life cycles that include *both* knowledge production *and* sharing. After all, valuable organizational knowledge presumably comes from somewhere, a fact that supply-side thinkers conveniently overlook. I call the more balanced practice of supply- *and* demand-side thinking, second-generation KM[5] (see Figure 9-1).

Given the prevalence of Taylorism[6] even in recent times, it should come as no surprise to anyone that knowledge management initially took the supply-side form that it did. Classical economics encourages us to objectify knowledge as if it were something that can be captured, codified, and distributed in discrete form. The suppliers in these schemes are, of course, managers who are presumed to possess the wisdom needed to determine *who* should have *what* knowledge, and *when*. This is the inspiration that lies behind the predominant mantra in first-generation KM: *it's all about getting the right information to the right people at the right time*. The unspoken assumption, therefore, is that *the right information already exists*.

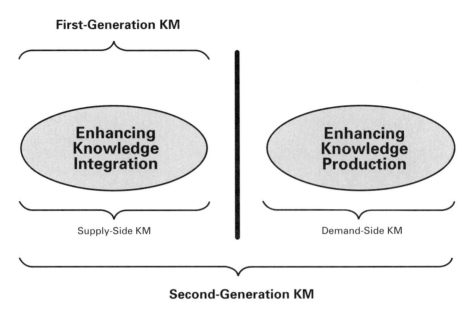

Figure 9-1
First- versus Second-Generation Knowledge Management

Demand-side thinkers, on the other hand, have stopped to question where existing knowledge comes from in the first place, and how it is that some firms manage to have more of it than others? How is it, in fact, that some firms seem more capable of engaging in effective organizational learning such that they adapt faster than their competitors and are more agile in the marketplace? In other words, how do firms innovate?

I have been fortunate to count myself among those of a small group of demand-side thinkers who have been wrestling with the question of organizational knowledge production for some time now. This group, the Knowledge Management Consortium International (KMCI),[7] is a nonprofit professional association that has declared its commitment to systems thinking as a foundation for practice in KM. As a result, KMCI has become the de facto center of thought for second-generation KM theory and practice. Moreover, in a reference to its views on complexity theory, KMCI was described in 1998 by *Knowledge Management* magazine as "the Santa Fe Institute for knowledge management."[8] Indeed, the KMCI's formulation of second-generation KM is worth noting because it signals the particular influence of systems thinking on a management domain of great contemporary importance: *organizational learning and business innovation.*

FRAMING THE DEBATE

In 2000, the *Wall Street Journal* ran a front-page article entitled, *"Self-Organization: The Next Big Thing?"*[9] Therein appeared the following words:

Today, self-organization is rapidly becoming a very hot idea, the essence of which is that top-down master plans aren't the only way to build something big and lasting. Unorganized assemblies of people can create everything from marketplaces to computer systems almost spontaneously, on the fly, from the bottom up.

In other words, creativity in human social systems often flourishes despite the absence of centralized planning or control. From this perspective, innovation can be seen as an emergent social process, not a rule-governed one.

The KMCI's study of competing theories on how innovation happens in human social systems quickly revealed the predominance of two distinctly different schools of thought. The first camp, the *reductionists*, view innovation as an administrative function managed by hierarchies. This approach to organizational innovation includes the use of such techniques as the so-called "stage-gate" method, now commonly employed by mainstream R&D shops. Also featured in the reductionist school are techniques designed for *individual use* (i.e., by sole inventors) such as the TRIZ[10] method, which looks to conceptual patterns found in prior inventions for inspiration in the development of new ones. The reductionist camp invariably views the challenge of innovation as an utterly top-down, manageable affair. Even a cursory look at the manner in which product innovation is organized and carried out in most firms offers ample evidence of the reductionist perspective at work. Its days, however, are arguably numbered.

The other prevailing school of thought in the innovation debate is the *adaptive systems* crowd—myself included. We begin by recognizing the fact that the current corporate form of business is a relatively new institution (only about a century old). Further, human social systems—indeed humanity, itself—have been producing new knowledge at impressive rates for *millennia* now, and have been doing so without the benefit of the kind of centralized planning and control schemes so prevalent in today's mainstream corporations.

According to the adaptive systems camp, human social systems survive by continuously adjusting, or *fitting*, themselves to their environments; and they do this by engaging in real-time, nonstop learning. In fact, adaptive systems theory for human settings holds that innovations are the product of *social systems*, not individuals. Although individuals certainly invent, only whole social systems can innovate, because innovation involves widespread adoption of validated new knowledge into social practice. And there can be no widespread adoption of new knowledge into practice until, and unless, widespread *acceptance* of such knowledge has first occurred. This is a social proposition, not an individual one.

The reductionist side of the debate is unquestionably treading on thin ice right now. In discussing the so-called "problem of [modern corporate] innovation," authors William Miller and Langdon Morris, in their book *Fourth Generation R&D*,[11] put it this way: "Although commonly denied in public, it [the problem of innovation] is discussed at length and deeply lamented in private, where top managers know that their corporations are failing at innovation and particularly at making the substantial leaps that are required for discontinuous innovation" (i.e., radical new innovations that break from the current trends). They later add, "It is clear that there is a serious problem with the practice of innovation, and it would not be an exaggeration to say that most corporations are pushing a rope at it without success."[12] In other words, their current methods are ineffective in terms of actually having impact on innovation outcomes. The title of the chapter in which these statements appear is "Innovation in Crisis."

The adaptive systems side of the debate sees the crisis of innovation as the result of a failure to recognize the fundamental nature of human organizations. Instead of turning to such reductionist stalwarts as Frederick Taylor for inspiration, the systems thinking camp has turned instead to the natural sciences for an understanding of how cognition happens in living systems. Perhaps their richest source of insight has been the science of complexity, which is more a branch of mathematics than a science per se. Complexity science focuses on the study of orderly behavior in what are otherwise decidedly *disorderly* systems. Of particular interest to some complexity scientists is the ontogeny of knowledge in living systems.[13] The theory of how knowledge unfolds in such systems—according to complexity science—is known as *complex adaptive systems theory* (CAS theory). CAS theory is the special province of the Santa Fe Institute in New Mexico, the citadel of thinking in the field.

CAS theory, for the second-generation, systems-thinking side of the KM industry, has emerged as the most respected, most credible model for representing the complex dynamics of knowledge-making and practice in human social systems. But to many of us involved in both the KM and OL (organizational learning) communities, it's not clear that CAS theory's relevance to management or to the conduct of human affairs is yet fully appreciated—much less understood—by members of either group. From here, then, I will try to explain what, to me, is the most profound implication of CAS theory as applied to organizational learning and business innovation.

COMPLEXITY THEORY AND ORGANIZATIONAL LEARNING

In the past, I have been mildly critical of the organizational learning community's failure to consider complexity theory as a sound basis for describing and modeling the dynamics of social learning and innovation. However, since I am a card-carrying member of that community, I see myself as no less responsible than others for this, a charge I now mean to confront by revealing the compelling facts of my own discoveries in this area. What I have to offer, then, is a fresh perspective on the ontogeny of knowledge in human social systems, and a means by which related insights can be parlayed into useful practice for the improvement of organizational learning and performance.

CAS theory can be summarized as follows: *living systems continuously fit themselves to their environments by determining how well competing strategies for survival work for them in practice, and then by choosing their future behaviors accordingly.* In other words, they learn. They have the capacity to detect conditions in their environ-

Complex Adaptive System (CAS) Model

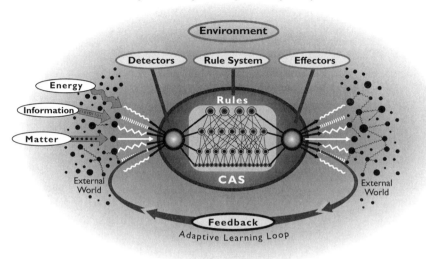

Figure 9-2
Complex Adaptive System (CAS) Model[14]

ments, and to further formulate coping strategies for themselves in response. Once experienced in the form of practice, the relative merits of different strategies are then assessed, after which they are either repeated, discarded, or modified for future use, depending on the kind of feedback received by the system. The "systems" in this case are living systems, which in a human context can be either individual people or whole social systems. Families, communities, nations, societies, organizations, businesses, clubs, groups, churches, and professional associations are all CASs operating at different levels of scale (see Figure 9-2).

Where OL theory has left off, then, CAS theory has picked up. In their combined form, the elegance and simplicity of the vision they evoke together is disarming. And so here it is.

THE "LEARNING DRIVE"

As every student of organizational learning knows, individual learning is an important element of mutual, collective, or organizational learning (OL). But it takes more than individual learning for OL to succeed. It takes *independent* individual learning. There's a big difference between learning about things *I* want to know because of *my* interests, versus learning about things I'm *required by others* to know. Here I point to the difference between learning and training. Learning in its purest form is a voluntary, self-directed act that follows from intrinsic motivation and is intended to solve a problem.[15] Training is something we endure in response to other people's views on what *they* think we should know (i.e., extrinsic motivation), whether or not it is relevant to any of our own problems.

In human social systems, people who learn and who hold knowledge about things that interest them deeply and personally tend to co-attract one another on the basis of their shared interests. This is not a managed process; rather, it's a natural one in the sense that its occurrence is self-organizing and emergent. No one forced me to join the Society for Organizational Learning. I did it voluntarily because of my desire to interact with kindred spirits who apparently share my passions and interests about the mysteries of learning. This is how communities form. Real communities, if you will, are self-organizing in origin.[16] You don't legislate communities; they spring forth from the mutual desires of independently motivated individuals to affiliate with one another on the basis of their shared interests.

Once formed, communities then act as the developmental breeding ground for new ideas, new knowledge, and potential innovations.[17] Inside communities, we share our individual ideas and subject them to group review, as even now I am doing in the production and publication of this book. Through dialogue and discussion in group contexts, ideas hatched in the minds of individuals become exposed to those of others, and are gradually refined, expanded, and integrated into forms that may meet with group, or community, approval. Many ideas as well are invalidated and discarded in favor of better ones. In these ways, ideas born in the minds of individuals are subjected in communities to scrutiny and evaluation. Communities, therefore, are of fundamental importance to the development of shared organizational knowledge. Without them, knowledge moves too quickly from the minds of individuals into the realm of organizational practice, a leap that undoubtedly accounts for the demise of authoritarian regimes throughout history. There's simply no denying the value of knowledge evaluation as performed by healthy and diverse communities in human social systems.

Just as people tend to collaborate and compete with one another for validation and acceptance of their ideas in communities, so do communities themselves collaborate and compete with each other for validation in the *communities of communities* we call organizations. The same principles that apply *within* communities are at work *between* them as well. The influence of adaptive system dynamics merely shifts in scale: from the individual to the community, to the community *of* communities, and so on. Even in the most rigidly managed command-and-control style organizations, ideas begin in the minds of individuals, migrate into groups or communities, and therein vie for favor and acceptance in the struggle for organizational adoption. In strict hierarchical regimes, there are simply fewer opportunities for individuals to participate in self-organized communities, and fewer communities to draw from in sourcing potential new knowledge. The adaptive capacity of organizations operating under such conditions suffers accordingly.

Now, here's the jaw-dropping insight gleaned from years of study by complexity scientists poring over the research on how knowledge happens in living systems. Their conclusions? It self-organizes.[18] And the form it takes as it does so expresses itself in precisely the same pattern of social processes I have sketched out above. Here it is again in more precise form: *independent individual learning; followed by group or community learning; followed by organizational adoption; followed, finally, by the integration of new knowledge into practice* (see Figure 9-3). That's the endemic pattern of knowledge processing found in all human social systems, and the beauty of it is that it's utterly emergent, self-organizing, self-propelled, and completely devoid of the Promethean hand of management—what complexity scientist Stuart Kauffman calls, "order for free."[19]

Now, burn that pattern indelibly into your mind's eye and then reread Thomas Kuhn's *Structure of Scientific Revolutions*.[20] What you will see is that Kuhn repeatedly invokes the same pattern as he skips across the centuries in his evolutionary account of scientific knowledge. First, the obvious role of *independent individual learning* by such luminaries as Galileo, Newton, Copernicus, Einstein, and many others looms large. Next, and just as conspicuous, are the many *self-organized communities* prominently featured within the revolu-

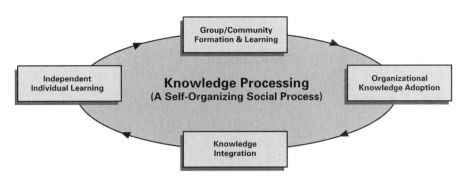

Figure 9-3
Self-Organizing Knowledge Processing

tionary structure that Kuhn writes of. In his own words, "Communities of this sort are the units that this book has presented as the producers and validators of scientific knowledge."[21] And finally, in a separate reference to what I refer to as *organizational adoption*—the organizational choice of knowledge that follows the intellectual competition between communities—Kuhn writes, "Competition between segments of the scientific community is the only historical process that ever actually results in the rejection of one previously accepted theory or in the adoption of another."[22]

These are very strong words, which on the basis of Kuhn's study of the manner in which scientific knowledge has evolved over the centuries, testifies to the irrepressible nature of self-organizing knowledge processes in social systems. This pattern—*independent individual learning; followed by group or community learning; followed by organizational adoption; followed, finally, by the integration of new knowledge into practice*—is undeniably at work under its own steam in human social systems at all levels of scale. It is as naturally present in the social milieu of organizational life as the sex drive is for individuals in the propagation of species. In this case, however, we're talking about the existence and influence of a *learning drive* as a basis for the propagation of knowledge and adaptive behavior in living systems. Both are self-organizing in their ontogeny, and both are undeniably at play in the affairs of human social systems.

That the learning drive exists, and that it expresses itself in the characteristic pattern I have described, are claims that I and others have made and that practically support themselves now on the basis of prima facie evidence alone. Once understood, the pattern can be seen everywhere in practice, expressing itself often, usually in the complete absence of management. A full appreciation of this phenomenon requires not only an understanding of organizational learning theory, but also a competent grasp of the role that complexity science has played in modeling the evolution of knowledge in adaptive systems. Think of it this way: the organizational learning movement now has a more granular and robust theoretical model to work with, one that offers a more detailed description of the dynamics of *mutual learning* in human social systems. Armed with such a plausible model of *how learning happens* in human social systems, practitioners now have something sufficiently tangible to work with—something they can easily see, touch, and feel as a concrete basis for action.

A FRAMEWORK FOR ACTION

Unlike the reductionist approach to managing anything, systems thinkers—and now the CAS-inspired OL crowd—understand that the behavior of complex systems can be traced to their structures. Thomas Kuhn knew this, and now we know this. What I have described above, then, is the *structure of learning*—knowledge production and integration—in human social systems. Listen to it again: *independent individual learning; followed by group or community learning; followed by organizational adoption; followed, finally, by the integration of new knowledge into practice.* Individuals engage in self-directed learning. They then co-attract one another and collectively form groups or "communities of knowledge." Mutually-held knowledge is then developed inside these communities and is evaluated by them as such. Communities then compete with one another in their shared *community of communities* and eventually come to adopt and integrate metacommunity knowledge (or organizational knowledge). When this happens, episodes of organizational learning can be said to have occurred.

But since all of this is self-organizing in its ontogeny, who needs management? You don't order social systems to engage in knowledge-making any more than you command plants to grow; they are both already predisposed to do so without the need for any management at all. But do all organizations learn equally well? Does my firm articulate these processes in the same way yours does? Probably not. In fact, most firms could be accused of actually *inhibiting* these processes, which after countless generations of human evolution unquestionably account for how we got this far, despite such inhibitions. God forbid we should get out of their way and let these social patterns of learning and innovation have their impact on the conduct of human affairs—*to help us adapt*! Indeed, you don't manage knowledge, you get out if its way. Better yet, you offer aid and support to its expression in human social systems. I will now try to explain how.

Reductionist dogma is predicated on the belief that people operating in human social systems can be manipulated and managed into following certain prescribed patterns of behavior. By refining those processes and managing people ever more efficiently, practitioners of reductionist thinking believe they can create human operating systems whose behaviors comply with management designs. This is vintage BPR (business process reengineering) and first-generation KM thinking. Interesting, but misguided. Reductionist thinking completely overlooks the fact that certain business-related behaviors are already present in human social systems and simply can't be ignored or wished away. It's the proverbial herding-of-cats problem. Cats will simply not be herded any more than people operating in human social systems can willfully disavow their tendency toward *independent individual learning; followed by group or community learning; followed by organizational adoption; followed, finally, by the integration of new knowledge into practice*. Any attempt to ignore these patterns or to replace them with artificially prescribed forms of learning and innovation only conflict with them in the long run, degrade along the way, and are therefore unsustainable. These patterns will simply not be denied, nor will they conveniently go away.

And why would we want them to? If it's enhanced organizational learning and business innovation we're after, we should embrace these patterns, roll out the red carpet, and grant them the keys to the kingdom. That, then, is the key to enhancing organizational learning and business innovation as inspired by complex adaptive systems theory. Unlike the conventional practice of management in which policies are prescribed in order to deterministically drive certain behaviors, wisdom in the practice of systems thinking suggests precisely the opposite. The policies we embrace, in this case, should be driven by organizational behaviors, not the other way around, because the behaviors of interest to us *already exist!* Therefore, on the one hand, we should go out of our way to avoid policies that either conflict with or inhibit the expression of these systemic behaviors, and on the other, we should aggressively seek to enact policies that will support, strengthen, and reinforce them. In this regard, the controlling orientation of conventional management is wholly inappropriate and self-defeating. What's required, instead, is a deferential approach, not a prescriptive one. Management policies, in this case, should follow from behaviors, not the reverse.

If the pattern of interest is *independent individual learning; followed by group or community learning; followed by organizational adoption; followed, finally, by the integration of new knowledge into practice*, then the kinds of interventions we should be considering are those that make its full realization and expression possible. The rest will naturally follow (see Table 9-1).

Some of the policy recommendations shown in Table 9-1 come directly from the "complexity" literature on complex adaptive systems. Of particular interest is the work of John Holland, professor at University of Michigan and a principal player in the early development of CAS theory at the Santa Fe Institute. According to Holland, the proper functioning of adaptive systems depends on "extensive interactions" and "the aggregation of diverse elements."[23] On the meaning of the term adaptation, Holland explains, "Adaptation, in biological usage, is the process whereby an organism fits itself to its environment. Here, we expand the term's range to include learning and related processes."[24]

To help simplify the matter of policy determination, I have found it useful to think in terms of the following framework, which practitioners can use as a normative guide in formulating potential policy interventions:[25]

1. *"Embryological" Policies*—This category of knowledge- and learning-related policies embodies policy decisions in two areas closely related to the formation of new knowledge in human social systems: individual learning and community formation. Policies that ensure opportunities for self-directed learning by individuals, and

Table 9-1
Knowledge Processes and Policies That Support Them

Knowledge Processing Behaviors	Supporting Policies
■ Independent individual learning	■ Support self-directed, self-managed learning programs for all employees ■ Recruit, hire, and retain workers with diverse values and worldviews ■ Facilitate omnidirectional communications
■ Group or community formation and learning	■ Embrace policies and programs that enable and support self-organized communities of knowledge ■ Formalize the inclusion of community-made knowledge in the politics of organizational knowledge-making ■ Facilitate omnidirectional communications
■ Organizational knowledge adoption	■ Enforce policies of transparency and openness in management deliberations and knowledge making ■ Facilitate omnidirectional communications
■ Knowledge integration	■ Enforce aggressive knowledge sharing ■ Facilitate omnidirectional communications

that also make it possible for communities of knowledge to self-organize and receive support for their activities, are important here. Policies adopted in this category therefore relate to the first two components of the self-organized pattern of knowledge-making (*individual learning* and *community formation*). They have their intended effects by determining the extent to which individuals in an organization can, in fact, engage in self-directed learning, and the extent to which conditions either inhibit or support community formation in a firm.

2. *"Politics" of Knowledge Policies*—This category deals with the manner in which new knowledge is produced and integrated in an organization. For the most part it deals with who gets to participate

in related deliberations, hence the political spin to its title. This category also involves policies related to knowledge entitlement, thereby incorporating corporate positions on such matters as intellectual property ownership and sharing. Policies adopted in this category determine the extent to which knowledge hatched by individuals and developed in communities can fairly compete for *organizational adoption* with the authority structures already in power in a firm. Whereas most firms tend to practice oligarchically-oriented politics in this space, highly adaptive organizations tend to be more open and democratic in their treatment of dissident views.

3. *Ethodiversity*[26]—Unlike most diversity programs in business, this category of knowledge-related policies has less to do with *ethnic* diversity than it does with *ethos* diversity, or *ethodiversity*. As such, its primary focus of interest is in the realm of policies that deal with managing the ethos demography, or *ethography*,[27] of a firm. Of particular interest here are policies that influence recruiting, hiring, and retention practices and the effects they have on the mix of values, worldviews, and outlooks embodied in the population of a firm. This is all about achieving a healthy mix of intellectual diversity by populating organizations with individuals who hold widely divergent philosophies and worldviews, as opposed to staffing an organization with people who all think alike. Again, this is *ethodiversity*, not ethnic diversity. Affirmative steps can be taken in this area, but only if the right policies and tools are in place to support them.

4. *Connectedness*—This last category deals with the extent to which information can flow throughout the organization in support of *individual learning*, *community learning*, and *organizational adoption*. Technology certainly plays a role here, but so do social rules in the culture of a firm, which very often conspire to inhibit free and open communication between people and groups. To the extent that these conditions inhibit the flow of information between people, communities, and authority structures, they frustrate, in turn, the emergence of self-organizing patterns of learning and innovation in organizations. Here again, affirmative steps can and should be taken to ensure that knowledge and information moves appropriately within the organization—or between it and others—as needed.

By synchronizing policies in each of the four areas described above with the known pattern-like complexion of self-organizing knowl-

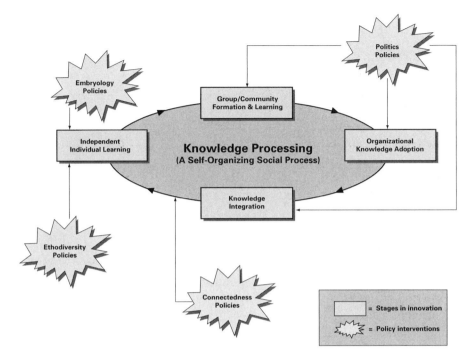

Figure 9-4
Management Policy Areas Related to Knowledge Processing

edge processes in human social systems, managers can willfully enhance both the rate and quality of learning and innovation in a firm (see Figure 9-4).

Because of this deliberate intent to synchronize policies with the emergent nature of knowledge-making in human social systems, I call the methodology described here the *Policy Synchronization Method*.[28] As such, it is the only method I know of that (1) predicates its interventions on the assertion that people in organizations tend to self-organize around the production and integration of mutually-held knowledge, and (2) claims that the most effective approach to improving organizational learning and innovation is one that affirmatively—and *deferentially*—embraces policies designed to strengthen and reinforce such (endemic) behaviors.

CONCLUSION

Complexity science has made it possible to see patterns of social processes involved in the production and integration of organizational knowledge. This pattern is predictable in the sense that it always tends to appear, or emerge, in a regular behavioral form in human social systems at multiple levels of scale, in the following way: *independent individual learning; followed by group or community learning; followed by organizational adoption; followed, finally, by the integration of new knowledge into practice.* By all accounts, this pattern of behavior has been deeply responsible for the evolution of human knowledge since time immemorial and is, itself, a product of evolution.

Managers in business who wish to improve their firms' performance in learning and innovation would do well to begin by recognizing that human social systems are already endowed with self-organizing patterns of related behaviors. Management in this arena, then, has a great deal less to do with the design of *new* business processes than it does with the support, strengthening, and reinforcement of *existing* ones. This can be achieved using a *policy synchronization method*, which advocates the adoption of organizational policies and programs in four critical areas: (1) embryological policies (individual learning and community formation); (2) politics of knowledge policies (governance of knowledge production, diffusion, practice, and entitlement); (3) ethodiversity policies (the distribution of worldviews or belief systems in a firm; ethos diversity, or *ethodiversity*); and (4) connectedness policies (enables natural rates of interactions between people and the proper flow of information and knowledge throughout an organization).

The use of the *Policy Synchronization Method (PSM)* for improving organizational learning and innovation offers the following key benefits:

1. Administrative and cultural barriers to individual and organizational learning are systematically broken down by focusing on related policies and programs in the four areas encompassed by the method. Both the rate and quality of adaptive learning and organizational innovation improve under such conditions.

2. The tendency of people and groups in organizations to self-organize around their own passions and interests is supported

and strengthened by embracing knowledge-related policies and programs that encourage and reinforce related behaviors. The best efforts and ideas of people thereby become more accessible, higher in quality, and more visible to the organization as a whole.

3. The PSM method turns learning and knowledge-making into a distributed enterprise-wide affair by formally embracing the learning and innovation interests of individuals and communities in all precincts. As a result, the creativity of *whole social systems*, not just their administratively anointed management teams, can be tapped for competitive and adaptive advantage. Although the vast majority of many firms' populations are effectively marginalized by overly-centralized, formal innovation programs, under the PSM method the totality of an organization's workforce becomes fully engaged in learning and knowledge production.

4. Because the policies advocated under the PSM approach are explicitly synchronized with endemic patterns of self-organized learning and innovation in organizations, the rate and quality of organizational learning and innovation not only improve but *remain* improved at sustainable levels. This leads to the notion of *sustainable innovation*. Knowledge processing policies that are *not* synchronized with self-organized patterns of learning and innovation in such systems inevitably conflict with those patterns and are eventually undermined *by* them. Artificial programs of this kind are therefore unsustainable. In contrast, policies and programs designed to explicitly support those patterns become locked in embrace *with* them in a mutually-reinforcing dance of sustainable innovation. In the jargon of system dynamics, this is known as a "reinforcing cycle" (see Figure 9-5). Organizational learning and innovation flourish under such conditions.

5. The PSM method is bottom-up, not top-down, in its orientation. It explicitly rejects the claim that people operating in a social milieu can produce and integrate knowledge on a sustainable basis via prescriptive management edicts, which seek only to command and control them at the expense of their intrinsic motivations and passion. By embracing the distributed learning capacity of whole social systems, the PSM method marks a radical departure from classical management dogma, according to which only a minority of a firm's individuals are seen as capable of engaging in worthwhile learning and innovation.

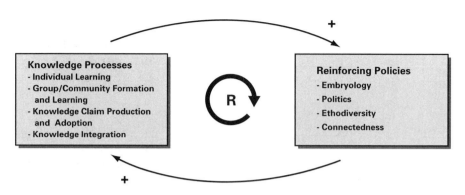

Figure 9-5
Management Policies Reinforcing Knowledge Processing

Strong anecdotal evidence exists in support of the kinds of policy interventions advocated by the PSM method. The so-called "Fifteen-Percent Rule" at 3M, according to which employees there can spend up to 15 percent of their time engaged in self-determined, self-managed *independent individual learning*, is widely seen as a major factor in what accounts for that company's industry-leading levels of innovation.[29] Elsewhere, at Deere and Company in Moline, IL, management has been working on the deployment of policies, programs, and infrastructures aimed at encouraging and supporting *self-organized communities* of practice.[30] As in the case of 3M, Deere is also taking steps to alter the politics of knowledge, so that community-made knowledge can play a more formal role in decision-making and in the development of business strategy, as promising new ideas rise to the fore.

These and other examples offer strong testimony to the effects that pieces and parts of the PSM method can have on organizational learning and innovation, but I know of no firms that have taken the whole step of transforming policies in all four areas. This, to me, represents a significant opportunity for practitioners involved in learning, knowledge, and innovation management, who may all "get" the vision thing, but who lack concrete steps for *how to get there from here*. By focusing on the development and implementation of specific knowledge processing policies and programs in each of the four areas described above, the rate and quality of organizational learning and innovation can be markedly improved on a sustainable basis.

Remember the pattern: *independent individual learning; followed by group or community learning; followed by organizational adoption; followed, finally, by the integration of new knowledge into practice.* Nurture the "learning drive," and sustainable innovation will follow.

Endnotes

1. Frederick W. Taylor was a late-nineteenth-/early-twentieth-century management theoretician best known for his reductionist approach to shop management, which he called "scientific management."
2. W. L. Miller and L. Morris, *Fourth Generation R & D* (New York: John Wiley & Sons, 1999), p. xiiii (using data from Value Line Publishing, Inc.); see also Figure 1-7 in this book.
3. M. W. McElroy, "The Second Generation of Knowledge Management," *Knowledge Management* (October, 1999), pp. 86–88.
4. Ibid.
5. Ibid.
6. F. W. Taylor, *Scientific Management* (New York: Harper & Brothers Publishers, 1947), pp. 40–41.
7. Knowledge Management Consortium International's website is www.kmci.org.
8. L. Mantelman, "KM Consortium Focuses on Complexity Theory." *Knowledge Management* (April, 1999), p. 12.
9. B. Wysocki, Jr., "Self-Organization: The Next Big Thing?" *Wall Street Journal* (July 10, 2000), p. 1.
10. The TRIZ method (pronounced "trees") is an invention facilitation technique created by a Russian patent-office worker, Henry Altshuller, in the former Soviet Union in 1947. TRIZ is a Russian acronym that stems from a phrase pertaining to the solution of invention problems.
11. Miller and Morris, p. ix.
12. Ibid., p. x.
13. See, for example, J. H. Holland, *Hidden Order: How Adaptation Builds Complexity* (Reading, MA: Perseus Books, 1995).
14. The KLC was developed by members of the Knowledge Management Consortium International (KMCI), a U.S.-based nonprofit association of knowledge and innovation management professionals from around the world (www.kmci.org).
15. See, for example, K. R. Popper, *Objective Knowledge: An Evolutionary Approach* (Oxford: Clarendon Press, 1979), Chapter 1; L. D. Kamada, "Intrinsic and Extrinsic Motivation Learning Processes: Why

Japanese Can't Speak English," a paper presented at the Japan Association of Language Teachers' International Conference on Language Teaching and Learning, November 22–24, 1986; E. L. Deci and R. M. Ryan, "Curiosity and Self-Directed Learning: The Role of Motivation in Education," in L. Katz, editor, *Current Topics in Early Childhood Education*, Vol. 4 (Norwood, NJ: Ablex Publishing Company, 1982); A. Maslow, "Self-Actualization and Beyond," from Proceedings of the Conference on the Training of Counselors of Adults, sponsored by the New England Board of Higher Education, and the Center for the Study of Liberal Education for Adults, held May 22–28, 1965; R. A. Zbrzezny, "Effects of Extrinsic Rewards on Intrinsic Motivation: Improving Learning in the Elementary Classroom," a dissertation submitted by its author in partial fulfillment of the requirements of a course (E591) at Indiana University of South Bend, April 10, 1989.

16. R. D. Stacey, *Complexity and Creativity in Organizations* (San Francisco: Berrett-Koehler, 1996).

17. E. Wenger, *Communities of Practice* (Cambridge: Cambridge University Press, 1998).

18. Stacey, pp. 23–45, 72–117.

19. S. Kauffman, *At Home in the Universe* (New York: Oxford University Press, 1995), Chapter 4.

20. T. S. Kuhn, *The Structure of Scientific Revolutions* (Chicago: University of Chicago Press, 1962).

21. Ibid., p. 178.

22. Ibid., p. 8.

23. Holland, p. 4.

24. Ibid., p. 9.

25. This framework is taken from the "Policy Synchronization Method," which is the subject of a U.S. patent application filed with the Patent and Trademark Office in September, 2000, by Macroinnovation Associates, LLC of Windsor, VT (www.macroinnovation.com). It currently holds patent-pending status.

26. *Ethodiversity* is a term I coined. It is a reference *not* to the ethnic diversity of an organization, but to its ethos diversity. I define this as *the distribution of values, dominant assumptions, worldviews, philosophies, and politics held by a collection of people in an organization, which, in turn, inform their attitudes, predispositions, beliefs, customs, and practices as they go about their daily affairs.*

27. *Ethography* is also a term I coined. It refers to the science of detecting, recording, and analyzing the ethodiversity of an organization. Further,

the linguistic or documentary representation of an organization's etho-diversity may take the form of an *ethographical description* or record.

28. See endnote number 24 above.
29. For a discussion of the 3M experience, see K. Baskin, *Corporate DNA: Learning from Life* (Boston: Butterworth-Heinemann, 1998), pp. 81–83.
30. From firsthand observations made by the author during visits to Deere and Company in Moline, IL.

Part IV

THE ECONOMICS OF KNOWLEDGE MANAGEMENT

"Every organization—not just business—needs one core competence: innovation. And every organization needs a way to record and appraise its innovative performance."

—Peter Drucker

"Intellectual capital is just as important for traditional businesses as for new economy Wunderkinder creating patents and intellectual property. It is the future of all business—literally. It is the only meaningful way to gauge the potential energy of a company. No innovation will ever take place without investments in intangibles."

—Leif Edvinsson

10

SOCIAL INNOVATION CAPITAL[1]

REDEFINING INTELLECTUAL CAPITAL

With companies around the world now routinely trading at levels far beyond their book values, senior managers, accountants, and other business executives have been increasingly focusing on the new field of intellectual capital. Intangible assets (or "goodwill," as it is sometimes referred to) have always played a role to some degree or another in corporate valuations, but the proportion of such intangibles in today's "market caps" has reached unprecedented levels. The aggregate price of the Dow Jones 30 Industrials in 1997, for example, exceeded the combined book values of the member companies by a factor of three-to-one.[2] For many companies today, this ratio is often much higher.

Not surprisingly, managers interested in getting their arms around intellectual capital are searching for ways to describe, measure, and manage their intangible assets with a particular emphasis on capturing their favorable effects on the bottom line and on shareholder values. Chief among these intrepid pioneers has been Leif Edvinsson, former corporate director of intellectual capital at Skandia AFS, who along with Michael Malone in 1997, coauthored the influential text entitled *Intellectual Capital*.[3] In their fine treatise on the sub-

169

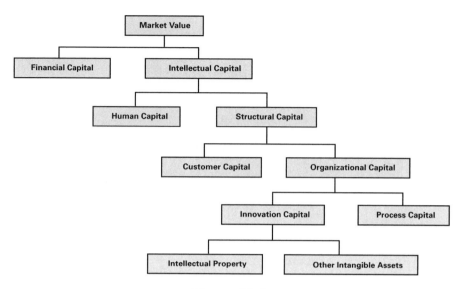

Figure 10-1
Leif Edvinsson's IC Model for Skandia AFS (Source: Intellectual Capital, by L. Edvinsson and M. Malone, New York: HarperBusiness, 1997)

ject, Edvinsson's experiences at Skandia in developing an intellectual capital (IC) management scheme are meticulously described. Of particular interest is the manner in which Skandia chose to map its IC territory (see Figure 10-1).

In Edvinsson's scheme, IC is composed of two major elements: *human capital* and *structural capital*. According to Edvinsson's view of IC shown in Figure 10-1, *human capital* refers to the value of knowledge, skills, and experiences held by individual employees in a firm; *structural capital* consists of what Edvinsson and Malone refer to as the "embodiment, empowerment, and supportive infrastructure of human capital."[4] As such, structural capital includes all the things that support human capital in a firm, but which are left behind when employees go home at the end of the day (i.e., *organizational capital*). And last, *customer capital* is the value of customer relationships.

Despite the groundbreaking advances made by Edvinsson and his team at Skandia AFS since they started in the early 1990s, their model fails to take into account another major component of intangible value now commonly recognized on other fronts: *social capital*. Unlike the other forms of IC, social capital points to the value of *relationships* between people in firms, and between firms and other firms. Trust, reciprocity, shared values, networking, and norms are all things that, according to social capital theory, add value in a firm, or between firms, by speeding the transfer of information and the development of new knowledge. In a sense, what Edvinsson refers to as *customer capital* is merely a form of social capital by another name, albeit only between a company and its customers. But social capital can take other forms, the combination of which unquestionably adds value to a firm, is intangible, and clearly warrants a prominent place in the taxonomy of IC.

Turning to the realm of social capital theory, then, we find two major schools of thought.[5] The first is the so-called "egocentric" perspective, in which social capital is seen as the value of an individual's relationships with other individuals in helping to get things done in a firm. The other is the "sociocentric" model, in which social capital is still held by individuals, but has more to do with the added value of *their position in the structure* of a firm than with their interpersonal relationships per se.

But there is arguably another form of social capital (one of many, I'm sure) that is of particular relevance to this discussion. I call it "social innovation capital" (SIC). Here, I use the term in such a way that the root concept is "innovation capital," which is modified by the adjective "social." In other words, the concept refers to innovation capital of a social kind (held by a collective), as opposed to, for example, innovation capital of an individual kind (held only by an individual). Social innovation capital, then, refers to the structural manner in which whole social systems (e.g., firms) organize themselves around—and carry out—the production and integration of new knowledge.

By recognizing such social innovation capital, managers not only can measure and value their firms' capacity to innovate, but can also enhance their performance and output as well (i.e., they can enhance their capacity to innovate *and* their innovations). In other words, by managing social innovation capital, managers can improve their rate and quality of innovation, as well as their competitive standing in practice. Indeed, this is the value proposition of managing social innovation capital, and is also the basis for advocating its inclusion in the formal typology of intellectual capital. Recognizing not only a firm's intellectual output but also its *capacity to produce* such output as a valuable intangible in its own right is wholly appropriate in a world where survival has everything to do with a firm's capacity to sustainably outlearn and out-innovate its competitors.

Although it is true that Edvinsson's scheme does already have a place for the notion of "innovation capital," he positions it as a subset of structural capital and defines it mostly in terms of intellectual properties or assets (i.e., patents, trademarks, and copyrights).[6] In doing so, Edvinsson places his emphasis on innovations as in *outputs*, but not on innovation as in *process*. Elsewhere in Skandia's model we see Edvinsson's reference to *process capital*, which at first could be interpreted as inclusive of innovation processes, but here again he defines his category in terms that have little to do with innovation per se.[7] Instead, Edvinsson's notion of process capital focuses mostly on operations or business processes, not the meta-operations or knowledge processes of interest to us in the context of innovation.

In sum, there is no place for the kind of social innovation capital I speak of anywhere in Edvinsson's model, much less a place for social capital of any other kind.

So, given the absence of social capital in Edvinsson's model, I propose a major modification to it—and to all others, for that matter—that includes the addition of both social capital and the underlying notion of social innovation capital (see Figure 10-2). In this modified IC model, I also fix what I believe is another shortcoming in Edvinsson's treatment of customer capital by placing it in context with other forms of "relationship capital," a term that Tom Stewart uses in his book *Intellectual Capital* (1997).[8] I accomplish this by repositioning customer capital as a subcategory under the heading of *social capital* where it belongs.

Finally, although there are many references in the social capital literature to notions of "networks" as instantiations of social capital,[9] the same literature fails to differentiate between one type of network and another in terms that might suggest different levels of value, or purpose, to different *kinds* of networks. Here, I propose the notion of *characteristic patterns of networks*, or archetypes, and suggest that one such pattern that has its own tell-tale identity is the kind that self-organizes around the production and integration of new knowledge. This is what I mean by social innovation capital: a particular archetypal social pattern that has as its aim the production and inte-

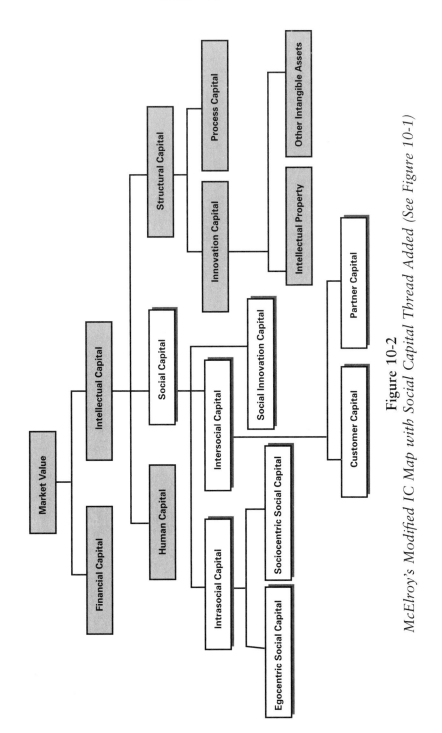

Figure 10-2

McElroy's Modified IC Map with Social Capital Thread Added (See Figure 10-1)

gration of new knowledge by, and for, the organization. Indeed, all firms produce new knowledge according to *some* such pattern(s), and so their SIC can, and should, be described accordingly.

Coauthors Janine Nahapiet and Sumantra Ghoshal point out in their very fine paper, "Social Capital, Intellectual Capital, and the Organizational Advantage,"[10] that "we use the concept of the structural dimension of social capital to refer to the *overall pattern of connections* between actors—that is, who you reach and how you reach them" (emphasis added). But although the same authors fail to *name* those patterns, I offer the following description of SIC: *a self-organizing social process in which individuals and groups collaborate with one another to solve problems by formulating, evaluating, and adopting new knowledge claims.* Groups, in this context, include communities of practice, interest, knowledge, and so on, as well as teams. Communities, groups, and teams are the wellsprings of knowledge in business, and it is their characteristic pattern of formation and behavior that contributes much to the shape and substance of social innovation capital. The relative health of an organization's *community of communities* is, therefore, one important measure of value in a firm's SIC.

That social capital theorists refer just to "networks of people" as social capital, but not to *specific patterns of networks* as such, is a bit like referring to the weather as "nothing but patterns of meteorological activity." Failing to differentiate between tornadoes, hurricanes, tsunamis, and heat waves leaves much to be desired. The same is true in human social systems. The manner in which people self-organize around the production and integration of new knowledge in organizations has a characteristic pattern like no other. It should be recognized, named, and approached as such. Indeed, the healthy presence of this pattern is of great value to a firm, and so I choose to acknowledge it as *social innovation capital.*

To successfully propagate these patterns of innovation—and thereby trigger improvements in the rate and quality of IC production—managers of SIC must focus on nurturing the elements, or subprocesses, of knowledge production and integration. By treating learning and innovation as social processes, not administrative ones, and by focusing on ensuring the health and well-being of related patterns of behavior, managers can markedly improve the value of their firms' IC and achieve *sustainable innovation* in the process.

PRACTICE IMPLICATIONS

Before continuing, I should take care to point out that the foregoing discussion of how best to characterize intellectual capital is based on only one such scheme: Leif Edvinsson's Navigator model, developed by Edvinsson and his team at Skandia AFS. There are certainly others as well. But since it was not my intent in writing this paper to perform a critique of all such methods—rather, only to spot the omission of social capital in *one* of them—I chose the Skandia model because of its hierarchical composition, and its apparently high standing in IC circles. That said, however, I would levy the same criticism at all other expressions of intellectual capital, which so far as I know all suffer from the same deficiency: the omission of social capital.

In their failure to embrace social capital, the Skandia model and others necessarily fail to address innovation per se, since innovation is without a doubt a social process. Knowledge production in human social systems has long been recognized as a function of collaboration between individuals in communities of interest, practice, and so on, as exemplified in Thomas S. Kuhn's study of the history of science in his well-known book *The Structure of Scientific Revolutions*.[11] For those who may still harbor doubts about whether or not innovation is a social process—that is, as opposed to an administrative one—I suggest a quick revisit to Kuhn's fascinating history of paradigm shifts, in which the social nature of knowledge production and integration is made abundantly clear.

From the perspective of intellectual capital management, the significance of seeing innovation as a social process is at least twofold. First, it tells us that one very important aspect of IC—if not *the* most important one—is the *social capacity to innovate* in a firm (i.e., to produce and integrate knowledge). Not all such capacities are equal across firms. Here, the importance of social capital in general really shines through, since trust, reciprocity, relationships, and norms all arguably enhance a firm's collective capacity to collaborate around the production of new knowledge.

Next, the view of innovation as a social process also helps us understand that in a very real sense, innovation is an unmanaged process. Indeed, it is a self-organizing one. This explains the very strong connections now seen between innovation and complexity theory, which is nothing if not the study of self-organization in dynamic systems. The management implications here are profound. Although there is certainly nothing wrong with current attempts to manage innovation in the administrative sense (i.e., managing R&D functions, etc.), tapping a firm's natural ability to self-organize around innovation on an *enterprise-wide basis* should be seen as a special source of competitive advantage. Why not engage the *whole* firm in the learning and innovation process? Why stop at the borders of the R&D function, or with the ranks of senior management?

I now assert that *social innovation capital* (SIC) is, in fact, the most valuable form of IC. I say this because it is the only form of IC that has as its purpose the creation of all other forms of IC, including itself. Social innovation capital is therefore a necessary precondition (or antecedent) to the production of *all* forms of IC, including valuable intellectual property (IP), such as patents, trademarks, and copyrights. In the absence of SIC—or in the presence of *weak* SIC—even the most valuable IP is merely ephemeral. Like all knowledge, its value eventually expires, or at least diminishes over time. Longevity in business therefore depends upon a continuous stream of new innovations, new patents, new ideas, new insights, and new bases of competitive advantage. Only investments in *social innovation capital* can deliver that kind of value in return because, after all, innovation is a social process.

I should now differentiate between the remaining issues of (1) how to establish strong social innovation capital, and (2) how to value both itself and its output. With this distinction in mind, I will only be dealing with the former issue for the remainder of this essay, since the latter one calls for its own, logically subsequent, treatment. Let us first discuss the composition of social innovation capital, what its drivers are, and how to manage it.

CULTIVATING INNOVATION

Over the past few years, I and several other members of Knowledge Management Consortium International, or KMCI,[12] have been working to articulate the assertion that *"innovation is a social process, not an administrative one"* in a way that would give managers a means of recognizing and nurturing the organizational dynamics of knowledge production and integration. Truisms are informative, but it takes more than provocative slogans to make a difference in business. If innovation is truly a social process, we argued, it probably takes the form of regular patterns of behavior in human social systems that can be recognized and described as such. Out of this effort came the depiction of organizational innovation shown in Figure 10-3.

Those of us responsible for producing this picture of knowledge processing have been careful to point out that it is more a "framework" than a model, since it is only meant to describe the broad pattern of knowledge production and integration in a firm (i.e., innovation), without necessarily attempting to put forth specific theories as to how, for example, groups or communities actually "evaluate" knowledge. The framework simply suggests, instead, that *evaluation happens* as a precursor to the adoption and integration of new knowledge at an organizational level.

In an effort to isolate the drivers of knowledge production and integration in a firm, I have found it useful to portray the life cycle in a slightly different and simpler way than previously shown in Figure 10-3 (see Figure 10-4). Here, the critical path of the KMCI life cycle is highlighted around the edge of a simple cycle in a sequential fashion. These are the key dynamics, I argue, in the self-organizing expression of innovation in human social systems. In other words, these are the fundamental steps that must be allowed to occur in order for enterprise-wide innovation to unfold to its full potential—its *critical path*.

In a sense, any organization left to its own devices will eventually start to display the pattern shown in Figure 10-4. This speaks to the tendency of human social systems to self-organize around the production and integration of new knowledge. The literature in anthropology, sociology, political science, social psychology, and the life sciences generally points to the role that such cycles play in group learning and adaptation as the raison d'être behind them.[13] Indeed, there's no shortage of explanations as to how these cycles account for learning, innovation, and adaptive behavior in human social systems. Listen to how Erich Jantsch put it: "The process of mentation originates in the individual, but the autopoietic structures of the neural mind form their own systems of relations which become translated into sociocultural macrosystems such as communities, societies and civilizations."[14]

The important point for us right now, then, is that these cycles invariably unfold under their own steam. Human social systems

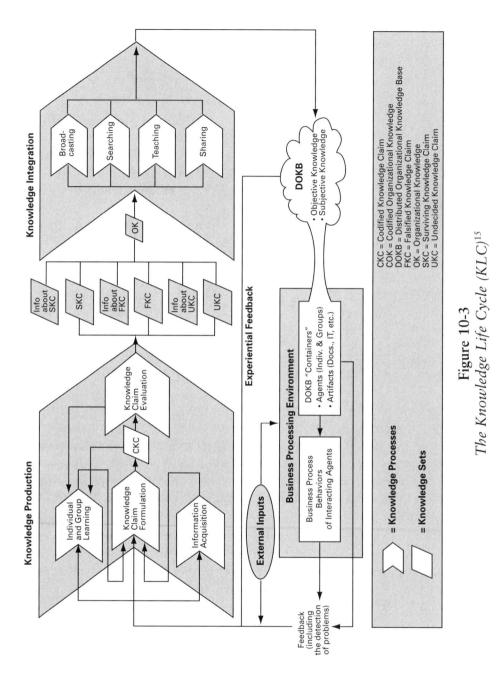

Figure 10-3
The Knowledge Life Cycle (KLC)[15]

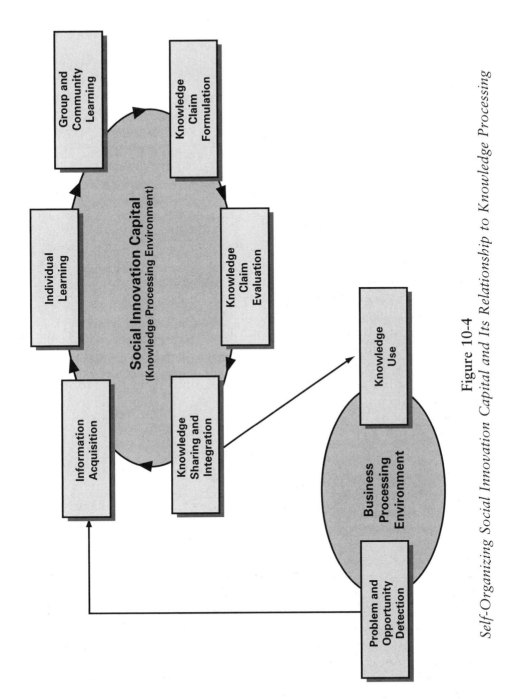

Figure 10-4

Self-Organizing Social Innovation Capital and Its Relationship to Knowledge Processing

want to express their innovation affairs in these ways, and always will, even—if not *especially*—in the complete absence of management direction. The self-organized expression of these patterns is ineluctable.

Fortunately for business, the full expression of these self-organized patterns of innovation is a good thing, because they lead to the production of new knowledge that has financial value implications. In some cases, the knowledge produced by healthy social innovation capital has direct value, as in the case of intellectual property such as patents, trademarks, and copyrights. In other cases, the value is indirect to the bottom line, such as well-crafted strategies, efficient organizational models, and flexible manufacturing schemes. What every business manager should therefore want is well-running social innovation capital that continues to supply its host organization with one new innovation after another, year after year.

But since social innovation capital of the sort I have described is self-organizing in its ontogeny, in what sense would a manager *manage* such a thing? The answer? By getting the hell out of its way! That's the flip response, for effect; now here's the practical one.

One of the key lessons from complexity theory is that visions of managing self-organizing systems are delusional and misinformed, especially when it comes to "managing" the biosphere. Innovation in human social systems is no less independent of outside intervention despite managers' best intentions, and so the best we can ever hope to do in encouraging its health is to manage its surrounding conditions—its climate, if you will. In this case, however, it's the *knowledge processing climate* that matters.

Within the knowledge processing climate of a firm—or what I call the *knowledge operating system*—there are eight variables, in particular, that have a direct impact on the degree to which self-organized learning and innovation can occur.[16] Depending on how well these factors are aligned (or *synchronized*) with the tendency of people to behave in the ways described in Figure 10-4, the overall level and quality of innovation in a firm will vary. Management policies in all eight areas can therefore be fashioned in such a way that they support, strengthen, and even reinforce knowledge production and integration in business.

The eight variables in an organization's *knowledge operating system* fall into two categories. First is the *structural* dimension of the system. In other words, we can describe the compositional and architectural aspects of the system, such as the makeup of its members and the degree of connectivity or connectedness between them. These two factors are, indeed, of interest to us here, since the diversity of backgrounds, values, and worldviews held by the members of an organization influence their range of collective creativity, as does the extent to which they have meaningful opportunities to interact with one another.

There is also the *operational* dimension of a system. This dimension is largely described by the diagram shown in Figure 10-4. From an operational point of view, we can describe the behavior of the system—what people actually *do* relative to learning and the production of new knowledge. Their behaviors in this case are described by the steps shown as we walk around the *knowledge processing* cycle shown in the figure.

Interestingly, in *knowledge processing* systems, we cannot completely specify or direct the operational dynamics of their inhabitants, since their behaviors are, after all, self-organizing and emergent. We can, however, have deterministic influence on their *structures*. For example, we can decide to hire more Democrats than Republicans, or more conservatives than liberals, or more people who simply tend to hold divergent views, vis à vis one another. The kind of diversity we're talking about here is not ethnic diversity but "ethos diversity"—or what I call *ethodiversity*.

Similarly, we can have deterministic influence on the density of interactions and communications between people in an organization by managing *connectivity infrastructures*. The goal of such efforts is to have an impact on the degree of *densities of connectedness* in organizations, which might involve the use of variable technology infrastructures as well as the social venues or rules people use to communicate with one another. For example, we can install technology-based networks, such as e-mail and the like, but we can also adopt different behavioral norms for interpersonal communications that make it more or less likely that people will, in fact, communicate with one another across, say, organizational or hierarchical boundaries. We can have more meetings, or less meetings; include more people in evaluating business options, or less people; and so forth.

Another structural aspect of organizations and their learning environments is the extent to which learning-related groups, or communities, actively exist. Managers can have impact in this area by setting the conditions in which communities are more or less likely to emerge, as well as the extent to which organizational resources are made available to support them (time, funding, infrastructure, facilities, business processes, etc.).

None of these structural interventions, of course, are determinative of operational outcomes, since, as we know, learning and problem-solving behaviors are emergent—just as their *knowledge claim outcomes* are. For the operational side of things, then, we must embrace learning-related policies and programs that are *permissive* in intent, but not *prescriptive*. As I have said, the behaviors of interest to us are already latently-held in the system (the organization); our job is to adopt policies and programs that support, strengthen, and reinforce these behaviors, and that effectively remove barriers to their fruitful expression.

These ways of describing the salient structural and operational aspects of an organizational learning system can inform us of how best to approach our choice of knowledge processing policies and programs. Here, then, are the eight variables organized into the two categories defined above.

Structural Dimension

- *Ethodiversity*[17]—Policies and programs that attempt to determine the degree of diversity in values and worldviews held by members of an organization. Impacts the range of perspectives and experiences available to an organization as it searches for solutions to problems and opportunities.
- *Connectedness*—Policies and programs that attempt to determine the density of opportunities for interpersonal communications between people and groups in organizations. Impacts the degree of interactions between people and the velocity of information flow.
- *Community formation*—Policies that determine the extent to which an organization will encourage and support the self-organized formation of learning-related groups or communities of learning, practice, and so on.

Operational Dimension

- *Individual learning*—Policies and programs that permit different degrees of freedom for individuals to pursue learning agendas of their own choosing. Impacts *knowledge claim formulation* activity.

- *Group learning*—Policies and programs that permit different degrees of freedom for groups or communities to pursue learning agendas of their own choosing. Impacts *knowledge claim formulation* activity.
- *Knowledge production*—Policies and programs that permit different degrees of openness and enterprise-wide participation in the formal *knowledge claim evaluation* stage of management's *knowledge processing environment*. Impacts organizational *knowledge claim evaluation* activities and outcomes.
- *Knowledge sharing*—Policies and programs that permit different degrees of openness relative to decisions made by a management regime, as well as the depth and effectiveness of knowledge diffusion throughout an organization. Impacts *information acquisition* and the scope and quality of *knowledge sharing* and *integration*.
- *Knowledge entitlement*—Policies and programs that permit different degrees of employee entitlement to the knowledge claim outcomes they help produce (e.g., patents, trademarks, copyrights, etc.). Acknowledges intrinsic motivation to innovate and has impact on *individual and group learning*, as well as *knowledge claim formulation* and *evaluation* activities.

What I am advocating here is the active management *not* of innovation per se, but of the policies that surround its effective practice in a firm. One can no more manage self-organizing processes than can a gardener order his or her plants to grow. But given the predisposition of human social systems to innovate in their own particular ways, it makes all the sense in the world to manage the conditions in which such behaviors can emerge, so as to support, strengthen, and reinforce their full expression (see Figure 10-5).

The methodology implied in the discussion above is called the "Policy Synchronization Method" (PSM).[18] Unlike other innovation management schemes, many of which rest on the view that innovation is a deterministic process, the PSM method offers a more effective prescription for *sustainable innovation*. This is because it is the only innovation management method extant that takes a deferential approach to self-organizing innovation in a firm. Rather

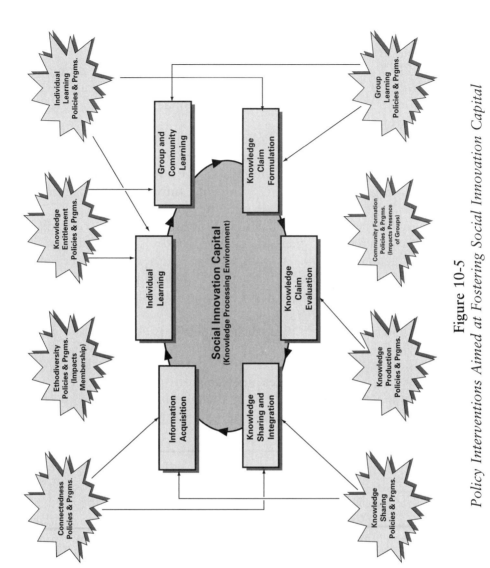

Figure 10-5

Policy Interventions Aimed at Fostering Social Innovation Capital

than compete with these forces or, worse yet, ignore them, the PSM method acknowledges their presence and focuses explicitly on their protection and support. Other innovation management schemes that fail to do this are ultimately unsustainable because they run counter to the predispositional tendency of human social systems to innovate in their own endemic ways. Over time, the friction between management policies and social tendencies actually undermines innovation.

In the practice of conventional management policies are used *to determine social behavior*, but in the case of the PSM method the reverse is true. Behavior drives policy. This is the key to *sustainable innovation*!

ENDNOTES

1. This chapter was originally published in March, 2002 under the same title: M. W. McElroy, "Social Innovation Capital," *Journal of Intellectual Capital* Vol. 3, No. 1 (2002), pp. 30–39.
2. W. L. Miller and L. Morris, *Fourth Generation R & D* (New York: John Wiley & Sons, 1999), p. xiiii (using data from Value Line Publishing, Inc.); see also Figure 1–7 in this book.
3. L. Edvinsson and M. S. Malone, *Intellectual Capital* (New York: HarperBusiness, 1997).
4. Ibid., p. 35.
5. E. Lesser, *Knowledge and Social Capital* (Boston: Butterworth-Heinemann, 2000).
6. Edvinsson and Malone, pp. 35–36.
7. Ibid., p. 36.
8. T. Stewart, *Intellectual Capital* (New York: Currency Doubleday, 1999), p. 77.
9. Lesser, pp. 4–6.
10. J. Nahapiet and S. Ghoshal, "Social Capital, Intellectual Capital, and the Organizational Advantage," *Academy of Management Review* Vol. 23, No. 2 (1996), pp. 242–266.
11. T. S. Kuhn, *The Structure of Scientific Revolutions* (Chicago: University of Chicago Press, 1962).
12. Knowledge Management Consortium International, www.kmci.org.
13. See, for example, F. Capra, *The Web of Life* (New York: Anchor Books, 1996); D. Stark, "Heterarchy: Distributing Authority and Organizing

Diversity," in J. H. Clippinger, III, editor, *The Biology of Business* (San Francisco: Josey-Bass Publishers, 1999); E. Jantsch, *The Self-Organizing Universe* (Oxford: Pergamon Press, 1980); H. R. Maturana and F. J. Varela, *Autopoiesis and Cognition* (Dordrecht, Holland: D. Reidel Publishing Company, 1980); M. Mead, *Continuities in Cultural Evolution* (New Brunswick, NJ: Transaction Publishers, 1999); E. Ostrom, *Strategies of Political Inquiry* (Beverly Hills, CA: Sage Publications, 1982), pp. 179–222; R. D. Stacey, *Complexity and Creativity in Organizations* (San Francisco: Berrett-Koehler, 1996); E. Wenger, *Communities of Practice* (Cambridge: Cambridge University Press, 1998).

14. Jantsch, p. 211.
15. The KLC was developed by members of Knowledge Management Consortium International (KMCI), a U.S.-based nonprofit association of knowledge and innovation management professionals from around the world (www.kmci.org).
16. This framework is taken from the "Policy Synchronization Method," which is the subject of a U.S. patent application filed with the Patent and Trademark Office in September, 2000, by Macroinnovation Associates, LLC of Windsor, VT (www.macroinnovation.com). It currently holds patent-pending status.
17. *Ethodiversity* is a term I coined. It is a reference *not* to the ethnic diversity of an organization, but to its ethos diversity. I define this as *the distribution of values, dominant assumptions, worldviews, philosophies, and politics held by a collection of people in an organization, which, in turn, inform their attitudes, predispositions, beliefs, customs, and practices as they go about their daily affairs. Ethography* is also a term I coined. It refers to the science of detecting, recording, and analyzing the ethodiversity of an organization. Further, the linguistic or documentary representation of an organization's ethodiversity may take the form of an *ethographical description* or record.
18. See endnote number 16 above.

11

RETURNS ON INVESTMENT FROM KNOWLEDGE MANAGEMENT

I begin this essay with a disclaimer: *investments in knowledge management (KM) can only have a direct impact on knowledge processing performance*, *not business performance*. But I also claim that the quality of business performance is heavily dependent upon the quality of knowledge processing, which means, of course, that to ensure top performance in business, organizations must invest in KM. Why? Because the purpose of KM is to enhance knowledge processing.

Are these conflicting statements? Not at all. Knowledge processing (i.e., knowledge production and integration) is a necessary condition for effective performance, especially market-leading or *top* performance. But it's not the only necessary condition. Businesses also need customers with money to spend, economies with suppliers to rely on, labor markets with people to hire, and many other things that add up to opportunity and success. Their capacity to process knowledge is just one of many such factors. So when we invest in KM and thereby improve knowledge sharing, learning, or innovation, how can we say that *it*, and only it, accounts for the enhancements in business performance that follow? We can't, of course.

The logical argument I am making here is that knowledge processing (the capacity to make and integrate knowledge) is a *necessary but insufficient condition* for positive outcomes in business. Contrast this with a popular definition of knowledge sometimes heard in organizational learning circles: *knowledge is the capacity for effective action*. Well, no, it's not. Effective action also requires the will and the means to do so, not to mention a supportive environment (social, legal, regulatory, etc.). Mere knowledge of what to do, or of what steps *might* fetch desired outcomes, is a far cry from having the will and the means and the environment required to *take* effective action. My knowledge of effective investment strategies, for example, is a necessary but insufficient condition to, in fact, make investments. I also need the will and the capital required to do so, as well as a market economy in which to invest (the environment).

Another way of saying this is that investments in KM can only have an *indirect* impact on business performance and, therefore, on business outcomes. Let's express this in visual terms (see Figure 11-1). We can differentiate between knowledge management, knowledge processing, business processing, and business outcomes in the following ways:

- *Knowledge Management*: A management discipline that focuses on enhancing knowledge processing.
- *Knowledge Processing*: In organizations, a social process that accounts for the production and integration of knowledge for, and in, business processing.
- *Business Processing*: The handling and management of transactions between workers, customers, suppliers, and other agents in a value chain, or network, aimed at satisfying customer demands for products or services.
- *Business Outcomes*: The state of affairs, or results, that follow from the business processing performance of an enterprise, such as its standing in sales, profitability, market share, quality, customer retention, employee turnover, and so on.

According to this model, business outcomes are three steps removed from knowledge management. So how can we say that

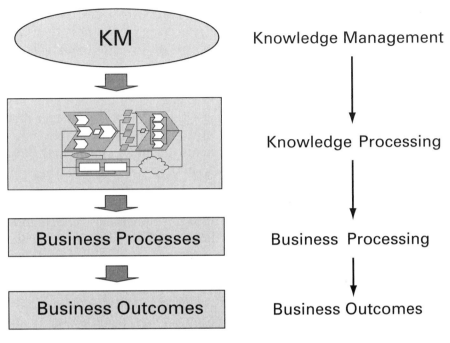

Figure 11-1
*The Indirect Impact of Knowledge Management on
Business Outcomes*

investments in KM can have a direct impact on business outcomes? The fact is we can't. What we can say, however, is that investments in KM can indirectly lead to improvements in business outcomes using the following kind of logic: *We can invest in KM, which, if done properly, should lead to improvements in knowledge processing, which in turn should lead to enhancements in our capacity to produce and integrate new knowledge. This, in turn, should lead to better business strategies and operating models, which in turn should lead to better outcomes.*

Here's another way of making the same point: *Our ability to choose the most effective strategies and operating models is heavily contingent upon our ability to learn and share knowledge effectively. Our business performance and outcomes are tightly coupled to the quality of our business processing decisions. Since the business processing choices we make through learning are themselves influenced by the quality of our knowledge processes, it is criti-cally important that our knowledge processes be the best they can be, and this is where investments in knowledge management come in.*

But there are no guarantees in any of this. This is why I use the word "should" instead of "will" in the first set of claims above. As a knowledge manager, even if I do everything "right," whatever that means, at the end of the day I'm still working with autonomous agents (people) in complex social systems (businesses) who may have more on their minds—or even less, perhaps—than satisfying my desire to be successful as a knowledge manager.

Still, although it's true that the impact of KM on business perfor-mance and outcomes is indirect, its impact is nonetheless undeniable. When we enhance our capacity to learn, and to integrate what we learn into practice, we increase the odds of our choosing the most effective behaviors which will, in turn, improve the quality of our outcomes.[1] Armed with these insights, any discussion of returns on investments (ROI) from investments in knowledge management should begin by recognizing that KM aims its interventions at the level of knowledge processing, not business processing, and certainly not at business outcomes. Its hope may be to enhance business pro-cessing and outcomes, but its power to do so is indirect, at best. Its power to have an impact on knowledge processing, however, is direct, and so that's where our discussion of ROI from investments in KM should be focused.

Now here, some colleagues of mine will protest, I'm sure—and many have. Some will say, *"Just because the impact of KM on busi-ness outcomes is indirect doesn't mean that it can't be measured, or that the connections can't be managed."* Another class of objections falls into the *"Nobody's interested in knowledge processing outcomes. If you can't show an impact on business processing and business outcomes, you're wasting your time."*

As for the latter class of objections, I make no apologies for point-ing out that a discipline designed to have impact on knowledge pro-cessing should be evaluated in terms of its impact on, well, knowledge processing, and that the scope of its direct impact is on nothing *but* knowledge processing. I cannot change the fact that discipline X, which is intended to have impact on Y, can only have *direct* impact on Y, since Y is the sole target of its reach.

But I can say from retrospective analysis that a business outcome Z might be causally related, albeit indirectly so, to a KM intervention X. For example, I can say, *"Forty percent of this year's sales came from products less than four years old, and the ideas for these products were hatched in learning and innovation programs that we launched as a result of specific KM interventions."* I can say all of that and more, but I can't say that any of it was predictable. I can explain it in retrospect, but I can't predict it in practice.

Indeed, I take exception to the implication that my theoretical ability to explain the indirect impact of X on Z means that I can predict such impacts. This, of course, is what we all want. We want to be able to say, *"If I increase the proportion of time spent by employees in learning by 5 percent, profit margins will increase by 10 percent."* This, of course, is nonsense. Any number of other variables, by themselves or in combination with one another, can account for an increase in profitability, and most of them are unpredictable. Maybe my chief competitor goes out of business, or a new market opens up, or my boss has a marital crisis and loses interest in the business. Who can say? Life, including business, is nonlinear. There are too many variables, too many uncertainties, and all of them combine to produce unpredictable outcomes. What we do as knowledge managers has a direct impact on knowledge processing only, and even there, as we shall see, its impact is not entirely determinative.

The former class of objections is another matter. I do not deny that science exists that allows us to determine the *indirect* impact of X on Z, even though the *direct* impact of X is restricted to Y.[2] But here is where we enter into the realm of nonlinearity, and at the same time exceed the scope of my current intentions. My intentions at this time are not to deny the existence of indirect impacts, nor the value of learning how KM interventions made three steps removed from business outcomes might, in fact, be made in a controlled fashion such that business outcomes could at least be *partially determined* within some range of known probability. Rather, my intentions are to discuss the direct impacts of KM, and the demonstrable value received from them. This necessarily restricts me to a discussion of KM impacts on knowledge processing, not on business processing or business outcomes. If we are to ever reach a point of competence with respect to managing the indirect impacts of KM interventions, we must first understand what the direct impacts are, how they are made, and what to expect from them—that is to say, we must understand what the direct impact of KM is on *knowledge processing*. That, then, is the subject of what follows.

KNOWLEDGE MANAGEMENT RETURNS ON INVESTMENT CURVES

By now, readers of this book will have come to appreciate the generational view of knowledge management. According to this view, knowledge management has evolved into two distinct styles of practice, one that places its emphasis on supply-side knowledge *sharing* goals (first-generation KM), and the other that focuses on demand-side knowledge *making* in addition to sharing (second-generation KM).[3] Although first-generation strategies are primarily concerned with enhancing the supply of *existing* valuable knowledge to workers, second-generation supply- *and* demand-side strategies also focus on enhancing an organization's ability to satisfy its demands for *new* knowledge.

This perspective on KM is clearly laced with value judgments and propositions, which differ depending on which generation of practice we're talking about. If it's first-generation KM, the purpose of making related investments is to enhance the distribution and use of valuable organizational knowledge in hopes that doing so will improve business processing performance. Although this is also of interest to second-generation thinkers, enhancing an organization's ability to produce new knowledge, or to innovate, is even more important. As Arie de Geus, former head of planning for Royal Dutch Shell, once said, "The ability to learn faster than your competitors may be the only sustainable competitive advantage."[4]

These intentions and expected outcomes from investments made in supply- and demand-side KM are important to bear in mind as we contemplate the kinds of returns we might expect to receive from them. But they are only starting points in the discussion, and they deserve to be more fully explored. To do this, I find it useful to think in terms of an organization's life cycle and the business processing performance of the people who inhabit it. As an organization engages in, say, successive projects from one year to the next, it can be seen as producing bodies of knowledge about the world, as well as its own

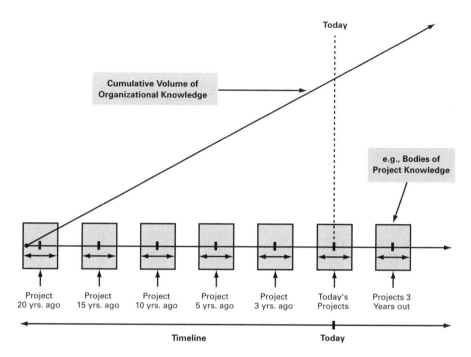

Figure 11-2
Scale for Representing the Accumulation of Organizational Knowledge over Time

history of learning, decision-making, and work. This, in turn, leads to a slowly increasing body of cumulative knowledge, that only grows in volume from one year to the next. This conception of gradually accumulating organizational knowledge can serve as an important backdrop to our discussion of returns from investment in KM (see Figure 11-2).

Next, if we orient ourselves in the timeline shown in Figure 11-2 to the "present" point in time, we can think in terms of either aiming our focus on knowledge and knowledge management retrospectively or prospectively in time. For example, we could make "retro" investments in KM by focusing on the capture, codification, and distribution of knowledge bound up in old files and databases (i.e., knowledge produced in the past), such that current and future generations of workers could search them. By contrast, forward-looking investments in KM (i.e., contemplated with future learning and sharing in mind) could be made by putting new knowledge capture

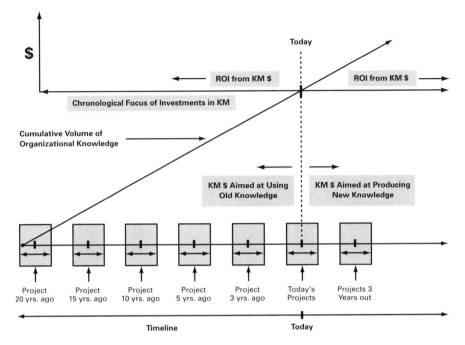

Figure 11-3
Bidirectional Scale for Plotting ROI in KM

or innovation systems in place that would seek to support, capture, and create new knowledge, and knowledge processing, for future generations of workers.

In the former case, the focus would be retrospective, with an eye toward capturing old knowledge; in the latter case, the focus would be prospective, with an eye toward producing new knowledge and information about it—or metaclaims—for future use. Investments made in only one way or the other would obviously have an impact on chronologically different bodies of knowledge, as well as on different generations of workers.

Using this "retro" versus "forward" perspective on the chronological target of supply- versus demand-side KM, we can envision an ROI scale for depicting the trajectory of returns from such investments as shown in Figure 11-3. We do this in a way that makes it possible to correlate returns from investments in KM with the chronological direction of related investments. This is achieved by first superimposing the ROI scale on the knowledge timeline scale, and second, by interpreting any rise either to the left or right of the "Today" line as a positive gain, or return, from investments in KM. This scale is therefore symmetrical in form, such that curves rising either to the left or right of the "Today" point in time represent increases in returns, and curves that decline either to the right or left of the same point represent decreases in returns.

More specifically, curves to the left of the "Today" point in time represent returns from "retro"-related investments in KM, but curves to the right of the "Today" point in time represent returns from "forward"-related investments in KM. It is the superimposition of the ROI scale on the organizational knowledge timeline (shown together in Figure 11-3) that allows us to visually correlate ROIs from "retro" and "forward" investments in KM this way. These tools, then, can be used to plot the ROI from investments in KM of any kind, using our generational view of KM and the chronological life cycle view of knowledge as it evolves in a firm over time.

To fully explore the kinds of returns we can expect to see from investments in KM, we need to take each of the possibilities and subject them to scrutiny in isolation from one another. Here are the five possibilities we will be discussing:

- **Supply-Side Retro Investments in KM:** Investments in KM aimed at the capture of valuable information and knowledge contained in an organization's historical files and databases, with expectations that access to such knowledge by present and future workers will enhance their business processing performance.
- **Supply-Side Forward Investments in KM:** Investments in KM aimed at the capture and codification of current and future information and knowledge for current and future generations of workers, again with expectations that access to such knowledge by present and future workers will enhance their business processing performance.
- **Demand-Side Retro Investments in KM:** Although this is a theoretical possibility, it is not a rational or practical one. Demand-side KM, by definition, is entirely forward-looking in scope. From where we stand today, we learn in the present and future, not the past. On the other hand, we can certainly learn *from* the past, but doing so requires making investments in cap-

turing and codifying information and knowledge from and about the past, which is really just another aspect of *supply-side retro KM*, already covered above. For these reasons, we will not be spending any more time on the notion of retro-oriented investments in demand-side KM.

■ *Demand-Side Forward Investments in KM:* This class of investments, unlike supply-side KM, is more concerned with the production of new knowledge than with the sharing of old. It seeks to enhance an organization's capacity to learn and innovate as a way of "outlearning its competitors." Here, the returns are measured in terms of an organization's impact on knowledge *making*, not knowledge *sharing*.

■ *Second-Generation Investments in KM:* Although all first-generation conceptions of KM were supply-side oriented, second-generation schemes reflect an intentional blend of both supply- and demand-side initiatives. This approach, therefore, deserves its own consideration in the form of examining what the blended shape of ROI curves would look like when investments in supply- and demand-side KM are made in a combined, concurrent way.

On the basis of the definitions above, we will only be looking at four of the five scenarios listed, since we have already decided to reject any further consideration of retro-oriented investments in demand-side KM. Let's begin, then, with the first scenario listed, *supply-side retro investments in KM*.

Supply-Side Retro Investments in Knowledge Management

This is by far the most common conception of KM. It usually takes the form of organized efforts to improve the capture, codification, and distribution of valuable organizational knowledge. This, by definition, means existing knowledge. We show the anticipated shape of the ROI curve from KM investments of this kind in Figure 11-4.

The usual goal of supply-side retro investments in KM is to enhance the reusability of existing organizational knowledge. This is typically considered with current business processing in mind. In other words, by enhancing access to existing organizational knowledge, we can reduce the time it takes for current workers to perform their work. In some cases, improving access to existing, or old,

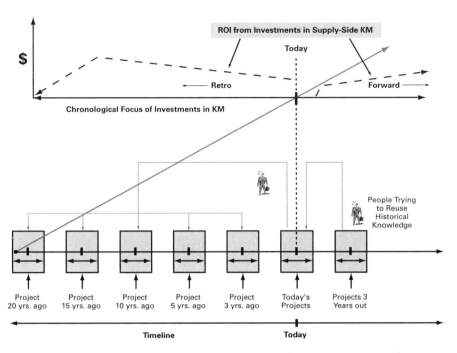

Figure 11-4
ROI from Investments in Supply-Side KM (Retro and Forward)

knowledge streamlines decision-making; in other cases it streamlines the performance of tasks. In all cases, however, the target of supply-side retro investments is old or existing knowledge. KM investments of this kind, therefore, are solely concerned with enhancing the integration of existing and past knowledge into current-day practice.

Because of its orientation, returns from supply-side retro investments are often immediate and, typically, escalate over time, but only to a point. They are immediate because they make previously inaccessible knowledge available to workers right away; they escalate because they continue to pay dividends as more and more users reach further back in time into deeper repositories of historical knowledge; but they decline after a point because of the eventual drop in relevance and applicability of old knowledge to current affairs.

The assumption here is that all knowledge declines in value over time. Indeed, much of our knowledge simply loses it relevance or is actually falsified. Either way, with the passing of time comes obsolescence in the value of knowledge, so investments in supply-side retro KM eventually lead to diminishing returns.

Although the purpose of supply-side retro investments in KM is usually to improve business processing performance, we can also acknowledge the value of having access to old knowledge for a different purpose: to support learning and innovation. Although true, the complexion and content of such systems would presumably be different in scope. Supply-side investments made with business processing in mind might focus more on providing access to historical transaction files, and investments made in support of innovation would be far less transaction-centric and broader in reach.

Supply-Side Forward Investments in Knowledge Management

Closely related to the retro variety discussed above, this form of supply-side KM typically involves efforts to improve the capture, codification, and distribution of valuable organizational knowledge *as it is produced in the present and future*, as opposed to *after* it was produced in the past. In other words, rather than subject current and future generations of workers to the tedious task of trying to mine old knowledge from historical sources, this form of supply-side KM attempts to institutionalize the *contemporaneous* capture of knowledge *even as it is being produced in real time* so that access to it in the future will be that much easier.

As shown in Figure 11-4, there is a delay in returns from investments in supply-side forward KM. This is because of the relatively low immediate value of capturing knowledge that is already fresh in the minds of current-day workers. In other words, capturing the lessons from today's experiences is arguably of greater value to future generations of workers than it is to today's generation, since today's generation of workers is already intimately aware of their own recent experiences.

With this in mind, we show a delayed, but continuously escalating rate of return from investments in supply-side forward KM. It continuously escalates because there will always be new current-day experiences and successive generations of workers who will need or want access to them.

In theory, investments made in supply-side forward KM will eventually make the need to invest in supply-side retro KM obsolete.

Why? Because with the passing of time, most historical knowledge of relevance and value will have already been captured proactively, as it were, thereby obviating the need to turn back and codify old knowledge. It will have already been rendered accessible for reuse by forward-looking programs years in advance. Indeed, the sooner we get started in making investments in forward-looking supply-side KM, the sooner we can dispose of the need to engage in difficult and costly retro-oriented initiatives.

Demand-Side Forward Investments in Knowledge Management

This is an extraordinarily promising area for investments in KM, as it can lead to improvements in the rate and quality of knowledge production, or innovation. In turn, firms that experience these kinds of returns are more adaptive, since their capacity to sense and respond to problems or opportunities in their environments can be greatly enhanced. We refer to this kind of KM as "demand-side" because of its impact on an organization's capacity to satisfy its *demands* for new knowledge.

Because innovation is fundamentally a social process, not an administrative—and much less a mechanical—one, demand-side investments in KM tend to be social in nature. This is not to say that technology-related investments in demand-side KM are not possible; they are. Rather, the point is that it is the social system in organizations that produces new knowledge, and so the greatest returns in the form of improvements in innovation come from social interventions aimed at improving the dynamics of knowledge production in organizational life.

Examples of interventions of this kind might include new or more formal programs for individual learning. Programs that make it possible, for example, for individuals to engage in self-directed learning, would support their ideas afterwards through funded research or development at an organizational level, and could be of enormous value to a firm. Similarly, the increasing popularity of "communities of practice,"[5] and programs that formalize them by providing time, funding, and other organizational resources to support their activities, can also be fruitful. Here, the communities of interest to us would be knowledge-producing groups, not just knowledge-sharing ones.

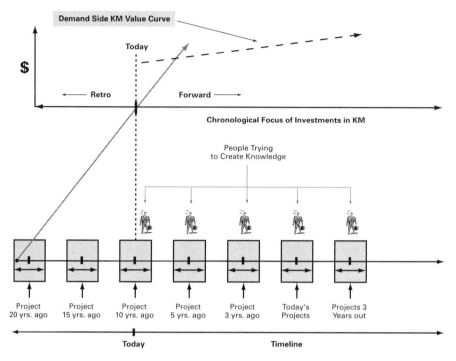

Figure 11-5
ROI from Investments in Demand-Side Forward KM

The shape of the ROI curve for demand-side forward investments in KM is shown in Figure 11-5. As we can see, investments in KM of this sort produce immediate and escalating—or "increasing"[6]—returns, thanks to the immediate impact on an organization's capacity to learn, innovate, and adapt. This is especially true in cases where the learning and innovation process becomes more distributed throughout an organization, and more inclusive of its whole population. When innovation becomes enterprise-wide in scope, as opposed to confined only to the purview of centralized groups like R&D or senior management, firms benefit accordingly by tapping into the creative capacity of their entire population. I call this *"wholescale" innovation.*

Whereas most investments in supply-side KM are aimed at improving current and future *business processing performance*, investments in demand-side KM are aimed at improving *knowledge processing performance*. In demand-side investments, it's not about *getting the right information to the right people at the right time*—the familiar mantra of supply-side strategies—rather, it's about *learning faster than your competitors* as a sustainable source of competitive advantage.

Second-Generation Investments in Knowledge Management

Each of the investment scenarios discussed thus far have been predicated on the assumption that they were being made in isolation from one another, but second-generation KM entails the coordinated investment in both supply- and demand-side KM, with enhancements to the complete knowledge life cycle in mind. In other words, unlike first-generation thinking (supply-side only) or even demand-side thinking by itself, practitioners of second-generation KM seek to have impact on the *whole life cycle* of knowledge production and integration, and, accordingly, they approach their work in a more holistic way.

Thus, when we talk about making investments in supply-side retro KM as second-generation KM practitioners, we not only consider the value of doing so as it relates to enhancing business processing performance, but we also contemplate its impact on knowledge production as well. Similarly, when we make investments in demand-side forward KM, we not only consider its impact on innovation, but also its impact on performance and the need to follow through on knowledge production with diffusion (i.e., the integration of knowledge into practice).

The shape of the ROI curves for investments in second-generation KM reflects a combination of the kinds of returns discussed above for each of the underlying scenarios (see Figure 11-6). But when we combine the investments in a coordinated manner, we can expect to see higher returns on both sides of the graph—higher returns for retro-aimed investments, and higher returns for forward-aimed investments. Why? Because the whole is greater than the sum of its parts. That is, strengthening the whole life cycle yields higher returns than when we only attempt to strengthen some of its parts.

To use a mechanical analogy, if I take an automobile and focus on enhancing the performance of only some of its parts, the best I can expect to receive in return is higher performance of the parts. But I should not expect to receive higher returns in the performance of the automobile if all I'm investing in is the performance of its transmis-

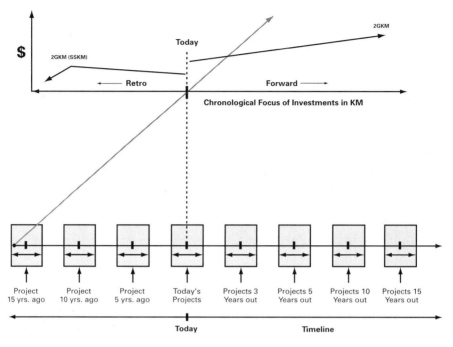

Figure 11-6
ROI from Investments in "Second-Generation" KM

sion. If, on the other hand, I take a holistic view and focus on managing the whole system, I not only see improvements in the performance of the individual parts, but I also note improvements in the performance of the whole system. This, in turn, enhances my ability to get around, which is of considerably higher value to me than a well-running transmission or a disintegrated collection of well-running parts. It is the performance of the whole system in its coherent form that matters most to me.

The same is true for the knowledge life cycle in human social systems. When we start from the perspective of seeing the whole social system as a knowledge processing system that has coherence to it, we can, and should, learn to think more in terms of getting the whole thing to run well, as opposed to only parts of it. Second-generation KM is *not* about *getting the right information to the right people at the right time*; it's about that *and* making sure the right information exists in the first place, by focusing on how to *create more of it* on an as-needed basis (i.e., as a response to when we encounter problems).

For these reasons, when we make investments in KM from a second-generation point of view, we should expect to see returns on both sides of the line, so to speak, rise in value over what they would have been had they been made only in isolation from one another. The key here is learning to start with a view of knowledge processing in organizations as a social system that has pattern-like regularity to it, followed by the recognition that the purpose of KM is to feed, strengthen, and support the pattern. This is utterly new thinking in KM—certainly when compared to first-generation, supply-side strategies—which is why many people are now referring to second-generation KM as "the new knowledge management."

NATURE VERSUS NURTURE

Everyone is familiar with the age-old debate over what really accounts for character in people: Is it the result of their environment and their genetic makeup (nature), or does it reflect the manner in which they were brought up, the values they were given by their parents, the lessons they were taught, and the care they received (nurture)?

Tom Stewart, the well-known journalist and author of *Intellectual Capital* (1997), asks the same question of knowledge processing in his subsequent book, *The Wealth of Knowledge* (2001). In discussing the literature on innovation, Stewart makes the following remarks:[7]

Innovation is either a machine or a magic garden. Because it is a machine, companies should design it, oil it, power it up, and manage it. Because it is a garden, companies should create the conditions under which it can flourish, stand back, and let the magic occur, then harvest it.

Innovation is both, of course. That's a management problem because the two ways of managing innovation seem contradictory.

If we define innovation as the entire life cycle of knowledge production and integration, not just knowledge production—and we *do* define it that way—Stewart's question can be applied to the entirety of knowledge processing, and certainly not just to *product* innovation or *product* design. But why would we do so? What does this have to do with making investments in KM?

Well, if your theory of practice is that innovation is a mechanical, administrative process, your investments in KM—and in particular, the kinds of interventions they lead to—will be crafted and chosen accordingly. That is, they will tend to be reductionistic and determinative in nature. On the other hand, if you see organizational innovation as a self-organizing social process, your investments and interventions will probably tend to be far less deterministic, and a great deal more deferential, in the sense that they will reflect your deference to the tendency of the system to express itself under its own steam, and in its own ways. So your theory of how organizations innovate is of foundational importance to the methods you choose to assist them or guide them in doing so.

This is why KM theory is so important to KM practice. But it also points the way to determining the kinds of returns we should expect to see from our investments in KM. If innovation is really a garden but I treat it like a machine, I should lower my expectations for returns. But if innovation is truly a garden and I treat it as such, my returns should reward me accordingly.

Indeed, I and many others—Ralph Stacey, for example[8]—hold the view that innovation is first and foremost a garden. People in organizations tend to self-organize around the production and integration of knowledge even—and especially, it seems—in the utter absence of management. This is particularly true in the case of the creative process. Back in the 1960s, a fascinating body of work took place in the form of several studies on teaching regimes and their impact on learning outcomes.[9] In particular, the studies of interest here focused on the differences in outcomes from learning driven by students' intrinsic interests, versus learning outcomes that followed from extrinsic interests.

Intrinsic interests lead to intrinsic motivation, which is a powerful driver of learning. Give me a budget to pursue my own learning agenda as opposed to yours, and I guarantee I'll come back with more effective learning. Force me to attend classes that *you* think are important, however, and I may still learn, but only from extrinsic motivation, which is always weaker in force than intrinsic motivation. Many of the studies referred to above further showed that extrinsically imposed motivations to learn actually *undermined* students' incentive to learn. Why shouldn't the same be true in business as well?[10]

From this, then, we can conclude that the most effective form of learning at the level of individuals is one that is driven by intrinsic motivation. The inspiration to learn is self-organizing and personal to the learner. We can have impact on it through extrinsic means, but the most powerful form of learning—and the most valuable form to an organization—is the learning that flows from the pursuit of personal interests and passions held at the level of individuals.

Similarly, people tend to co-attract one another on the basis of their shared interests and passions. Informal groups and communities of practice form in such ways. Individuals, groups, and communities then compete and interact with one another in a swirl of conjecture and refutation. New ideas are formulated and evaluated by peer groups. Problems are solved; inventions are made—all without any management oversight at all, just people doing what they naturally do.

Can we enhance these things? Absolutely. Should we? No question about it. The good news to KM is that people and organizations are already fundamentally predisposed to do what we want them to do: *to learn with passion and to commiserate with their peers in a mutual process of detecting and solving problems, and to innovate for the collective good.* As the great early-twentieth-century philosopher Karl Popper put it, "It is clear that the method of trial and error-elimination is largely based upon inborn instincts."[11] These are behaviors that people simply *come with*—no extra management required. It's what we fundamentally do. We're built that way.

Moreover, the patterns we form as we engage in these behaviors have regularity to them. The pattern goes something like this:

1. Individuals tend to engage in self-directed learning as they go through life in response to gaps they encounter between their current states and their goal states.
2. As individuals formulate potential solutions to their gaps (i.e., as they formulate theories on what actions to take in order to close these gaps), they sometimes commiserate with their peers in a process of error elimination or testing (i.e., they seek to validate their *knowledge claims*).

3. Groups that commiserate in these ways give rise to shared knowledge claims, which in turn are often practiced by their members, but which may also conflict with, and attract the attention of, authorities in the larger organizations they inhabit.
4. Some knowledge claims are then evaluated at an organizational level, after which they may be adopted for wider implementation. *Organizations learn* in such ways.
5. Ideas adopted for widespread use spread, or diffuse, throughout the organization and are integrated into practice by and for other groups and individuals.
6. Knowledge integrated in such ways is routinely practiced until such time as its use or potential use gives rise to new gaps in current and goal states; then the cycle starts all over again. Individual learning leads to group learning, which leads to organizational learning, which leads to the organizational integration of new knowledge into practice.
7. This cycle repeats itself endlessly, and is completely self-organizing in form.

Armed with this theory of how people in organizations tend to self-organize around the production, diffusion, and use of knowledge, we can begin to formulate a KM intervention strategy that will yield positive returns in ways that are specific to the nature of the beast, as it were. In my own approach to doing so, I developed (with the support and assistance of my friend and colleague, Dr. Steven A. Cavaleri of Central Connecticut State University) a KM methodology that currently holds patent-pending status in the United States. I called this method the "Policy Synchronization Method,"[12] or PSM.

THE POLICY SYNCHRONIZATION METHOD

The PSM method reflects a point of view that is supported by Tom Stewart's claim that innovation is both a machine and a garden. It is a machine in the sense that its processes can be administratively supported and reinforced, but it is a garden in its most fundamental sense, because it is a natural feature of human social systems. Innovation predates management.

In formulating the PSM method, I began by providing myself with a reference model that would allow me to show the points of entry,

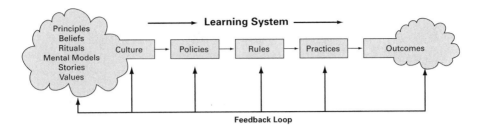

Figure 11-7
Learning System Reference Model for "Policy Synchronization Method"

so to speak, for potential management interventions, while illustrating the garden-like backdrop of organizational learning (see Figure 11-7). According to this model, learning "outcomes" follow from learning "practices," which, in turn, follow from learning "rules." Learning rules might consist of, say, a corporate program for training that specifies what classes to attend and how many hours per year an employee should receive in continuing professional education.

Learning "rules," in turn, are driven by learning "policies." In the case above, for example, the learning policy in use might be one that states that all employees shall be expected to receive continuing professional education, which the company will support and make possible. The training program, or rule, is then nothing more than a fulfillment of policy. And there may be many more such programs, or rules, that fulfill the same policy in different and complementary ways.

Learning policies, on the other hand, are expressions of culture in the sense that they reflect the principles, beliefs, norms, values, and so on held by a collective population of people on how learning should happen and what its importance is to the organization. A firm that supports policies aimed at making continuing education possible clearly shares a value for education and expresses that value in the form of policy. Policy, in this sense, can sometimes be interpreted as *the voice of culture*, but not always.

As I studied this model, I concluded that there were only two places where management could make effective interventions in the learning system of an organization: *policies* and *rules*. Why? Because policies and rules are human artifacts. We make them. Culture, practice, and outcomes, however, are emergent. We can have impact on them, but we cannot determine them. As a manager, then, I can make policies and rules, and I can enforce them, but I can't make culture; nor can I make practices or behavior, because I can't be there to make everybody's decisions or take their actions for them. People make their own decisions about practice and behavior, but always under the influence of culture, policies, and rules. Outcomes, of course, are downstream from everything else—they are the states of affairs that follow *from* behavior or practice.

So this leaves us with policies and rules as potential points of intervention for making investments in KM. My definition of policies in this "learning system" context is slightly different from the usual use of the term. What I mean by policies in this case is meta-rules, which are intended to specify the nature and range of knowledge processing rules acceptable to a management regime in an organization. What I mean by "rules" in this case is programs, initiatives, or other activities carried out by managers in order to fulfill knowledge processing policies, or meta-rules. Further, the intent of the PSM method is to specify meta-rules that will foster the adoption of programs, initiatives, and other activities of a sort that are *synchronized* with the self-organizing pattern-like dynamics of people in organizations, as they attempt to express their knowledge processing behaviors in the ways summarized above—hence, the title I gave to the method. It's all about choosing meta-rules (i.e., policies) that will give rise to rules (learning programs, etc.) that are synchronized with the behaviors of interest to us, which we hope our policies and rules will support and reinforce.

Use of the PSM method, a second-generation KM type of intervention, can lead to higher returns on investment for all of the reasons covered earlier for second-generation KM interventions. But unlike other approaches to second-generation KM, the PSM method not only tackles knowledge processing in holistic terms, it does so in a deferential way. Whereas in the conventional use of policy by management, policies are intended to *cause behaviors*, in the PSM method, we start with an understanding of endemic behaviors (i.e., those that stem from endogenous rules), and we then adopt policies that we feel will permit and protect them, but not cause them (i.e., by enforcing exogenous rules that are inspired by knowledge of the endogenous ones). Under this approach, policy follows from behavior, not the reverse.

In the end, the PSM method may prove to be one of the more valuable kinds of KM interventions available for practitioner use. Why? Because the only thing more valuable than valuable intellectual capital, or knowledge, is the organizational capacity to produce it—*sustainably*. That, then, is the promise of second-generation KM—its central value proposition—and *that*, therefore, is the *new* kind of ROI that we can expect to receive from investments in *the new knowledge management*!

ENDNOTES

1. A. D. Ellinger, A. E. Ellinger, B. Yang, and S. W. Howton, "The Relationship between the Learning Organization Concept and Firms' Financial Performance: An Empirical Assessment," *Human Resource Development Quarterly* Vol. 13, Iss. 1 (Spring 2002), pp. 5–21.

2. See, for example, T. L. Saaty, *The Analytic Hierarchy Process: Planning, Priority Setting, Resource Allocation* (New York: McGraw-Hill, 1980).

3. M. W. McElroy, "The Second Generation of Knowledge Management," *Knowledge Management* (October, 1999), pp. 86–88.

4. Quoted by P. M. Senge, *The Fifth Discipline* (New York: Currency Doubleday, 1990), p. 4.

5. E. Wenger, *Communities of Practice* (Cambridge: Cambridge University Press, 1998).

6. B. W. Arthur, *Increasing Returns and Path Dependence in the Economy* (Ann Arbor: University of Michigan Press, 1994).

7. T. A. Stewart, *The Wealth of Knowledge* (New York: Currency Doubleday, 2001), p. 183.

8. R. D. Stacey, *Complexity and Creativity in Organizations* (San Francisco: Berrett-Koehler, 1996), p. 256.

9. See, for example, L. D. Kamada, "Intrinsic and Extrinsic Motivation Learning Processes: Why Japanese Can't Speak English," a paper presented at the Japan Association of Language Teachers' International Conference on Language Teaching and Learning, November 22–24, 1986; E. L. Deci and R. M. Ryan, "Curiosity and Self-directed Learning: The Role of Motivation in Education," in L. Katz, editor, *Current Topics in Early Childhood Education, Vol. 4* (Norwood, NJ: Ablex Publishing Company, 1982); A. Maslow, "Self-Actualization and Beyond," from Proceedings of the Conference on the Training of Counselors of Adults, sponsored by the New England Board of Higher

Education, and the Center for the Study of Liberal Education for Adults, held May 22–28, 1965; R. A. Zbrzezny, "Effects of Extrinsic Rewards on Intrinsic Motivation: Improving Learning in the Elementary Classroom," a dissertation submitted by its author in partial fulfillment of the requirements of a course (E591) at Indiana University of South Bend, April 10, 1989.

10. A. Kohn, *Punished by Rewards* (Boston: Houghton Mifflin, 1999).

11. K. R. Popper, *Objective Knowledge: An Evolutionary Approach* (Oxford: Oxford University Press, 1979), p. 25.

12. The "Policy Synchronization Method" is the subject of a U.S. patent application filed with the Patent and Trademark Office in September, 2000, by Macroinnovation Associates, LLC of Windsor, VT (www.macroinnovation.com). It currently holds patent-pending status.

Appendix

A PRESENTATION ON SECOND-GENERATION KNOWLEDGE MANAGEMENT

Second-Generation Knowledge Management

Mark W. McElroy
Macroinnovation Associates, LLC

KM World
October 30, 2001

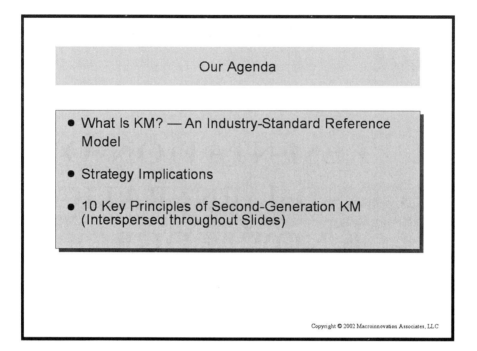

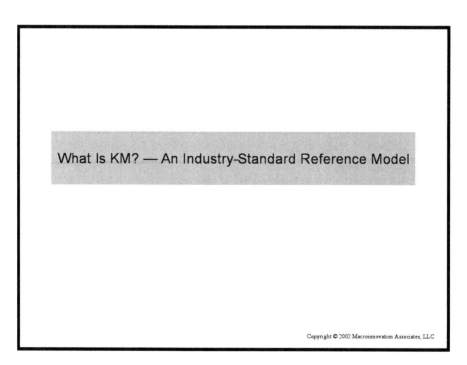

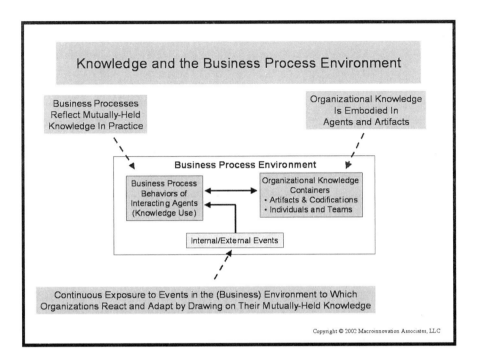

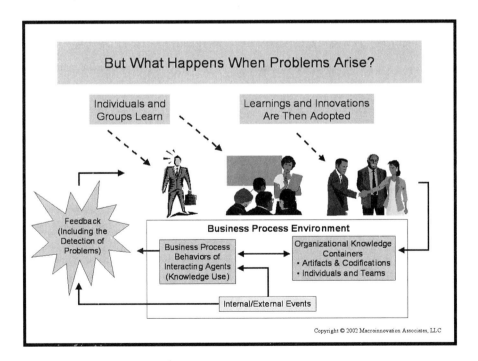

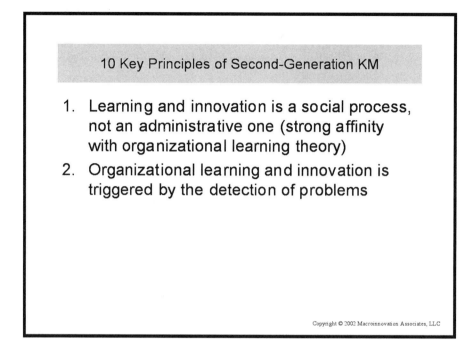

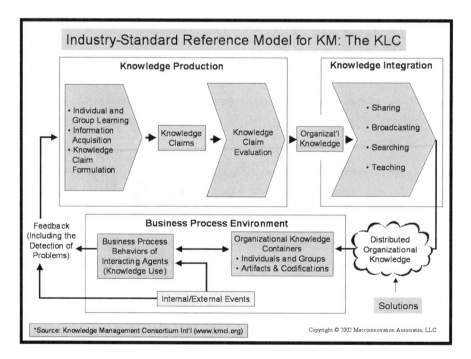

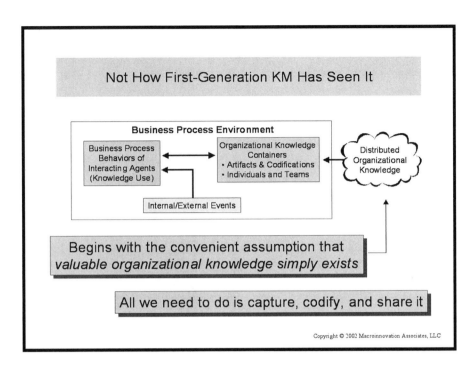

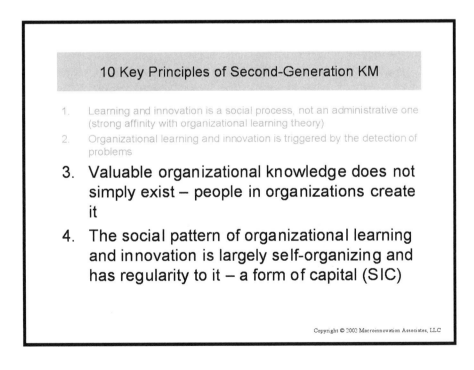

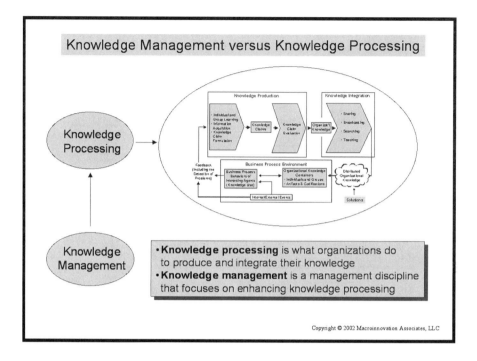

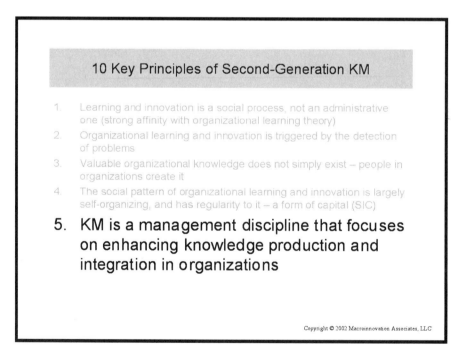

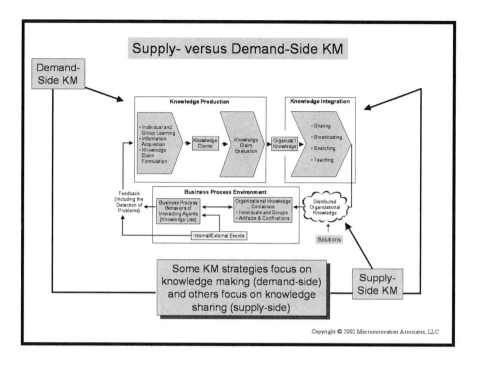

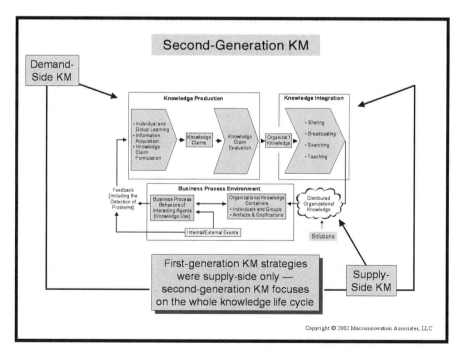

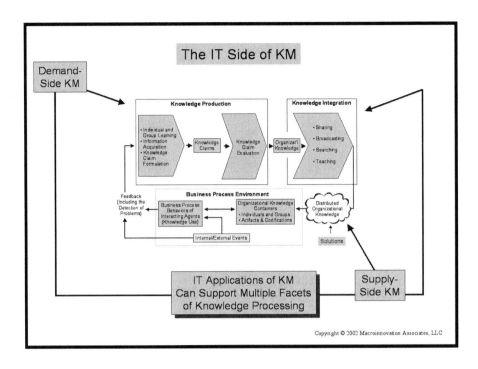

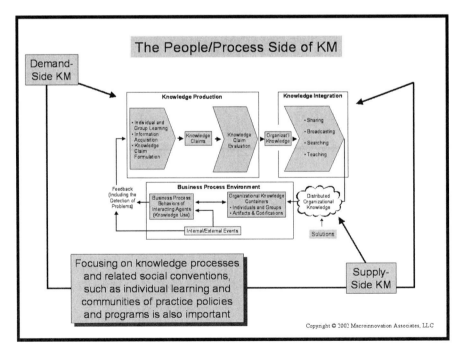

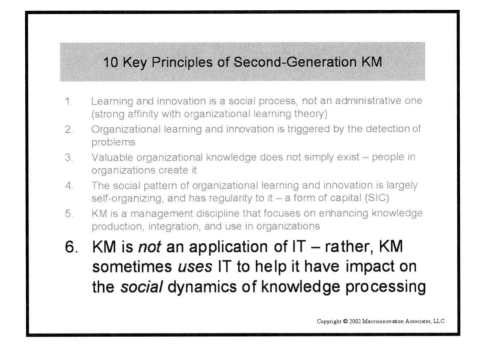

10 Key Principles of Second-Generation KM

1. Learning and innovation is a social process, not an administrative one (strong affinity with organizational learning theory)
2. Organizational learning and innovation is triggered by the detection of problems
3. Valuable organizational knowledge does not simply exist – people in organizations create it
4. The social pattern of organizational learning and innovation is largely self-organizing, and has regularity to it – a form of capital (SIC)
5. KM is a management discipline that focuses on enhancing knowledge production, integration, and use in organizations

6. KM is *not* an application of IT – rather, KM sometimes *uses* IT to help it have impact on the *social* dynamics of knowledge processing

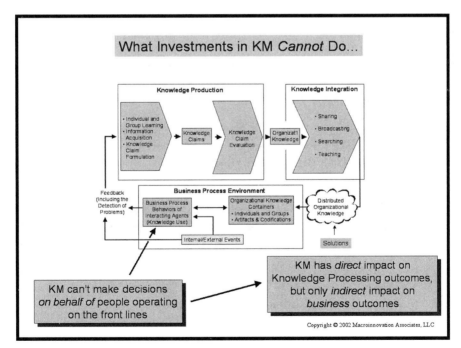

What Investments in KM *Cannot* Do...

KM can't make decisions *on behalf of* people operating on the front lines

KM has *direct* impact on Knowledge Processing outcomes, but only *indirect* impact on *business* outcomes

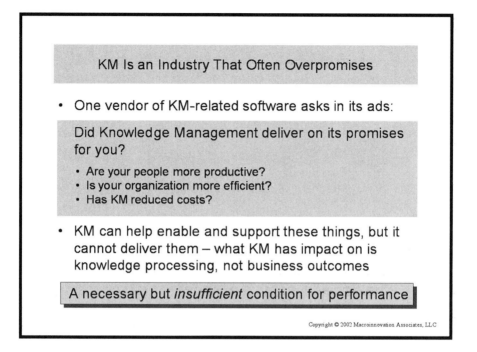

KM Is an Industry That Often Overpromises

- One vendor of KM-related software asks in its ads:

Did Knowledge Management deliver on its promises for you?

- Are your people more productive?
- Is your organization more efficient?
- Has KM reduced costs?

- KM can help enable and support these things, but it cannot deliver them – what KM has impact on is knowledge processing, not business outcomes

A necessary but *insufficient* condition for performance

Copyright © 2002 Macroinnovation Associates, LLC

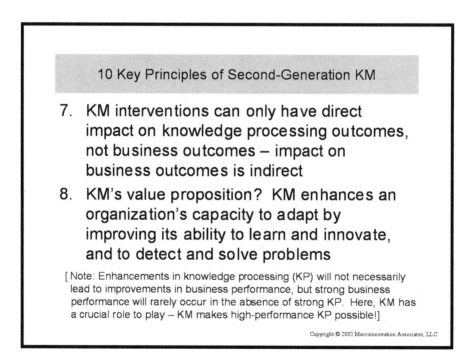

10 Key Principles of Second-Generation KM

7. KM interventions can only have direct impact on knowledge processing outcomes, not business outcomes – impact on business outcomes is indirect

8. KM's value proposition? KM enhances an organization's capacity to adapt by improving its ability to learn and innovate, and to detect and solve problems

[Note: Enhancements in knowledge processing (KP) will not necessarily lead to improvements in business performance, but strong business performance will rarely occur in the absence of strong KP. Here, KM has a crucial role to play – KM makes high-performance KP possible!]

Copyright © 2002 Macroinnovation Associates, LLC

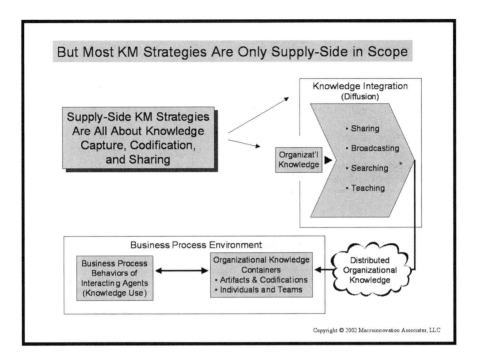

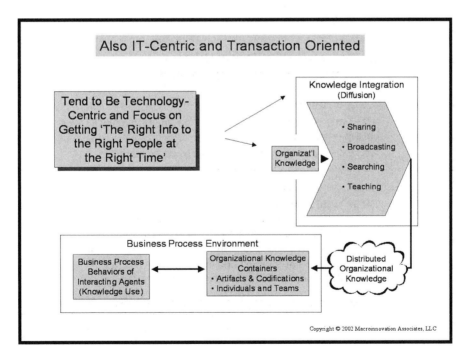

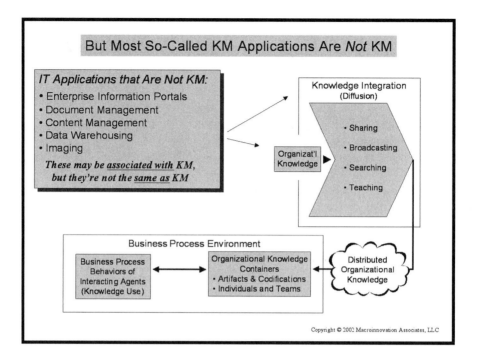

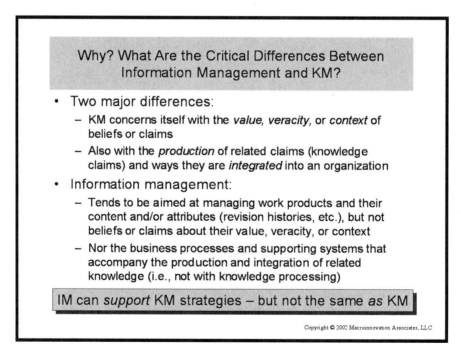

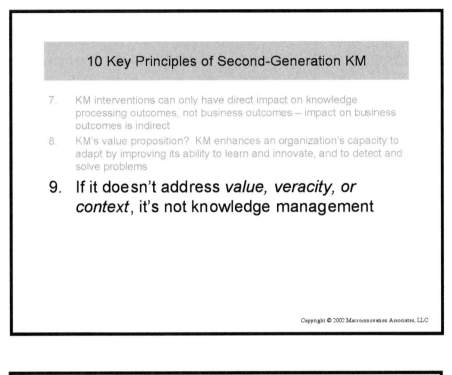

10 Key Principles of Second-Generation KM

7. KM interventions can only have direct impact on knowledge processing outcomes, not business outcomes – impact on business outcomes is indirect

8. KM's value proposition? KM enhances an organization's capacity to adapt by improving its ability to learn and innovate, and to detect and solve problems

9. **If it doesn't address *value, veracity, or context*, it's not knowledge management**

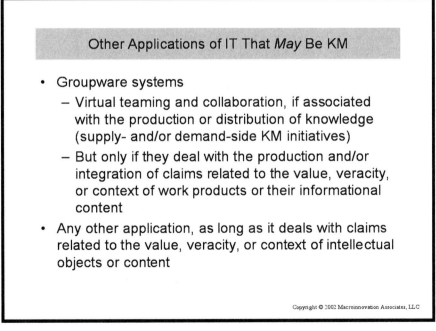

Other Applications of IT That *May* Be KM

- Groupware systems
  - Virtual teaming and collaboration, if associated with the production or distribution of knowledge (supply- and/or demand-side KM initiatives)
  - But only if they deal with the production and/or integration of claims related to the value, veracity, or context of work products or their informational content
- Any other application, as long as it deals with claims related to the value, veracity, or context of intellectual objects or content

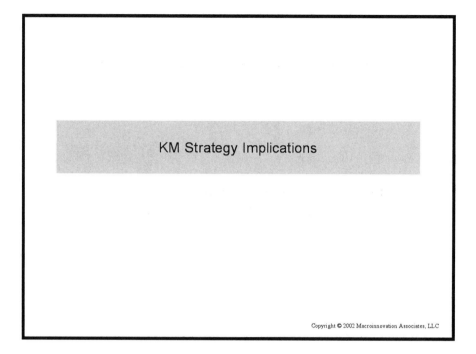

KM Strategy Implications

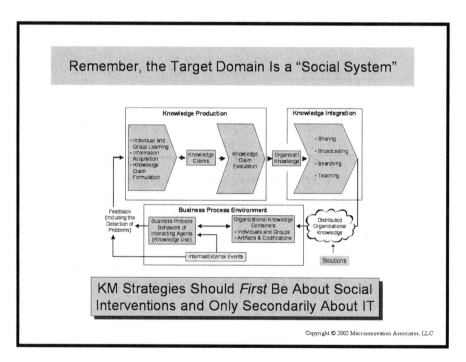

Remember, the Target Domain Is a "Social System"

KM Strategies Should *First* Be About Social Interventions and Only Secondarily About IT

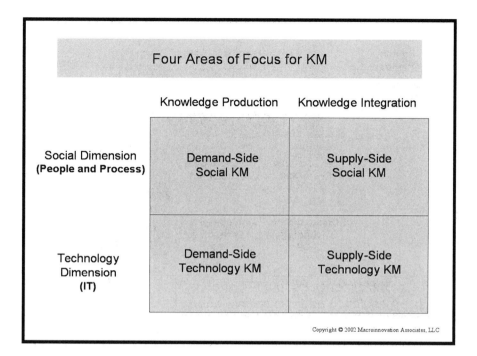

Four Areas of Focus for KM

	Knowledge Production	Knowledge Integration
Social Dimension (People and Process)	Demand-Side Social KM	Supply-Side Social KM
Technology Dimension (IT)	Demand-Side Technology KM	Supply-Side Technology KM

Copyright © 2002 Macroinnovation Associates, LLC

Some Examples of Common KM Initiatives

	Knowledge Production	Knowledge Integration
Social Dimension (People and Process)	• Individual Learning • Group Learning • Innovation & IC Mgmt. • Communities of Inquiry • KAIZEN Events in Mfg. • Think Tanks • Management Planning	• Training Programs • Communities of Practice (CoP) • Knowledge Capture • Storytelling • KM Cultural Initiatives • Operations Mgmt.

Technology Dimension (IT)	• Knowledge Portals
	• Innovation Mgmt. Tools
	• Groupware
	  - Collaboration Apps
	  - Virtual Teaming Tools
	  - E-mail
	• Listserv Discuss'n Grps.
		• Information Portals
		• Intranets
		• Information Mgmt.
		• Work Product Mgmt.
		• Content Mgmt.
		• Imaging
		• Groupware

Copyright © 2002 Macroinnovation Associates, LLC

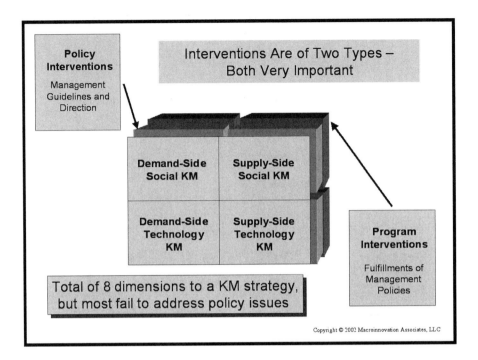

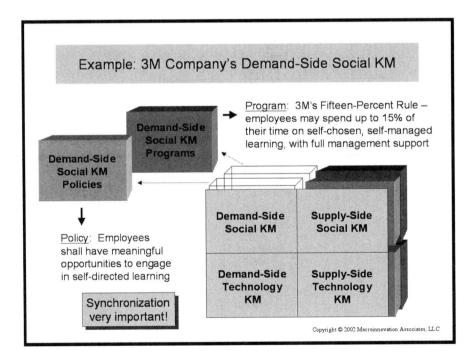

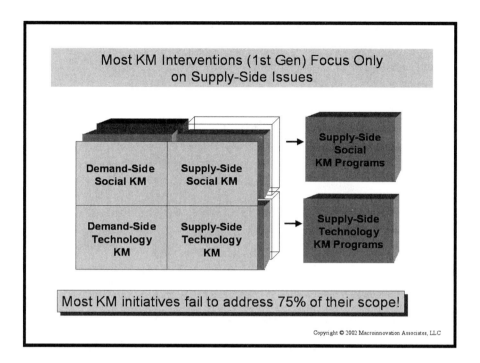

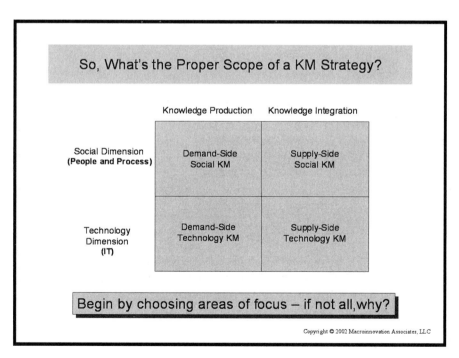

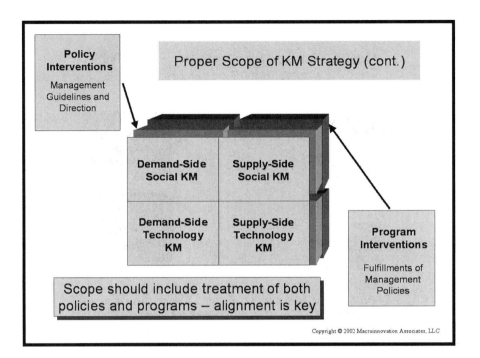

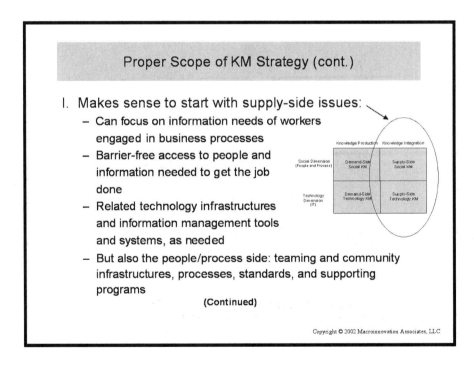

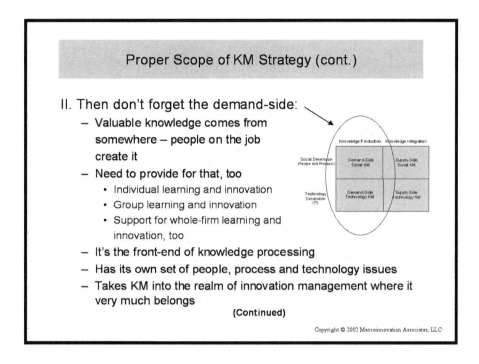

Proper Scope of KM Strategy (cont.)

II. Then don't forget the demand-side:

- Valuable knowledge comes from somewhere – people on the job create it
- Need to provide for that, too
  - Individual learning and innovation
  - Group learning and innovation
  - Support for whole-firm learning and innovation, too
- It's the front-end of knowledge processing
- Has its own set of people, process and technology issues
- Takes KM into the realm of innovation management where it very much belongs

(Continued)

Copyright © 2002 Macroinnovation Associates, LLC

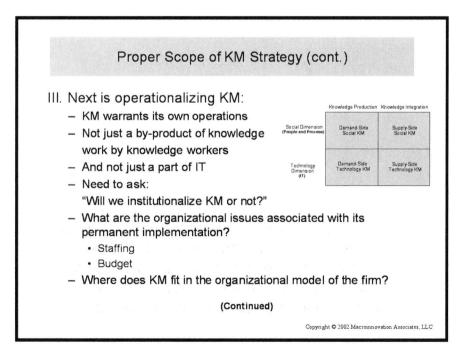

Proper Scope of KM Strategy (cont.)

III. Next is operationalizing KM:

- KM warrants its own operations
- Not just a by-product of knowledge work by knowledge workers
- And not just a part of IT
- Need to ask:
  "Will we institutionalize KM or not?"
- What are the organizational issues associated with its permanent implementation?
  - Staffing
  - Budget
- Where does KM fit in the organizational model of the firm?

(Continued)

Copyright © 2002 Macroinnovation Associates, LLC

Proper Scope of KM Strategy (cont.)

IV. Finally, reconciling KM vs. business strategy:
  – Most KM methodologies begin with commission of a first-generation sin
    • Business strategy knowledge exists
    • Purpose of KM is to serve the supply-side interests of existing business strategy knowledge
    • KM reduced to a knowledge capture, codification, and sharing plan for a set of existing knowledge (this is IM*; supply-side KM at most)

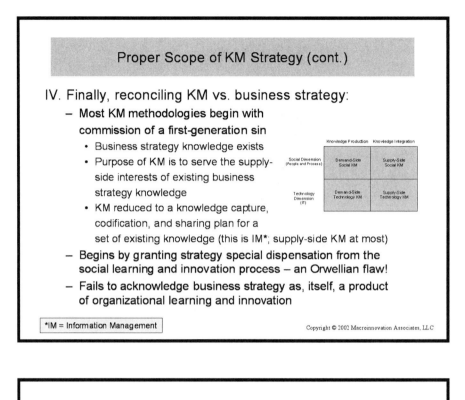

  – Begins by granting strategy special dispensation from the social learning and innovation process – an Orwellian flaw!
  – Fails to acknowledge business strategy as, itself, a product of organizational learning and innovation

*IM = Information Management

---

10 Key Principles of Second-Generation KM

7. KM interventions can only have direct impact on knowledge processing outcomes, not business outcomes – impact on business outcomes is indirect

8. KM's value proposition? KM enhances an organization's capacity to adapt by improving its ability to learn and innovate, and to detect and solve problems

9. If it doesn't address *value, veracity, or context*, it's not knowledge management

10. **Business strategy is subordinate to KM strategy, not the reverse, because business strategy is itself a product of knowledge processing – KM is not an implementation tool for strategy; strategy follows from KP and is, therefore, *downstream* from KM**

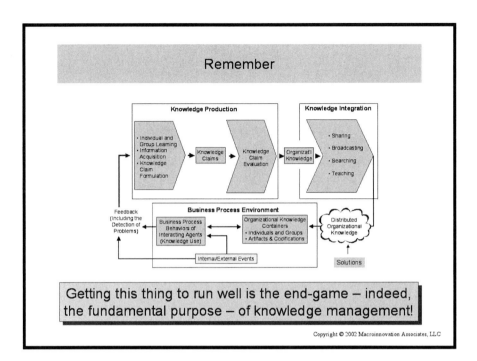

Getting this thing to run well is the end-game – indeed, the fundamental purpose – of knowledge management!

Thank You!

Contact Information

Mark W. McElroy
Macroinnovation Associates, LLC
10 Ogden's Mill Road
Windsor, VT 05089

mmcelroy@vermontel.net

(802) 436-2250

www.macroinnovation.com

INDEX

Note: Page numbers followed by the letters *f* and *t* indicate figures and tables, respectively; page numbers followed by *n* indicate endnotes.

Mark W. McElroy is a thought leader, consultant, and award-winning author in the fields of knowledge management, organizational learning, intellectual capital, and innovation. He is a twenty-five year veteran of management consulting, including time spent at Price Waterhouse and KPMG Peat Marwick. While at KPMG, he served as U.S. National Partner-In-Charge of the Enterprise Networks practice. He was also a Principal in IBM's Knowledge Management practice in Cambridge, MA.

At present, Mark is President and CEO of Macroinnovation Associates, LLC, a business innovation consultancy based in Windsor, VT. He is the principal developer of the "Policy Synchronization Method" (PSM), a patent-pending technique for enhancing business innovation. The PSM is based on a unique blend of organizational learning and complexity theory, and is offered to end-user organizations around the world through free and perpetual licenses.

Mark is also President of the Knowledge Management Consortium International (KMCI), the largest professional association of KM practitioners in the world. He serves on the board there, as well, and has been affiliated with KMCI since 1998.

Mark can be reached by e-mail at mmcelroy@vermontel.net.

Macroinnovation Associates, LLC
10 Ogden's Mill Road
Windsor, VT 05089
(802) 436-2250
(802) 436-2275 (fax)
www.macroinnovation.com

kmci

KNOWLEDGE MANAGEMENT CONSORTIUM INTERNATIONAL

Thought Leadership in *The New Knowledge Management*

Knowledge Management Consortium International (KMCI) - The leading non-profit professional association of knowledge and innovation managers dedicated to the ongoing development and practice of *The New Knowledge Management.*

The New Knowledge Management - KMCI is the cradle of thought leadership for *the new knowledge management,* a body of theory and practice that sees organizations as adaptive systems, whose capacity to adapt is driven by the quality of their social *knowledge processing* systems and the degree of *openness* within them.

A Balanced Approach to KM - KMCI advocates *a balanced approach to KM* in two important ways. First, it promotes KM strategies and interventions aimed at not just knowledge sharing, but *knowledge production* as well. Second, it argues for the use of *social interventions* - and not just IT - in KM strategies.

The KMCI Network
Information and Resources for a Competitive Edge

KMCI is your leading resource for professional development, offering special training and certification programs, as well as access to the latest news, conferences, and education events for today's knowledge and innovation managers.

Our on-line journal *Knowledge and Innovation Management* published jointly with the Institute for Knowledge Management, The George Washington University, offers a unique perspective which draws together the concepts and processes of *Knowledge Management, Innovation Management, Intellectual Capital Management, Organizational Learning Theory, Transparency Management, Systems Thinking,* and *Complex Adaptive Systems Theory.*

We offer a range of membership levels. Benefits include discounts on *KMCI Institute's* CKIM certification courses, other training programs, and books from *KMCI Press.* Members can also participate in KMCI's on-line discussion groups, and have exclusive access to the "Members Only" portion of KMCI's website. Visit our website for these and other features including links to our affiliates and corporate sponsors, job postings, and more.

www.kmci.org

General Inquiries (703) 461-8823 KMCI P.O. Box 191, Hartland Four Corners, VT 05049